Adolescents, Music and Music Therapy

of related interest

Microanalysis in Music Therapy
Methods, Techniques and Applications for Clinicians,
Researchers, Educators and Students
Edited by Thomas Wosch and Tony Wigram
Foreword by Barbara Wheeler
ISBN 978 1 84310 469 8

Improvisation
Methods and Techniques for Music Therapy
Clinicians, Educators and Students
Tony Wigram
ISBN 978 1 84310 048 5

Receptive Methods in Music Therapy
Techniques and Clinical Applications for Music
Therapy Clinicians, Educators and Students
Denise Grocke and Tony Wigram
Foreword by Cheryl Dileo
ISBN 978 1 84310 413 1

Songwriting
Methods, Techniques and Clinical Applications for Music
Therapy Clinicians, Educators and Students
Edited by Felicity Baker and Tony Wigram
Foreword by Even Ruud
ISBN 978 1 84310 356 1

The Theory and Practice of Vocal Psychotherapy
Songs of the Self
Diane Austin
ISBN 978 1 84310 878 8

Melody in Music Therapy
A Therapeutic Narrative Analysis
Gudrun Aldridge and David Aldridge
ISBN 978 1 85302 755 0

Adolescents, Music and Music Therapy

Methods and Techniques for Clinicians, Educators and Students

Katrina McFerran

Foreword by Tony Wigram

Jessica Kingsley Publishers
London and Philadelphia

First published in 2010
by Jessica Kingsley Publishers
116 Pentonville Road
London N1 9JB, UK
and
400 Market Street, Suite 400
Philadelphia, PA 19106, USA

www.jkp.com

Copyright © Katrina McFerran 2010

Library of Congress Cataloging in Publication Data
A CIP catalog record for this book is available from the Library of Congress

British Library Cataloguing in Publication Data
A CIP catalogue record for this book is available from the British Library

ISBN 978 1 84905 019 7

Printed and bound in the United States by
Thomson-Shore, 7300 Joy Road, Dexter, MI 48130

Contents

Acknowledgements

The decision to write this book was a swift response to the arrival of a Jessica Kingsley catalogue in my mailbox at the end of 2007. As I scanned the huge number of music therapy texts with excitement I realized that there was still a gap to be filled on the topic of music therapy with adolescents. I had dreamt about writing such a book at some time in the future, but suddenly I felt ready. I wrote to my friend and mentor Tony Wigram with a suggestion. Did he think there was a need for such a book? Would he be prepared to write it with me?

It is hard to believe that two years have passed since that idea was born. As the idea grew and developed into a book of my own, I was supported by many colleagues who did think that a book on music with adolescents would be useful. Tony Wigram has continued to be a guide and inspiration for me in terms of developing a way of writing accessible texts that talk about the music – how we do it and why we do it. Brynjulf Stige has challenged me to work hard on the theoretical underpinnings of my ideas and to locate my opinions so that I could make a rigorous contribution to the debate on what music therapy could be. Felicity Baker provides me with continuous support by meeting and matching me with her energy and enthusiasm, and helping me feel comfortable about fitting so many exciting opportunities into my life.

In addition to these more nebulous influences, I am grateful to a number of colleagues who read chapters of the book and took the time to offer honest and much valued feedback. Lucy O'Grady, Cheryl Dileo, Freya Dalgleish, Astrid Notarangelo, Brynjulf Stige, Carolyn Hart, Katie Lindenfelser, Nadia Millar and Jason Kenner all spent time and energy in this way. Katie and Freya also made additional contributions to the book by collecting and compiling literature and song preferences into databases for me to analyse. Lucy's contribution is also greater than her feedback on only one part of the book. She is a constant source of support and a valuable companion with whom to explore what music therapy can be. Her influence can be felt in many of the ideas that are posed here.

Other influences have been less personal. The work of the great humanists such as Carl Rogers, Abraham Maslow and Rollo May, as well as Irvin Yalom, have always underpinned my approach to music therapy. Community music therapy theory has provided me with a stimulating set of ideas with which to challenge the more conventional models that I had been stretching well beyond their limits. The concept of mind-mapping has supplied me with a much needed visual tool for developing writing ideas. And a reignition of my relationship with God has been a welcomed surprise during the writing of this book.

Many influences have been important, but the inspiration of Denise Grocke can be felt in every sentence in this book. Not only has she read and commented on each word, but she has been my teacher and mentor from the moment I arrived in the world of music therapy as a 17-year-old classical pianist – still a teenager myself. It is Denise's teaching in class, discussions in supervision, and more recently her thoughtful comments over a cup of coffee or glass of wine at the end of a day that have shaped my understanding of music therapy. She is careful and perceptive, creative and rigorous, a colleague, leader and a great friend. It is fair to say that none of this would have been written without her.

My family has also been deeply involved in the creation of this book as well as the career that sits behind and beneath it. My laptop has been a constant companion in the lives of Liam and Imogen, and they have grown skilled in dragging me away from it as well as generous in allowing me to play with it. The last months spent at the beach house will always be remembered not only for finishing the book but also for finding a real shark and seeing more sunrises than I care to remember. The number of times we have run or skipped (never walked) up and down that beach, singing and playing in the freezing cold waves are beyond counting. It was the perfect complement to staring at a screen, which I did at every opportunity. My husband Kevin has also been an important source of support in co-parenting our gorgeous children and accepting my decision to undertake such a mammoth task at a busy time in our lives. I continue to rely on the love and support of my parents in everything I do.

There is no doubt that the real inspirations for this book are the many, many teenagers with whom I have worked over the years. Some I have come to know extremely well and they taught me about how I could, and could not, be of assistance. Others I met only once and will never see again, but they touched and surprised me in their willingness to use music as therapy during such brief encounters. Some could speak, some could not. Some liked rock, some pop, some hip-hop. These young people continue to energize me and to introduce me to new music across a vast range of genres.

And last, but not least, I would like to thank pop music for being so, well, popular. I have an innate ability to recognize a Top 10 song as soon as I hear it and I am one of the enthusiastic masses who will enjoy it – although I spent my own adolescence pretending that I preferred classical music. Since then I have broadened my tastes to keep up with the many different genres preferred by my teenage clients, but my heart is still very clichéd. Before anyone else influenced my thinking, there was Madonna. 'Music makes the people come together (never gonna stop)' (Madonna 2000). She is so right.

Author's Note

Please note that the methods described in this book are used by qualified music therapists and should be used with caution by untrained professionals.

Foreword

I am greatly honoured to be invited to write the Foreword for this book for two very special reasons. First and foremost, the content excites and inspires me, and without any doubt provides a most unique and comprehensive array of methods, techniques, experiences and guidance for people who want to work with adolescents. The way this book starts immediately makes you want to read more, and Kat McFerran establishes in the first two paragraphs not only her experience with adolescents, but her attitude, and approach and affinity for them, which leads me to my second reason. I have immense confidence and very high regard for Kat McFerran, whose genuine attitude, and her caring and authentic feelings towards adolescents, ring out in every chapter, page, paragraph and sentence. So while I can say with my academic hat on that this book makes a very significant contribution to the literature from the perspective of clinical practice and research, with my therapist hat on I was filled with a very real sense of understanding and insight into the complex and fascinating world of adolescence, which reached me at all levels – as a therapist, a researcher, teacher, and as a parent. I would also like to comment that this book further adds to the high quality of music therapy literature representing both research and clinical practice that has been coming out of Australia, particularly over the last ten to fifteen years.

What, then, has this book to offer our discipline and where does it stand in the wide range of theoretical, clinical, research and methodology texts? It actually has a unique position, and I will explain why. Music therapy has developed as an intervention in health care, education and the social services for populations within clinical areas such as developmental disability, mental health, elderly care, and more recently neuro-disability, oncology and acute medicine. Adolescence is not a 'pathology', it is a vital and complex stage of human development that moulds and prepares us for our adult life. There is surprisingly little literature directed specifically to adolescents in our field, and this book definitely fills this gap. I say surprisingly, because who could be a more accessible group for the power and inspiration music offers as a medium for engagement, creativity, identity formation and an equal-terms relationship with others, than adolescents? We exist in a world where there is an increasing group of disillusioned youngsters whose ideals and aspirations are damaged by the world around them, with everyday evidence presented of the selfishness, greed, immorality and lack of personal integrity in the adult world of which they stand at the threshold. Music is an integrating, emotional and highly attractive art form, and Kat McFerran demonstrates here with all her exciting ideas and methods how the power and value of music can be a positive force in the lives of adolescents. This positive force can build identify formation, self-esteem and healthy peer relationships and feelings of both relationship with and responsibility to others. Music has the power to evoke and promote pleasure and motivation, but equally has the capacity to contain all the conflicting emotional feelings felt acutely during adolescence – confusion, frustration, anger, isolation, helplessness. In this book, Kat McFerran has addressed all of these issues, writing personally and profoundly about her experiences with this group, seeing the feelings behind the defences, potentials behind the resistance, and the demands for understanding behind the anger. The many examples from her own sessions with adolescents are a testament to this, and bring remarkable relevance and illustration to the approaches she is explaining.

A part of my own clinical experience over the last 33 years has been working with adolescents in the field of autism, intellectual and developmental disability, and much earlier in the field of special education, working with emotional and behavioural disturbance. It is a population where I had to work hardest to hold back, wait, listen, think about their motivations and interests, and nuture their healthy autonomy and independence. Adolescents are inevitably suspicious of adults and I reflect on many cases where improvisational strategies allowed both a transfer and a balance of power – perhaps a key factor in the development of a working therapeutic, or even just musical, relationship. Perhaps the most care I took was to avoid overtly trying to 'help' – an approach they both saw through and ran away from with inevitable damage to the working alliance. We cannot escape symbolizing authoritarian figures, but we can reduce the impact. Perhaps we have knowledge, experience and wisdom to offer, but far rather with this population we wait to be asked than to use it in order to drive forward our therapeutic agenda. Kat McFerran's thinking simply reinforces all these ideas, and adds so many realistic dimensions to the personal attitude needed to engage and support adolescents successfully.

This book follows a concept developed some years ago in articulating methods and techniques in music therapy, to provide both the clinicians and students in training with tried and tested tools for a working practitioner. From that perspective, the content of this book provides very rich material, brilliant ideas and exciting techniques which will inspire those in the clinical field. Kat McFerran has gone further than previous texts by adding in comprehensive clinical vignettes that make concrete and real the ways of working she is proposing. You will find the relevance of songwriting in the story of Grace, a young Sudanese girl experiencing isolation in her school life. Thematic group improvisation provides the focus and inspiration for generating an exciting and meaningful group process for five young men with muscular dystrophy – a container and the tools for expressing strong emotional feelings safely. The group experiences continue with the rock 'n' roll band, with a strong sense of fun leading to motivation for a group of kids trying to re-engage into the school system through a community programme. In all cases, the rationale behind the experiences is clearly explained, and most importantly the types of activities being used. The examples range from work in a hospice to adolescents with profound and multiple learning disabilities, from youngsters with emotional and behavioural problems to the sadness and grief experienced through the loss of loved ones – approaches the author very sensitively explored in her own doctoral research. These examples are beautifully constructed and explained, and those of us who work with adolescents will no doubt all recognize people we know in the characters Kat McFerran has taken from her own experiences.

The driving force for the structure and materials in this book is found in the introduction which demonstrates the author's intention to address fundamental questions such as why, how, and in what way music therapists can work with adolescents. It starts by suggesting that the ideas in the book are written 'for those interested in exploring the purpose of music therapy for adolescents', and then goes on to say that this could be for music therapists, 'as well as professionals who work with adolescents'. Okay – so is it a book just for music therapists? I don't think so, as there is a wealth of information that will be of great help to anyone using music (rather than exclusively music therapy) with adolescents. This raises the question of whether the caution that is put into the front of this and the other methods books (*Songwriting, Receptive Methods in Music Therapy* and *Microanalysis in Music Therapy*) should really be here – i.e., that you should be a trained music therapist to use these methods. Yes, this book is primarily focused on music therapy – but again there are some great examples of how to approach and work with adolescents that could be really well understood and used by secondary (11–18) education music teachers, not to mention community workers and perhaps even parents working through difficult relationships with their son or daughter. What really are the boundaries when we want to meet and be with adolescents? The boundaries are perhaps governed by a sense of responsibility about our own understanding and competencies, and there can be experienced clinical practitioners from not only music therapy, but teaching, psychology and other fields who need to think carefully about their attitudes and biases before tackling the challenge of adolescents. Kat McFerran places those issues firmly on the table, and makes you think about your motivations and your potentials – can you step outside the box, can you find your way inside the thinking processes and needs of adolescents? What do you understand about healthy adolescence?

The most valuable and vital material in this book is directed towards the music Kat has used over so many years of experience. Immediately she focuses on songs – probably the most relevant and understandable music activity for adolescents, culturally. While improvisation is present throughout for use in many forms, Kat McFerran explores popular music as the most meaningful genre for the work, and gives a very extensive range of styles and cultures. For me as a good old classical music addict, I recognize immediately a knowledge and expertise I would need to expand to engage with adolescents in the way she does. For the acquisition and application of this knowledge and expertise, Kat creates a model where each method has a 'Setting and purpose', 'Illustrative vignettes' and 'Evaluating effectiveness' section and, at the end, 'Key points'. This works very well, and is applied to all of the explanations of method.

When people write books from a clinical or research perspective, they use a lot of impressive 'jargon' to demonstrate their theoretical foundations and clinical skills. The most impressive experience that I had from reading this book is Kat McFerran's ability to speak from the perspective of the adolescent, and her use of language immediately shows her intimate knowledge and understanding of the way of thinking and doing with this population. This is very special, and endears the reader to really understanding what a working alliance should be like when engaging adolescents. She really knows them, and when they present her (intentionally or unintentionally) with their challenges – especially the challenge of 'you never know what's going on' – she really gets it! This book gives us something you simply cannot find purely by reading clinical articles or studying theory – working methods that are firmly grounded in a remarkable insight into the population and years of experience. It continues the process of documenting methods and techniques so necessary to define our work and help to train the new generations of music therapists, and should become a standard text for us all whether we are working with adolescents now or in the future.

Tony Wigram
Professor of Music Therapy and Head
of PhD Studies in Music Therapy
Department of Music Therapy and Music
Aalborg University, Denmark
November 2009

Introduction

I really enjoy working with adolescents using music. If you are reading this book then I suspect you either feel the same way, or perhaps completely the opposite. The idea of walking into a room full of teenagers with drums either makes you smile or makes you want to turn around and run. The feeling of the bass line pumping through the floor as you walk the last few steps to reach the music room either energizes you or makes you feel tense. The size of the young men who seem poised to jump from the table to the floor is either overwhelming or amusing. As I sit at my computer typing this book, hour after hour, I think of both these reactions and I write for both types of reader. The question that I have tried to answer with this book is the one that I have been asked many times in the past 15 years – why work with adolescents using music? Sometimes this question is asked with an incredulous tone – why on earth would you want to work with teenagers using music? Sometimes it is asked with sincere curiosity – what is the point of using music with teenagers?

I understand why some might question my desire to work with adolescents. They can be intimidating and abrupt, particularly when they are approached en masse. Each time I begin work in a new setting I experience the same sense of trepidation. I am conscious of a sense of paranoia about whether they will like me. The particular way that teenagers in this situation either stare at me or, alternatively, casually ignore me, reignites my adolescent self. The feeling usually passes within a few moments, but it returns me immediately to the years of my own adolescence. I have discovered that when I am working with teenagers I need to have a secure sense of myself as an adult who is comfortable with my memories of the teenage years. I suspect that many of those who ask me 'why?' with an incredulous tone find this initial experience off-putting.

By way of an answer, I have included detailed case descriptions within the methods chapters of this book that show how I approach teenagers. I have depicted the nuance of my experiences with individuals and groups of teenagers through rich illustrations that convey both the thoughts and actions of the music therapist. These case studies flowed from my fingers to the page and as an author I thoroughly enjoyed caressing the detail from each memory and blending different experiences together to tell the stories that you will find. The feedback I received from generous colleagues who read various draft chapters consistently reinforced that these were helpful and stimulating. I hope that this will also be your experience.

The descriptions contained in the methods chapters are framed by a rationale that I have developed for the more curious reader. These ideas are written particularly for those interested in exploring the purpose of music therapy for adolescents. This includes music therapists who already have a natural and easy rapport with adolescents, as well as professionals who work with adolescents or who manage organizations that service adolescent clients. The rationale surrounding the descriptions grew out of a systematic review of the literature on music therapy with adolescents (presented in Chapter 1). After gathering together every article and chapter that I could find on this topic, I set about interrogating the material, examining it from every direction to answer my question about why we should work with adolescents using music. A number of answers were provided by this review, including information about where music therapists work, the stance they take and the methods they use, the condition of the adolescents they work with and the outcomes that they anticipate. All of this is interesting and useful, but the most striking feature of the analysis was the powerful influence of the music therapist's approach. In attempting to identify patterns between each of the various elements, it became clear that there were no straightforward links between different variables. The teenager's diagnosis was not a good indicator of therapeutic outcomes. The setting did not lead to the consistent use of particular methods. The young people were sometimes contextualized in reference to their 'adolescence' and sometimes their condition. In contemplating what music therapists might be able to grasp as they approach a teenager, it became clear that it was, quite simply, themselves. This idea is central to the examples provided in Parts Two, Three and Four of this book, and the illustrative vignettes and key points provide guidance about locating oneself while forming relationships with teenagers in music therapy.

BUT FIRST, WHAT DO I MEAN BY 'ADOLESCENCE'?

Stanley Hall (1904) was the first person to suggest that a distinct stage of life exists between childhood and adulthood. The research upon which he based this proposal would not stand the test of evidence-based standards today and even at that time was not replicable because of his highly subjective approach. Nonetheless, something about his assertion that adolescence is a time of 'storm and stress' held immense appeal within American culture and continues to do so internationally. Despite the popularity of his idea, Hall's depiction of adolescents as experiencing mood disruptions, being involved in risky behaviour and causing conflicts with parents is not universally applicable (Epstein 2007). As described in Chapter 3, many non-Western cultures do not expect adolescence to be a turbulent period of development. Indeed, there are many individual adolescents in Western cultures who are neither rebellious nor particularly moody.

A more internationally relevant approach to defining adolescence is to attach it to the concept of being a teenager. To be aged between 13 and 19 provides straightforward boundaries for a definition. The World Health Organization suggests that adolescence is more comprehensive, however, including 10–19-year-olds in their definition, but extending the upper limit to 25 such that it is expanded to include three stages: early, middle and late adolescence. The physical milestones that mark adolescence also provide relatively uncomplicated parameters for definition. The influx of hormones that mark the journey through puberty are an important influence on how adolescence is experienced. Paul Van Heeswyk (1997) insightfully describes adolescence as being 'kick-started by puberty and cruising slowly to a halt at adult identity, the point at which the petrol is getting low and we need to think about saving it for the long, straight road ahead' (p.3).

Concrete markers such as age brackets and physical development provide signposts for what it means to be an adolescent. Political correctness dictates what language can and cannot be used. The term 'young people' is currently the most politically correct phrase in the Australian context, since the word 'adolescent' has taken on the implication of delinquency to some degree. 'Young person' is a useful term because it describes an age bracket, not a series of characteristics, and therefore avoids associations such as 'storm and stress'. But it is a clumsy phrase and for the purposes of this book young people and adolescents will be used interchangeably, along with teenager and sometimes even teen or youth where it suits the rhythm of the sentence. One word was simply not enough to capture the various reflections on adolescence in this text.

The use of gender also deserves a brief commentary. I have occasionally used the terms young man and young woman where it felt appropriate. The gender of the music therapist is consistently female, however, since the examples are drawn from my own work and I invariably pictured myself as the therapist being described. The wide variety of names that I have selected for the teenagers in the illustrative vignettes are not a reference to young people I have worked with, however. On the contrary, I amused myself by using the names of music therapists from around the globe within each example. At no point did I stop to consider whether the music therapist was well suited to the particular adolescent condition being described; instead I was more interested in achieving a cultural blend within and across the examples. Any similarities between the name and the characters they have been attached to are purely coincidental.

Another way of understanding adolescence is that it provides the opportunity to answer the question 'Who am I?' as part of a process of identity formation (Erikson 1963). Although this is another culturally constructed concept, it is a useful framework for understanding the role of music therapy with adolescents – we can help the adolescent to answer the all important question, 'Who am I?' If this is accepted, then one part of our role as therapist is to stay out of the way of the client's journey – it is not about us, after all. Some therapists do this by being conscious of projections and counter-transference. Others attempt to maintain an objective stance, where the personal is kept quite separately to the therapeutic encounter. Each therapeutic approach has its own principles about how to focus on the client. When that focus is helping a teenager discover his or her identity, it is very useful for the therapist to have a strong sense of their own personal identity, both as a professional and as an individual. The chosen therapeutic stance of each professional is grounded in a therapeutic approach. The importance of therapeutic approach is supported by research that has identified the therapist's allegiance to a particular therapeutic approach as linked to successful outcomes for clients (Hubble, Duncan and Miller 1999). Although the particular therapeutic approach is not of significance, it is important that the therapist is committed to and supported by a theoretical framework. This matches with my interpretation of the music therapy and adolescents literature. A strong sense of therapeutic intention provides the best framework for how to work with adolescents in music therapy. This is congruent with my own experience as a music therapist, where I have learned that it helps to have a strong sense of my own identity when I am working with teenagers. At an inter-personal level, authenticity is the key. At a planning level, being commited to a therapeutic approach is the most helpful guide.

This emphasis on approach is more thoroughly explained in Chapter 2, where I piece together the inter-personal and the intra-personal to provide a Map for how music therapy can be with adolescents. The development of these ideas has been painstaking work because some of the more simplistic explanations I had developed to explain why I make particular decisions in music therapy with adolescents did not withstand the interrogation to which I subjected them. It would have been convenient to explain my approach to adolescents with reference to the various models of music therapy that exist. The blended, eclectic approach that I have adopted and that is common practice in Australia does not stay within the boundaries of a particular model, however. A logical relationship between the condition of the adolescent, selection of method, and outcome achieved was not forthcoming from the literature and nor is it so simple in my own clinical experience. All teenagers have different needs based on who they are, where they are and what they are grappling with. The way that we use music together varies depending on the kind of music they like, how active they are willing to be and what I am capable of providing. Each of these things can vary between sessions and even within sessions. I longed to be able to provide a simple explanation, but it was not possible. Chapter 2 is my attempt to provide a rationale for the rest of the book. I hope that it makes sense to you.

All of these ideas are grounded in a theoretical framework that outlines a relationship between adolescence, music and health (Chapter 3). I have read across each of these fields over the duration of my career and followed the development of ideas that have piqued my interest. Four broad concepts are most relevant to the practical nature of this book – identity formation, resilience, connectedness and competence. In the field of adolescent health, ideas about resilience have always caught my attention, strongly influenced by trends in social work practice with young people. More recently, the concepts of connectedness and participation have stimulated my thinking about young people in community settings and have gradually infiltrated all of my clinical practice and research. My early experiences of working with teenagers in special education led me to value the development of competencies and the ways that music can motivate learning and improvement. In addition, the regular function of music for adolescents is an important framework for understanding, since young people are also members of their community and their culture. The ways that healthy teenagers use music has been a source of interest and investigation and I attempt to incorporate what I know of these fields. Chapter 3 can be seen as a brief introduction to my favourite ideas about adolescents and music.

Parts Two and Three comprise very practical chapters, consisting of descriptions of the use of songs and improvisations with individuals and groups of adolescents. A brief theoretical rationale is provided in the introduction to each section; however, the chapters themselves are unapologetically free of references in the main.

This book forms part of a series of texts by Tony Wigram and a string of Australian collaborators that outline the relevant music therapy methods in more detail. *Improvisation* (Wigram 2004) is the first in the series, and is the foundation from which I teach music therapy students at the University of Melbourne to improvise at the piano, on guitar, with their voice and using a range of instruments. *Songwriting* (Baker and Wigram 2005) was edited by Tony Wigram with Felicity Baker and provides an invaluable overview of various approaches to this method, all of which may be used with adolescents and some of which are specifically described as such. Receptive methods have been insightfully documented by my colleague Denise Grocke with Tony Wigram (Grocke and Wigram 2006); their book addresses the nuance of methods such as song sharing in greater detail than I provide here. This book focuses on the music therapist's approach to adolescents. The unique attitudes and needs encountered with this age group are at the centre of each of these practical chapters.

The final section of this book provides an overview of contemporary approaches to working with adolescents. Many of the ideas documented in Part Four have not been thoroughly documented in the literature and therefore a more rigorous rationale is provided for each. The illustrative vignettes are framed by theoretical elements, rather than being straddled by the music therapy treatment programme. Community music therapy is an exciting development in music therapy practice, the empowering nature of which is well suited to fostering identity formation (Chapter 8). In Chapter 9, grief and loss are examined in relation to bereavement, but also as underpinning many other circumstances faced by the adolescent. Part Four concludes with a commentary on the increasing use of performances in contemporary practice with adolescents. Pros and cons are outlined in Chapter 10, and successes and failures presented.

It has been a great pleasure to document my experiences with adolescents. I hope and pray that they have some relevance to you and welcome any feedback that you are inclined to offer. Enjoy.

PART ONE

Background

Chapter 1

Taking a Systematic Look at the Literature

Music therapists have been singing with and for clients for over five decades. This chapter provides a systematic synthesis of what has been documented about music therapy with adolescents. It does not attempt to convey the rich work that is taking place every day around the globe; these descriptions are left for subsequent sections of this book. This chapter provides a jumping off point for the material that follows about how music therapy can be with adolescents.

Music therapists have been describing and documenting their work with teenagers for more than five decades – making the field more than twice as old as adolescents themselves. The existing literature is therefore an appropriate place to begin a book on music and adolescents, answering the question of 'What do we know already?' We know that at least 140 music therapists have taken the time to contemplate and write about their work with teenagers in articles published in refereed journals, books and theses. What these authors have put forward forms the basis of this chapter; however, it is important to recognize that this information is a small indication of the knowledge held by music therapists who have worked with adolescents over the decades. It is inspiring to realize that the voice of adolescents has grown stronger in the literature over time, with an increasing number of music therapy publications being produced that specifically nominate teenagers within their descriptions: 11 in the 1970s; 25 in the '80s; 37 in the '90s; and already 67 in the 2000s. This increasing tendency to distinguish teenagers from children reflects the development of the adolescent health field more broadly. It is more common in contemporary thinking to understand adolescents as facing unique challenges in relation to their physical or psychological conditions rather than to depict them as older children or younger adults. This is a welcomed development.

The overview presented in this chapter focuses exclusively on the discipline of music therapy, not delving into the array of material from other fields that discusses the application of music with teenagers. Restricting the search to material written by music therapists makes it easier to identify patterns and therefore make a useful contribution to knowledge. It is possible to make generalizations about the value of music therapy for teenagers through this restricted process, and this information may be useful for other professionals such as youth workers, educators, social workers, occupational therapists, psychologists, psychiatrists, paediatricians, and other allied health clinicians, as well as to music therapists who will know individual pieces of information already. The fact that the vast majority of the literature was found in music therapy-specific journals and books reflects this focus, although some literature on the topic of music therapy and teenagers was uncovered in refereed journals of allied disciplines.

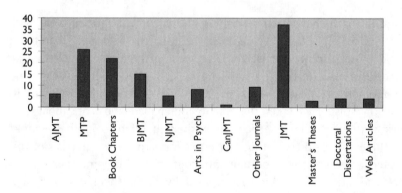

AJMT = Australian Journal of Music Therapy
MTP = Music Therapy Perspectives
BJMT = British Journal of Music Therapy
NJMT = Nordic Journal of Music Therapy
Arts in Psych = Arts in Psychotherapy
CanJMT = Canadian Journal of Music Therapy
JMT = Journal of Music Therapy

Figure 1.1: Source of identified publications on music therapy and adolescents

Figure 1.1 graphically suggests that the United States of America is the dominant influence within the literature, seen particularly by the number of publications in the two major music therapy journals of the US (*Journal of Music Therapy*; *Music Therapy Perspectives*). Eight of the 22 book chapters are also of American origin, plus two of the Doctoral dissertations and two Master's theses – accounting for more than half of the total publications. Relatively few publications about music therapy were identified outside the discipline and this suggests that little may be known about the practice of music therapy with adolescents beyond our own boundaries. It further justifies the need for a systematic review such as that presented in this chapter.

In the following sections a range of information will be provided, answering questions about the logistics of music therapy practice, the orientation of the professionals who are providing the services, the purpose of their work and the particular methods they use to achieve these intentions. Not all of the articles in the review provide information about all of these areas and therefore the analysis is limited by what authors have considered important in presenting their clinical work and/or their research. Since the identified literature includes a combination of case descriptions, research and theoretical musings, this varies significantly between them. The difference between practice and discourse also needs to be considered, since there may be a gap between the two. Not all music therapists write about their work, in fact very few do, and articles are not always direct reflections of clinical practice. They may have been altered to fit into research designs, or the author may be offering theoretical reflections based on a range of work over a number of years. Most authors present their favoured work, in the form of significant clinical breakthroughs or novel ways of working. It is not usual to write up the nuances of a daily clinical load, although it would probably be very useful. The review is therefore limited by these qualifications, but sustained by a significant variety of contributions.

The literature reviewed was drawn from the entire history of music therapy published in English up until early 2008. Searches were carried out using a range of databases, with the 'Music Therapy Research' database being used to explore the American literature in *Music Therapy Perspectives*, *Journal of Music Therapy* and *Music Therapy*, supplemented by hand searches of publications between 2004 and 2008 that were not included on the available version. A guided keyword search was undertaken using CAIRSS for Music (CAIRSS 2009) and Meditext (National Library of Australia 2008), and advanced searches were conducted on Medline (US National Library of Medicine 2009), ERIC (Institute of Education Sciences and US Department of Education 2009) and Web of Science (Thompson Reuters 2009). The *Australian Journal of Music Therapy, British Journal of Music Therapy, Canadian Journal of Music Therapy, New Zealand Journal of Music Therapy* and *Nordic Journal of Music Therapy* were hand searched, as were music therapy textbooks held in the comprehensive collection at the University of Melbourne. Although this review of the literature has been undertaken in a systematic way, the goal has not been to determine whether or not music therapy works. Instead, the review provides a synthesis of the literature that answers the following questions:

- Where does music therapy happen?
- What stance do music therapists take in working with teenagers?
- What music therapy methods are used?
- What challenges are faced by the young people we work with?
- What is the purpose of music therapy for young people?
- What can we learn from this?

Each of these questions is explored in this chapter.

WHERE DOES MUSIC THERAPY HAPPEN?

Information about the setting in which music therapy takes place was extracted from the 140 articles identified for review and this is represented in Figure 1.2.

In contemplating the most likely setting for music therapy with teenagers, the school would appear to be the logical location. In theory, teenagers spend around 30 hours a week at school, taking classes as well as breaks. School takes up most of the hours of their weekdays, while homework and other school-related activities, such as sport and creative arts activities, may take up further time after school and across the weekends. Yet analysis of the literature shows that the majority of music therapy work does not take place in educational settings, which comprised only 21 per cent of the articles. Music therapy in educational settings is mostly provided for young people who have disabilities, although this

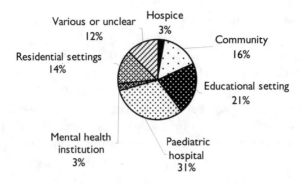

Figure 1.2: Music therapy settings for adolescent clients

group does not always receive music therapy in schools since these young people access different types of support settings dependent upon their cultural context. In many countries, young people with disabilities tend to live at home with their families and travel to school on a daily basis, in line with their able peers. In other countries, different models are utilized. In some, the educational programmes do not occur in schools, but rather in centres, or even hospitals. In some countries children may reside in an institution where they receive their developmentally-oriented services. Half of the venues classified as residential settings in this review were also described as educational facilities, and adding residential settings to educational settings brings the total to just over a quarter (26%), which is similar to the largest category, hospitals.

It is interesting to note that the vast majority of music therapy work still takes place with young people who are institutionalized in either hospital, inpatient mental health institutions, residential settings or hospices (51%). This means that they are spending both day and night in the setting where they receive music therapy. This phenomenon matches with traditional music therapy practice as an intervention for clients who are 'unwell'. These vulnerable clients require a high level of inpatient support, either because of nursing care requirements or because their home alternatives are not suitable. If family is assumed to be the natural source of support for many young people, the need for institutionalization indicates a serious health challenge. It also suggests developmental challenges, with separation from peers and educational opportunities (with some exceptions, noted above). The emphasis on music therapy services for institutionalized teenagers suggests that music therapists are frequently working with young people in crisis.

The knowledge that music therapy is servicing young people with high needs has implications for the likely length of programmes, assuming that most young people do not remain institutionalized for long periods of time. In paediatric hospitals, the emphasis is on brief and efficient stays, sometimes occurring over multiple admissions. Contemporary models of hospital care focus on returning patients to their home for the majority of the recovery period, for both psychosocial and economic reasons. Short stay implies brief music therapy interventions within the hospital. Brief does not imply single sessions, however, and extended therapeutic relationships can be established with irregular contact based on sporadic returns to the hospital environment, both scheduled and unexpected. In comparison, some of the residential treatment programmes described in the literature offer intensive programmes of limited duration. Very few programmes are described as residential and educationally oriented in this century, with the vast majority of contemporary residential programmes for adolescents being due to behavioural disorders – related to emotional or mental health conditions. Programmes in these facilities seek long-term benefits from concentrated interventions. Although inpatient mental health facilities operate differently, the long-term model of institutionalization fashionable in previous decades has been replaced in many countries with an emphasis on a return to community living in the shortest feasible timeframe. The literature suggests that music therapists are not working with adolescents so much in community settings, and this fact emphasizes the unusual circumstances in which young people are engaged in music therapy services.

This distance from typical everyday existence is also captured in the data on hospitalized teenagers, with brief hospital stays often being used to support young people struggling with mental illness. Twenty-three of the 44 articles describing work with adolescents in paediatric hospitals referred to those with eating disorders or other forms of psychiatric disorder requiring medical treatment. In the case of adolescents with eating disorders, this was usually due to the low weight or electrolyte imbalances that make them medically unstable and leads to extended hospital stays if the patient continues to refuse to eat and restore a stable weight.

Alternatively, patients may have injuries from suicide attempts or other accidents that have led them to the hospital system. Within this type of institution, professionals have the opportunity to access vulnerable young people who are subsequently offered a range of therapeutic opportunities during their usually brief stay. In previous decades, these patients would have been immediately transferred to inpatient psychiatric facilities that would have emphasized their mental health while also addressing medical needs. However, the changing nature of mental health interventions has led to a decrease in the amount of medical services provided as a regular part of treatment, meaning that higher levels of medical support cannot easily be catered for. The diminishing number of mental health institutions also means that there are fewer places available and hospitals often provide institutional care for these young people out of sheer necessity. Many young people will therefore experience a medical focus during hospitalization for injuries sustained as part of their mental illness.

The low number of programmes identified in this review as community-based suggests that music therapy has been used infrequently for prevention or rehabilitation. This may be related to the fact that training of music therapists has traditionally emphasized learning how to develop treatment programmes that are mandated for attendance by institutionalized populations. In fact, many of the programmes in the community-based category are actually only a small step away from this traditional model, seen as day programmes that clients attend in full-time capacities. Thirteen of the 22 community articles were written in the past decade, forming the majority. A further eight articles were contributed in the early 1990s, potentially a reflection of the deinstitutionalization movement that took place in many Western countries around that time. Another explanation for the limited descriptions of community-based programmes may be found in the early discourse of community music therapy. Gary Ansdell (2002) highlights that although many music therapists have been adjusting programmes to suit community-based populations for years, this has been in a pseudo-secretive manner that has not been documented alongside more traditional models of institutionalized practice. Music therapy with people in the community whose diagnoses are not known, or who experience music therapy without documented treatment programmes or measures of outcome, has been sparsely documented. Prior to the popularizing of community music therapy in this decade, many professionals had questioned whether this kind of work really was music therapy. Yet the earliest article included in this review was Zane Ragland and Maurice Apprey's innovative work with at-risk adolescents in 1974, an article that has many similarities to the model of community music therapy being posed since 2002. The roots of community music therapy are found even earlier in the work of Florence Tyson (McGuire 2004), also in the United States. It seems likely that a greater number of articles, chapters and books will emerge on community music therapy with teenagers now that it has achieved some acknowledgment within the profession (see Part Four of this book).

WHAT IS THE STANCE OF THE MUSIC THERAPIST?

The discipline of music therapy embraces a range of approaches to practice, and has typically adopted various psychological theories to this end. Even Ruud (1980) was the first to clearly detail music therapy in this context, particularly emphasizing the relationship with psychoanalytic, existential and behavioural theories. Kenneth Bruscia's (1987) *Improvisational Models of Music Therapy* also required each of the approaches to be located in terms of theoretical orientation; however, this clarity/transparency has been an exception rather than a rule. It is uncommon for music therapy authors writing about their work with adolescents to articulate their orientation clearly. Nonetheless, it is often possible to discern the dominant theoretical influence on their practice based on the kinds of programmes described and the cultural and locational influences that the author is representing. This approach was used to uncover three theoretical orientations that dominated the music therapy literature, as seen in Table 1.1.

Table 1.1: Theoretical orientation of music therapists working with adolescents

Primary orientation		Blended with another model
Behavioural	12	4 of the 12
Humanistic	44	26 of the 44
Psychodynamic	52	23 of the 52
Unclear/unknown	32	–
Total	140	53

The most obvious trend in this analysis is the tendency towards blended, or eclectic, approaches to practice (seen in column 3). An eclectic approach is also common across most practising psychotherapists, who tend to draw on whatever strategies best suit the person in front of them in that moment (Miller 2008). Contemporary understandings of therapeutic effectiveness are grounded in the knowledge that the greatest influence on the success of therapy is actually outside of the therapy itself, namely the client's life. Other common factors of successful therapy include the quality of the alliance between the therapist and client, and allegiance to a theoretical model of the therapist's choice (Hubble *et al.* 1999). The trend towards eclectic practice may be even greater than the literature suggests, since some authors may have described their work as clearly aligned with one particular model, but this may not represent all their work in the field, or even all their sessions with that client or group. Some authors were very clear as to what approaches to practice they took, however, and those maintaining a behavioural orientation were more likely to present their work in purist ways.

A psychodynamic orientation to practice was most popular in the literature on music therapy and adolescents that was reviewed (37%) and was clearly related to increased personal understanding. A broad definition of psychodynamic practice was utilized in attributing literature to this category, essentially including articles that described the unconscious influences acting upon the young person. Psychodynamic practice is an approach that has evolved out of psychoanalytic traditions, and involves the interpretation of the client's behaviours as rooted in previous experiences, particularly early family experiences (Hadley 2003). In the context of music therapy with adolescents, this is enacted in a number of ways that often involve the interpretation of musical choices made by the young person. For example, a preference for certain genres of music can be understood as symbolizing more than musical taste, as it may refer to psychological needs or defences. The instruments selected by clients may hold symbolic meanings, and are considered as representing the projection of feelings when they are played strongly, softly, in a repetitive way, or freely. An emphasis is placed on insight-oriented discussions in a psychodynamic model of practice, with the aim of assisting the teenager to better understand his or her unconscious motivations and needs. If young people are not willing, or not able, to participate in these kinds of dialogues, the therapist continues to interpret meaning from behaviours and to respond in ways consistent with these meanings, particularly being aware of the repetition of relationship patterns. The focus of therapy in a psychodynamic model is towards resolution and developing insight into conflicted ways of being that may be rooted in past experiences.

Behavioural approaches were not as strongly represented in the review of music therapy literature (9%), and often incorporated cognitive behavioural therapy (CBT) as well as more applied strategies. A behavioural stance is aligned with learning theories where the inner life of the teenager is not of primary concern (Ruud 1980), and the therapist instead emphasizes increasing competence in observable behaviours. These behaviours can be taken to represent emotional experiences or cognitive understandings and it is on this basis that the therapist targets behaviours to achieve therapeutic outcomes. In music therapy, this is most easily achieved through the use of music as a positive reinforcer. At the most basic level, demonstrating the requested behaviour results in being able to choose an instrument, listen to selected music, or some other musical reward. Failure to behave in the expected way leads to withdrawal of the music until the required behaviour is achieved. Cognitive behavioural strategies are suitable when a higher degree of intellectual functioning is possible, and music is used to clarify the teenager's intended approach to a challenging situation, providing positive reinforcement of positive thinking. Songwriting can be used to articulate a strategy for action and music making is used to help focus on appropriate social interactions and identify less useful patterns of interaction. Contemporary application of behavioural strategies is usually within a more eclectic framework, where it is not uncommon to require young people to stop playing because their behaviour is out of control, or where particular behaviours result in having more, or fewer, opportunities to control the session. Improvements are usually the focus of sessions and these are closely monitored through observable responses.

In between a focus on observable behaviours and unconscious workings is the middle ground of broadly humanistic approaches. For the purposes of this review, articles that appeared to have a developmental focus were classified as an adaptation of humanistic thinking for young people with developmental challenges, taking into account their curricular and social needs. According to Kenneth Bruscia (Bruscia 1998a), a developmentally-oriented stance is particularly appropriate when a client's development has been thwarted and the focus of therapy is on facilitating the achievement of all potentials. There is a clear overlap here with the traditional tenets of humanism that emphasize a belief that each person contains the potential and desire for growth as an inherent predisposition (Maslow 1968). Creative Music Therapy and its recent evolution as a music-centred approach (Aigen 2005) has also been classified as broadly humanistic because of its alignment with the ideas of Steiner and the anthroposophic movement in humanistic psychology (Wigram, Pederson and Bonde 2002). Creative experiences are highly regarded in humanistic approaches, and in music therapy this is often seen in a free session plan where the interests of the individual or group dictate the direction of the encounter on any given day. A wide range of musical experiences are available and appropriate on each day, from songwriting to improvisation to shared music listening. There is a lack of judgement or expectation on the part of the therapist, who creates conditions that are supportive of personal growth. The particular way that clients play will be seen as expressive of their unique characteristics and they will be encouraged to develop ideas and skills as a result of that interaction. The clients' choices guide the therapeutic process, from musical interests to particular activities that hold appeal.

HOW IS MUSIC BEING USED IN SESSIONS?

The adolescent music therapy literature review canvassed articles and chapters from a range of countries, and although all had been published in English, this did include authors from Europe and Asia. As a result of this diversity, there was little consensus about the labels used in describing different (or the same) music therapy methods. In addition, the most common music therapy methods are used differently depending on the abilities and interests of the client as well as the orientation of the therapist. Despite these linguistic challenges, an inductive analysis revealed that four main groups of methods could be identified based on the type of musical material used:

- musical games
- live songs – including choosing, singing, playing and writing
- improvisation – including instrumental and vocal
- pre-recorded music – including listening, discussion and relaxation.

It is not possible to provide a consensus definition for each of these categorizations, or even for each element of them. Improvisation, arguably the most common method in music therapy practice, is an excellent example of how complex this classification can be. At a technical level, improvisation can be explained as the use of instruments, the voice and other media for spontaneously creating musical sounds (although non-musical sounds are also acceptable). It contrasts with the approach to musical playing used in the classroom to emphasize perfecting pre-composed musical material – 'playing by heart' as it is often called in English (Wigram 2004). In the therapy context, improvisation does not require improvement and practice; instead, it utilizes the freely expressive capacity of music. Because of this, clients often use untuned or modified instruments in order to achieve immediate success in their music making (Bruscia 1987). At the very least, traditional notions of harmony are frequently discarded. However, music therapists use this method differently depending on their orientation. For those identifying with a psychodynamic approach, improvisation provides material for interpretation and projection of unconscious drives. From a humanistic perspective, it provides opportunities for success because it is not possible to play a 'wrong' note and therefore complete acceptance is guaranteed. The use of improvisation by a behaviouralist is based on opportunities to play freely that have been earned through other achievements. It is clear that the definition of improvisation used by each of these practitioners would vary. The methods chapters in Parts Two and Three of this book acknowledge these distinguishing influences and discuss musical strategies in terms of the therapist's approach rather than proposing different methods based on the challenges faced by the client.

In identifying the methods used in the articles reviewed, the descriptions were deductively classified into the four categories noted, based on the use of live songs, improvisation, pre-recorded music and musical games. It is important to note that most music therapists were not describing the use of only one method in their sessions with adolescents. Of the 110 authors that disclosed their methods, two methods were used on average. This most commonly involved a combination of songs (found in 65% of the articles) and improvisation (found in 63% of the articles). Pre-recorded music was also used quite often (found in 46% of articles), while music and movement or musical games were less frequently documented (12%). The lesser emphasis on this final categorization can be seen as a strength of practice, since the research of Christian Gold and colleagues (2007)

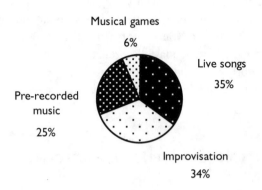

Figure 1.3: Range of music therapy methods used with adolescents

shows that the use of discipline-specific music therapy techniques is more effective than the inclusion of other play-based strategies.

In terms of how these methods were used in music therapy sessions with adolescents, the literature reflected an emphasis on individual rather than group work. Of the 96 articles that were specific about this, 59 per cent described individual work compared to 38 per cent that described group work. A combination of both, or family and individual work, represented the remaining 3 per cent. In the individual sessions, 27 articles described using only one method, and this was fairly evenly spread over songs (9), improvisation (11) and pre-recorded music (7). For groups there were some differences, the most noteworthy being that pre-recorded music was the most common strategy when the articles focused on using only one, with very few (2) describing a purely improvisational focus. Improvisation was more commonly used as one in a number of methods, and the use of improvisation, songs and pre-recorded music being nearly equal when more than one method was used. The use of dance and musical games occurred only in group, rather than individual, contexts.

The emphasis on individual work is surprising given the importance of peer relationships to teenagers. The knowledge that music therapy authors are publishing on highly vulnerable, institutionalized young people may impact on this figure. Working in hospitals often occurs bed-side for example, making group work difficult to coordinate, particularly in an ongoing way. There is also a trend within the field of eating disorders to reduce inter-personal contact between young women in institutions since there is a documented tendency to share secrets about hiding food and foiling weight gain attempts (Beaumont, Russell and Touyz 1993). The emphasis on individual work may also reflect a desire to communicate the nuance of work with one fascinating client, where group work with teenagers can be challenging to describe, particularly in terms of outcomes.

WHAT CONDITIONS CHALLENGE ADOLESCENT CLIENTS IN MUSIC THERAPY?

It has been established that many of the clients we work with are 'in crisis' or grappling with the serious impact of ongoing illness or disability. In examining the different conditions challenging adolescents in the music therapy literature, it was possible to discern five main categories. These were:

- physical illness

- mental illness

- disability

- emotional and behavioural problems

- 'at risk' teenagers.

As with previous classifications, there were some difficulties related to the language used in different cultures for describing various challenges. In addition, depending on the nature of the setting in which a young person was described, there was some overlap, particularly between emotional and behavioural problems and mental illness. The first episode of psychosis is likely to occur during adolescence, and may have been pre-dated by a range of unusual behaviours that were considered to be problematic, or classified as emotional behavioural disorders prior to a diagnosis of mental illness. Another linguistic challenge is that a learning disorder can also be classified as either a disability or a behavioural disorder, and in this review such disorders were classified along with the emotional and behavioural problems because of the similarity of presentation, despite the fact that these young people were often seen in school settings. Different groups of professionals also perceive more or less value in the use of labels such as diagnosis – for some they are a useful tool in providing access to the most helpful services, for others they reduce the individual to a code and fail to account for the unique variations experienced by that person, not to mention his or her family, cultural and historical context. Some of the literature described a range of challenges within one article, and others described adolescents generally, without relating the material to any particular group. The strongest influence on the establishment of the categories was to make them as broad and generic as possible. The following table describes which specific disabilities/illnesses/disorders and circumstances were categorized together.

Table 1.2: Classification of challenges faced by adolescent clients in music therapy

Category	Number of articles	Range of conditions classified
Disability	31	Developmental disability/intellectual disability, Down's syndrome, physical disability such as cerebral palsy, multiple and profound disabilities, vision impairment, autistic spectrum disorder, hearing impairment, brain injury
Mental illness	28	Eating disorders (including anorexia, bulimia, body image issues), pervasive refusal syndrome, elective mutism, borderline personality disorder, post traumatic stress disorder, depression, anxiety
Emotional and behavioural problems	25	Behaviour disorder, 'maladjusted', juvenile delinquency, emotional behavioural disorder, conduct disorder, sex offence, substance misuse, aggression, learning disabilities including attention deficit hyperactivity disorder and school phobia
Illness	22	Cancer, coma, rehabilitation, traumatic brain injury, burns, chronic illness, terminal illness, muscular dystrophy
At-risk	21	Experience of trauma, dislocation, abuse, bereavement, unplanned pregnancy

The expectation that most of the adolescent clients who access music therapy are in crisis was supported by this analysis, with mental illness and illness making up nearly 40 per cent of those described. Young people with disabilities and behavioural problems make up another significant group (44%). In each group a range of severity is represented, from mild to profound, and this has a significant impact upon the setting in which teenagers are seen.

This review confirmed what most music therapists might expect to see as the most traditional client groups – teenagers with disabilities and those with mental illness – as seen in Table 1.3 where the reviewed articles are split by both setting and condition. What is surprising is the number of young people with mental illness that are being served (and written about) in hospital settings. The medical orientation of paediatric hospitals is not ideal for these young people and yet it is clear that there is both increasing need and increasing interest on the part of professionals to support teenagers in crisis within the hospital system. The demise of institutionalization for young people with mental illness has been an important achievement in many countries; however, the economic rationalism of the time has been less helpful in providing responsive and supportive services in the community. Other institutions may have therefore taken up the slack.

Table 1.3: Settings and conditions for music therapy work with adolescents

	Disability	Mental illness	At-risk	Illness	Behavioural problems	Total
Educational settings	19	1	4		7	31
Hospital		20	4	23		47
Institutional programmes	7	4			14	25
Community programmes	4	3	10		3	20
Total	30	28	18	23	24	123

WHAT IS THE PURPOSE OF MUSIC THERAPY?

The literature on music therapy with adolescents has many functions and each piece of literature provided different types of information. Relatively few focused on the treatment plan, in which assessment, planning, treatment and evaluation strategies are outlined (Davis, Gfeller and Thaut 1999). More articles focused on case studies with descriptive outcomes, and some combined knowledge from clinical practice with external theories without using a single case to illustrate. In order to ascertain the clinical purpose of music therapy, the goals, aims, outcomes and intentions described in

101 articles were pooled. Most of this material described working towards a number of outcomes for clients, rather than focusing on only one goal, and even within the categories created it was common for at least two types of outcomes to be sought. In analysing this information as a whole, the two main foci of music therapy work appear to be deeply personal, involving both inter-personal (social) and intra-personal (identity formation) dimensions. Summed together, aims that were focused toward either social or identity formation outcomes were documented in 57 per cent of the articles, with 46 per cent of all articles identifying both purposes. This dominant focus was not dependent on the orientation of the therapist. Social and identity related goals comprised 75 per cent of the goals of pure behaviouralists;[1] around 58 per cent of the goals of the psychodynamic therapists; and 38 per cent of the humanistic and developmentally oriented therapists (whose intentions were more evenly spread across physical, cognitive and creative goals as well). Taken together, this shows that many music therapists of all orientations were focusing on their clients achieving goals that improved their understanding of themselves and/or their relationships with others. Further cementing the centrality of social and identity driven goals is the fact that this was evenly spread across the different client groups – being the first and second most common goal across each categorization of the conditions challenging teenagers, except those with disability, where physical and cognitive goals were described as equally important.

The purposes classified under the label of identity formation were often easily recognizable by the use of the word 'self'. Different authors expressed the nuance of this focus in varying ways – self-expression, self-concept, self-esteem, self-awareness, self-confidence, self-knowledge, self-regulation and sense of self. The orientation of the therapist had some influence over the detail of this description, as did the setting where music therapy took place and the type of information being shared. Yet the dominance of 'self' is clear and neatly aligned with the psychosocial task of adolescence proposed by Erikson (1963) of identity formation. Although this was the most common type of purpose across all client groups (except teenagers with disabilities, where it was third), it was clear that this was the goal of choice for 'at-risk' teenagers, being noted in 88 per cent of articles on this topic. It was also significant in mental health, with 85 per cent of the articles

---

1   Remembering that many of the therapists had a blended or eclectic orientation to practice, so only those who were firmly grounded in one approach have been included in these figures.

about teenagers who were challenged by mental illness rating identity formation as the purpose of music therapy.

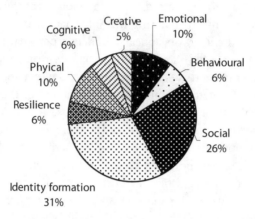

Figure 1.4: The purpose of music therapy with adolescents

Although slightly less commonly noted than identity, social goals were also evenly spread across all types of clients. More than 50 per cent of all articles noted this purpose, with the exception of teenagers facing medical challenges, where their illness suggested a stronger focus on individual identity and physical improvements. Overall, the types of goals classified as social were more varied, and incorporated achievements ranging from basic communication to group cohesion. The conditions challenging the adolescents had a much stronger influence over the nature of these purposes. Teenagers who had multiple and profound disabilities needed to focus on the achievement of awareness, eye contact and vocalizations as precursors to more complex communication. In contrast, the nature of social interaction for teenagers who were more cognitively capable was relationship oriented and included achievements such as engagement, cohesion and awareness. These more advanced inter-personal dynamics have political, rather than functional dimensions, and mirror the kinds of social achievements that adults strive for in the workplace, in families and within communities.

Physical and emotional purposes were equally represented in the data, and often overlapped. Both anxiety and relaxation have physical and emotional dimensions and for the purposes of this review were classified into one or the other grouping, depending on the specific nature of the outcomes expressed. When described in the context of pain reduction and motor control, the anxiety- and relaxation-related goals were categorized as physical. In addition, many of the descriptions of relaxation and physical well-being in the psychiatric context emphasized the physical dimension. Other kinds of physical goals included physical control and coordination for teenagers with disabilities, those in rehabilitation programmes, and for the babies of young mothers who were also accessing social supports through music therapy programmes. Physical goals were addressed by therapists from all orientations and comprised a significant proportion of the goals in music therapy with teenagers who had both disabilities (43%) and physical illness (47%).

When the purpose of music therapy was categorized as 'emotional', the most common explanation was linked to expression of emotions related to the challenges faced by the adolescent clients. This was almost exclusively identified in the intentions of psychodynamic therapists, and it was rare for emotional goals to be addressed outside this approach. The specific emotion being targeted was sometimes named, and was most often anger or sadness, but interestingly, never happiness. Emotional goals were also related to improving and regulating mood and affect when described in a psychiatric context. As noted above, anxiety and relaxation were classified as emotional when the descriptions were related to specific experiences and the psychological context.

Cognitive and behavioural purposes were each represented in 6 per cent of the articles that articulated clinical intentions, indicating a far lower priority within music therapy programmes. Cognitive purposes were most often related to attention and focus, which could equally be classified as behavioural, potentially increasing the behavioural category to around 12 per cent. The other behavioural purposes varied between settings, with hospital-based professionals emphasizing compliance, those based in educational settings focusing on increasing tolerance and impulse control, while socially-oriented improvements were sought in the context of mental illness. It is noteworthy that when clients were classified as having behavioural problems, behaviourally-oriented goals were only noted in 27 per cent of those articles.

The various goals and outcomes drawn together under the topic of creativity were equally divided between general descriptions of creative expression and the achievement of musical skills. Creative expression was never listed as the primary focus; however, it was sometimes central to more behaviourally-oriented programmes where the acquisition of musical skills was the targeted behaviour. Learning to play an instrument is not a common goal in music therapy, and none of the authors saw this as an end unto itself. Acquiring musical skills was seen as a means to achieve psycho-social goals. This is one of the main ways that music therapy differs from both community music and music education.

The purpose of music therapy as enhancing 'resilience' was almost exclusively noted by therapists who maintained a psychodynamic orientation and was noted in only 6 per cent of the total literature. Although resilience is a prominent topic within adolescent health, analysis of the literature suggests that music therapists have not drawn extensively on this construct. Yet music has consistently been identified as one of the main strategies that teenagers use to cope (Frydenberg 2008), along with sport, friends and television. Access to resources that assist the young person to cope is seen as one of the major influences on coping, outside of individual traits. It may have a more relevant role to play than music therapists have considered thus far.

WHAT CAN WE LEARN FROM THIS?

The literature on music therapy with adolescents seems to represent a very conventional model of practice. The finding that most adolescents are seen in institutional settings is remarkable within a social context that emphasizes de-insitutionalization. This finding is matched by the emphasis on psychodynamic practice, a model which feminists argue represents a further power imbalance between the therapist – who is more skilled in making 'interpretations' – and the client – who needs the therapist's help (McLellan 1995). In contrast, contemporary models of practice that have been popular in the adolescent literature emphasize ideas such as resilience, strengths-based practice, and the pursuit of happiness. These concepts are aimed towards fostering internal and enduring capacities in the young person that are not dependent upon an ongoing therapeutic relationship. Randi Rolsjvord's model of resource-oriented music therapy practice (Rolvsjord, Gold and Stige 2005) addresses many of these ideas within an institutional context and provides a relevant framework for music therapists. Her model also helps to address the lack of indigenous theory[2] that is available about how music therapy works with adolescents.

The focus on identity formation and social skills is a positive outcome of this traditional orientation to music therapy with teenagers. 'Who am I?' is an important question to be addressed throughout life, but it gains prominence during this stage of peak intellectual and physical capacity. The emphasis on the unique adolescent, as seen by the use of the word 'self', is a direct response to this question and it is a clear priority from the perspective of music therapists. Music has a natural role to play in this process and has long been used by teenagers as a way of expressing themselves and asserting their identity (see Chapter 3 for further discussion). In envisaging more contemporary developments in the music therapy discipline, this aspect could be even more heavily emphasized in the literature.

The dominance of individual work also reflects a traditional approach to practice, once again emphasizing the importance of private relationships with the therapist over peer-oriented relationships. Group work is a powerful model of work in adolescence, but it does come with many challenges, not least of which is dealing with the chaos of a group of teenagers making music. The crisis model that is being presented in this body of literature probably explains the emphasis on individual work, and the most vulnerable clients are perhaps not ready to consider how their crisis exists in context until they have grappled with its personal repercussions.

Eclectic practice is strongly represented in all aspects of the literature review. Blended orientations, multiple methods, numerous purposes and various settings constitute the discussion of music therapy practice with adolescents. A recent meta-review of the literature on children and adolescents with psychopathology (Gold, Voracek and Wigram 2004) associated an eclectic approach to music therapy practice with the most significant results, suggesting that this is best practice in the field. Although a blended, eclectic model is both best practice and a true representation of music therapy practice, it is not useful in answering the question of how best to work with adolescents in music therapy. The systematic review of the literature outlined here provides a foundation for approaching this question.

---

2   This phrase was coined by Aigen (1991) to describe theory that has emerged from understandings of music therapy rather than from allied fields such as psychology and medicine.

Music therapy methods provide the means with which we work with adolescent clients. They distinguish our professional practice in contrast to our colleagues, and as far as most adolescents are concerned, they are quite simply *what* we are there for – to do music, or what Christopher Small has labelled 'musicking' (Small 1998). As a discipline, music therapy is more focused on *why* we do what we do – what is the purpose? The way that we understand *how* to combine what we do (methods) with why we do it (intentions) is impacted upon by our orientation as a music therapist. This incorporates our essential beliefs about the value of therapeutic relationships. This review identified three traditional theoretical approaches from the discipline of psychology that were relevant for categorizing the orientations of music therapists as described in the literature. In the following chapter, and for the remainder of this book, these orientations will be clearly linked to the intention of individual music therapists and the stance that they adopt in their approach to teenagers – how they act. A largely psychodynamic orientation will be linked to an intention to foster understandings in the young person in order to promote resilience; a humanistic orientation will lead the music therapist to offering acceptance to the teenager in order to encourage identity formation; and a behavioural orientation will focus the music therapist on facilitating the adolescent's development in order to increase competence (see Figure 2.1 in Chapter 2). It is my view that clarity of intention is essential in 'doing' music therapy with teenagers. With this in hand, music therapists can decide *how* to do music on a given day in response to a given client. *What* they do will be grounded in their beliefs about *why* they are doing it.

Chapter 2

The Real Deal on How to Work with Adolescents

Developing a trusting relationship with teenagers is the focus of this chapter. I have adopted a personal and casual voice for this discussion, because I consider authenticity and transparency to be critical to this approach. The opinions offered are based on my clinical work, research and discussions with teenagers in music therapy. They are mostly designed for those who are unsure about how to approach young people. They are in no way meant to represent 'best practice'; merely my practice and experiences.

Working with teenagers is a messy business. Trying to simplify the way that this work takes place is neither authentic nor feasible. Synthesizing the literature on music therapy with adolescents is a straightforward process yielding interesting results that should inform practice. An approach to being a music therapist who enjoys working with teenagers is a separate discussion. It is raw and real. In my experience, there are four things to keep in mind:

- You never know what's going on.
- The only thing you can know is yourself.
- It helps to put yourself on the Map (explained below).
- Where you locate yourself on the Map can vary (on a given day, with a given teenager, with the same teenager on the same day...).

This chapter will provide a Map for doing music therapy with adolescents. The Map is more of a security blanket than a guarantee. It can provide much needed reassurance in moments of crisis and then be discarded completely on the days when you are striding ahead, full of confidence, with destination in sight and mind. The Map supports the provision of blended, eclectic practice with adolescents that is ultimately grounded in flexibility and creativity. Professionals who enjoy working with teenagers are usually accomplished in both of these attributes.

Working with teenagers is dynamic work. One definition of dynamic is 'active and changing: characterized by vigorous activity and producing or undergoing change and development' (UK Encarta Dictionary 2009). This definition captures a session with adolescents for me. An alternative definition from the same source captures what is critical for me as a professional working with teenagers: 'vigorous and purposeful: full of energy, enthusiasm and a sense of purpose and able both to get things going and to get things done.' In this section, I will reflect on the first definition and in the following I will focus on the second. Both are very important.

YOU NEVER KNOW WHAT'S GOING ON

In my experience of working with teenagers it is rare to have a firm and confident sense of what is going on. I frequently leave a session wondering 'what just happened?' and it is only in writing up progress notes that I begin to see patterns or make interpretations that restore my confidence. This has been a constant state over my years of working with teenagers. The big picture of working with teenagers is very positive. Music rarely fails to engage their interest, at least momentarily. The musical material in sessions is constantly changing and it is stimulating to work with popular and contemporary genres. The young people I have worked with have a lot in common, despite the various conditions they are challenged by. They are initially defensive, then quickly open and vulnerable. They enjoy attention and praise. The energy, or 'vigorous activity', of teenagers is inspiring and the older I get, the more I admire it. But if I reflect on individual moments, normal moments in the non-extraordinary weeks of working with groups or individual teenagers, I feel less settled. It is common for me to feel as though nothing is being achieved. There are long patches in my work with teenagers where I struggle not to take it personally. I can be plagued by insecurity. Perhaps they hate me. Perhaps I am boring.

'Miss, this is boring. Can I go now?'

In short, working with teenagers means that I am constantly returning to my own adolescence. There is nothing in the adult world that quite matches the intensity of being with adolescents. An act as simple as 'entering a room' is enough to trigger a whole range of self-conscious responses in the land of teenagers. Actually having a meaningful interaction without the safety net of teasing and joking is nearly impossible to conceive, at least in the Australian context. To be with adolescents in their normal state demands that the therapist is comfortable to re-engage with these experiences. This sense is particularly strong in groups, but it is also present to some degree in individual interactions. Conceptually, I enjoy working through issues related to my own adolescence on a regular basis. Sometimes this is in formal supervision, sometimes in peer debriefing, and sometimes inside my own head. After 15 years of working with teenagers, this part of the experience has changed very little and yet the constant state of adolescents as self-conscious and paranoid (in a non-pathological way) is wearing. This aspect of adolescence means that teenagers do not usually indicate whether sessions have been helpful. As Bilides (1992) says, 'Few of them will come up to you and say, "thanks, that was a really good group, I got a lot out of it"' (p.143). It can be difficult to observe and assess the change and development that is anticipated. Teenagers are usually pretty busy being cool.

Although the value of music therapy is not always obvious in daily work with adolescents, I have been convinced over time that it definitely is worthwhile. As a clinical researcher, I have interviewed a large number of adolescents about their experiences of music therapy. Some of these young people have been my own clients and I have drawn upon the trust built up in our therapeutic relationship to encourage them to be honest and authentic in their sharing with me. They have made many touching statements, some of which are listed here.

> 'Music therapy helps to get it off my chest, it's a truth serum.' (15-year-old girl)

> 'The group gave me a lot more spirit 'cos I got to be destructive and express my feelings.' (14-year-old boy)

> 'It just basically broke the seal on the fridge that's closed until somebody decides to open it.' (15-year-old boy)

> 'It was important to just keep together to make the music sound better and there were times where we sort of actually made

> something that was really good – like a really famous person.'
> (15-year-old girl)

> 'You could tell that they were feeling like you when we made the
> music and you didn't have to worry about whether or not people
> will think it was any good.' (16-year-old boy)

> 'Music therapy lets your expression come out.' (14-year-old girl)

> 'I didn't like the girls' music and if they didn't like mine, well they
> can go jump.' (15-year-old boy)

In other projects I have had no existing relationship with the young people
I am interviewing and I have taken the opportunity to really dig into
the authenticity of their responses. I have asked what they didn't like
about music therapy. I have challenged their positive interpretations and
suggested that it sounds too good to be true. Invariably they refuse to
concede. They highlight the importance of the opportunities for emotional
expression. They describe feeling connected to other people in their music
making. They describe how much fun it was. They say that it has changed
their life.

> 'I used to keep a lot of things in, just to myself … And I think
> I did it all the way up until the three weeks of the music group.'
> (14-year-old boy)

> 'I was amazed. And I said to Mum "this music group's really, really
> helped me a lot".' (14-year-old girl)

> 'It was really good. I wasn't concentrating on anything that was
> going around outside of school and I was just concentrating on
> what's happening and since I've been going to music therapy I've
> realized that "what's the point?" It's over, it's my life now. I can do
> whatever I want and concentrate on the future.' (15-year-old girl)

Young people do not make comments like these in music therapy sessions.
I have only rarely had the opportunity to work with an individual teenager
who has engaged in an insight-oriented discussion and shared reflections
on the therapeutic process, and this has never happened in any group
that I have facilitated. Yet some of these comments were shared in focus
group interviews, with two or three teenagers present. Scott Miller and
colleagues suggest that psychotherapists should solicit this information
from clients more regularly (Duncan, Miller and Sparks 2007). It is useful

not only to get the kind of positive feedback that will not be forthcoming in the session itself, but also to see if there are changes that could be made to improve the quality of the programme. Seeking client feedback is not common practice in music therapy, or in psychotherapy, but research suggests that it may be more feasible than it appears.

THE ONLY THING YOU CAN KNOW IS YOURSELF

The teenager is determined to be masked, but the music therapist is transparent. For every inch of defence held by young people, the music therapist should be prepared to reach forward dynamically, with 'vigor and purpose' to engage them. Teenagers are not holding back because they do not need help, they are trying to work out if you can be trusted. Teenagers have good reason to behave like this. The school ground is a complicated place where bullying and betrayal occur regularly (known as politics and business in the adult world). They need proof, and all the music therapist has to offer is a clear sense of purpose and a willingness to get stuff done. This needs to be made clear through a consistent and authentic presentation of self. Not unflappable. Not in control. Not cool. Just real.

When a music therapist is responding to a group of young people, there are a number of valid choices available that reflect an authentic state:

- Stay calm – don't get caught up in the fact that the chaos and lack of clarity is vaguely disturbing. Just set up the musical interaction and then watch, listen and interact.

- Go with it – match the energy and enjoy the ride. Bounce ideas around and be a part of the experience. Be prepared, because things may get a little out of control.

- Stay one step ahead – use the music to keep them interested and engaged. Intuit the challenges as they emerge on the horizon and take steps to keep things on course. Music is a flexible friend that way.

I suspect that each of us has a natural affinity with one of these ways of responding to adolescents. As therapists, we have the full repertoire of responses available to us and we will draw on different ways of being depending on our judgement in any given moment. Being consistent and authentic is not about being rigid; it is about being responsive. But there will be one way of responding that occurs more often and feels more comfortable.

Clarity regarding a preferred way of being with teenagers is the greatest asset a music therapist can have in working with adolescents. It is the first clear sign on the Map. The teenager does not particularly care which one of these stances is adopted, as long as it is clear and respectful of them. They will trust you more quickly if it is flexible but consistent. Andrew Malekoff describes this as being both 'fluid and grounded' (Malekoff 1997, p.20) and recommends that adolescents need a worker who does not give up. 'As much as they love to dish it out, teens appreciate an adult who, if momentarily rattled, can take it in their stride and in good humour' (p.22). What many teenagers have not experienced is an adult who can engage with adolescents without behaving like a parent or a teacher; after all, most adolescents have ample access to parental and teacher responses. The music therapist's role needs to be different. It is creative of course, but many people who work with teenagers are creative. What music therapy offers is the combination of those two words – music and therapy. This book addresses *how* to do the music side of things. But a confident understanding of one's own therapeutic stance fundamentally informs *why* these musical interactions take place. It is important that music therapists do not forget that whatever is going on in their music therapy session with teenagers – it is probably not about them.

A good example of why this is true is related to the myth that you need to be young and hip to work with teenagers. This could not be further from the truth. For a start, no one over 25 is young or hip. It is simply impossible from the perspective of a 13-year-old. The music therapist simply needs to be authentic. Just as sharks can smell blood in the water, so a teenager can smell an adult who is trying to be cool. It is quite a different thing to be confident, however, and teenagers appreciate an adult who is comfortable with him or herself and is young in spirit. Andrew Malekoff (1997) also has a memorable way of describing a way of being with adolescents. He suggests leaving one's ego outside the door and picking it up on the way back out. All that is needed in the room is a good sense of humour, an ability to not take oneself too seriously and a genuine intention to be helpful. I would add that it helps to take some music in there too.

IT HELPS TO PUT YOURSELF ON THE MAP

It helps to be authentic and to know your own most preferred way of being with teenagers. This is the first position on the Map. The second position locates that way of being within a theoretical framework. The different responses outlined above can be aligned with the three psychological theories identified as most influential in the music therapy literature – psychodynamic, humanistic and behavioural. Placing yourself on the theoretical territory of the Map can be useful at times, particularly on the days where your own adolescent insecurities are making you question yourself.

'What am I doing here? This isn't working at all. I am hopeless. Maybe I should quit.'

Psychodynamic therapists maintain a calm stance in order to provide a blank slate for the client to project upon. Although the old-fashioned approach of sitting quietly and waiting for the client to speak is extremely unpopular with teenagers, a more active engagement that still offers containment and stability can achieve the same results.

Stay calm – Psychodynamic orientation

Humanistic therapists are much more focused on being present with the client and offering unconditional positive regard. Once again, this looks different in music therapy with adolescents. Instead of listening and agreeing, it involves energy and creativity in order to meet the clients where they are. Depending on the teenager, this may be loud or quiet, but it is always about being right there.

Go with it – Humanistic orientation

Behavioural therapists have more of a plan and they take purposeful steps towards achieving their target. Music is a powerful motivator for teenagers and utilizing this capacity does not feel mechanical or dull. Musical engagement is fun but organized.

Stay one step ahead – Behavioural orientation

It also helps to know what you are offering the teenager. Clarity about what the young person may be able to achieve from music therapy is critical in shaping the session to accomplish such outcomes. Taking the connection between orientation and stance one step further, it is possible to suggest a dominant intention for each perspective.

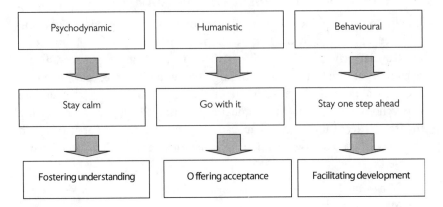

Figure 2.1: A Map of the relationship between the therapist's orientation, stance and intention in conventional music therapy

The intentions suggested here are broadly aligned with the purposes of music therapy identified in the review of the literature. Music therapists traditionally work towards deeply personal outcomes that involve the adolescent self as well as adolescents in relation to their peers, and occasionally their families. What is missing from the Map is a fourth strand of therapeutic approach that is grounded in an ecological orientation (Bronfenbrenner 2005). This involves seeing adolescents as embedded in more distant layers of meaning, from friends and family to the institutions that they are connected to, the culture and community that they exist in, as well as the expectations of adolescence that they are subjected to. This theoretical approach to practice has been noted (Bruscia 1998a; Stige 2002a), but it does not yet have a conspicuous presence in the music therapy literature. When added to the Map it can be expanded to encompass not only what music therapy with adolescents *is* according to the literature, but also what it *can be* at a theoretical level (Stige 2002a, 2003b, 2009), or how it can be at a practical level.

One final dimension completes the 'Map of how music therapy can be with adolescents'. Four popular constructs from adolescent health have been included in Figure 2.2 to clarify what outcomes result for teenagers as a result of the particular approach adopted by the music therapist. These will be detailed in the following chapter through the presentation of defining features as well as identifying how music, in particular, is utilized to achieve these outcomes in everyday life.

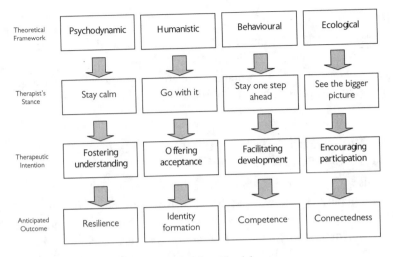

Figure 2.2: The Map of how music therapy can be with adolescents

WHERE YOU LOCATE YOURSELF ON THE MAP CAN VARY

Positioning on the Map is a personal decision and it can vary between teenagers, for the same teenager on different days and even for the same teenager at different points of the session. Each individual music therapist will also have her or his own inclination and this may also vary somewhat over time and in response to the work setting, as well as in direct relationship to the teenager or group. In this way it is informed by one's own natural stance and beliefs about what works in therapy, and should be combined with an assessment of the most relevant model to the teenager or the group of adolescents in question. My own personal inclination is towards offering acceptance, since I believe in the inherent potential of individuals to grow given supportive conditions. This is undoubtedly informed by my training under Denise Grocke at the University of Melbourne during the early 1990s, who previously trained under Professor Bob Unkefer at Michigan State University in the late 1960s and whom she describes as humanistic in orientation. Training has an impact on the beliefs that we develop about how music therapy works. So does our prior education, our familial beliefs and our experiences, all of which occur within a cultural context. In fact, it is simplistic, but possible, to make an educated guess about what orientation a music therapist is most likely informed by based on the nation he or she trained in. But of course, there are many exceptions to these kinds of broad cultural generalizations, and they are only of passing interest. What is most important is the capacity for the teenager and the therapist to establish an affiliation. Brynjulf Stige (2002a, 2003a) describes music therapy as 'the performance of relationship' and when working with teenagers, this performance involves negotiation and collaboration.

THE BLENDED ECLECTIC MODEL OF MUSIC THERAPY WITH ADOLESCENTS

The use of psychological models as the structure for the 'Map of how music therapy can be with adolescents' is neither new, nor perfect. Even Ruud first identified the three conventional 'treatment models' in 1978 when he described how music therapy was related to psychoanalysis, existentialism and behaviouralism. Models specific to the discipline of music therapy have been proposed since that time, some of which are indigenous[1] to music therapy practice, and some which are appropriations of models from psychology, social work or education. Kenneth Bruscia outlined 25 music therapy models in 1987, and an attempt to create a taxonomy of contemporary models of music therapy in the first decade of the twenty-first century would easily double this number. Despite the fact that some music therapy textbooks explicitly link models and theoretical frameworks (e.g. Wigram *et al.* 2002), it seems likely that the degree to which individual music therapists are familiar with each of these models may be closely related to their cultural background (Schapira 2003). Many models are well known locally, but few have gained wide acceptance and understanding across the discipline internationally. Some indigenous models are delineated by music therapy theorists who provide rigorous rationales for their proposal. Others are practical models that rely on explanations of what to do and draw loosely on theories from other fields to explain their approach. It is possible to attach some music therapy models to the Map provided above (Figure 2.2), although it is unapologetically limited by my own interest in, and familiarity with, different ideas (Table 2.1).

---

[1]   This phrase was coined by Aigen (1991) to describe theory that has emerged from understandings of music therapy rather than from allied fields such as psychology and medicine.

Table 2.1: Illustrating how some music therapy models can be understood in context of the 'Map of how music therapy can be with adolescents'

Psychodynamic	Humanistic	Behavioural	Ecological
Analytic music therapy	Music-centered music therapy	Neurologic music therapy	Community music therapy
Bonny method of guided imagery and music	Free music therapy	Cognitive behavioural music therapy	Feminist music therapy
Benenzon's music therapy	Resource-oriented music therapy	Medical music therapy	Culture-centred music therapy

As noted in Chapter 1, the meta-analysis conducted by Christian Gold and colleagues (Gold *et al.* 2004) leads to the conclusion that an eclectic, blended model is the most effective approach to music therapy with adolescents. This confirms that there is no need for a music therapist to identify purely with one approach in practice. It suggests that we should be guided by what best suits the adolescent in the moment. As an experienced clinician, I can honestly say that I may foster understanding, offer acceptance, facilitate development or encourage participation depending on my assessment of the adolescent in context in any given moment. This does not mean that I rigidly adhere to a single approach once I have assessed it as most suitable for the individual or group, nor do I switch between approaches at a rapid tempo. I adopt a dominant orientation that is informed by my initial assessment of their needs and the ways that I am best able to address them within the bounds of my own resources and limitations. This often changes over time as our relationship improves and I acquire a better understanding of their capacity and interests and what music therapy may be able to offer. This may be regarded as an Australian perspective, since Ruth Bright (2002) has advocated for an eclectic, supportive approach to grief and loss work, and Jane Edwards (2002) has briefly noted a pluralistic approach to practice as common in Australian contexts. However, a 'plurimodal' method is also advocated in South America by Diego Schapira and Mayra Hugo (Schapira and Hugo 2005), which suggests that eclecticism has international relevance.

Flexibility and creativity in our approach to working with adolescents is the trademark of music therapy. What is important to note, however, is that when adopting an eclectic approach it is relatively easy for the music therapist to write a set of goals and objectives for a treatment plan that facilitates development, and then act in a way that fosters understanding of unconscious influences within a session. This is not a disaster, particularly if the change of approach is responsive to the presenting needs of the teenager. However, when the time to evaluate the programme arrives, the music therapist may find that there is no development in observable skills, since these were not actually the focus of the sessions. Music therapy can be very effective, but the mere presence of the music therapist does not lead to the development of skills. A well designed and rigorously implemented music therapy treatment programme certainly can.

An example can be drawn from work with adolescents in special education. This setting typically has an overarching behavioural orientation, and assessment strategies are usually focused on observable outcomes as evidence of achievement. A music therapist in this setting will usually develop goals and objectives that focus on the *development* of said observable skills – for example, increased attention span as seen by greater lengths of time spent playing instruments or without moving from seats. But what happens when teenagers leave their seats to participate on unexpected instruments in the corner of the room? Does the music therapist stop playing, ask them to return to their seats, and offer to provide the second instrument at the conclusion of the song (a behaviourally informed response)? Or does the music therapist note the time spent in the chair prior to the action and consider strategies for increasing this in future sessions, such as making the desired object available within the activity (a cognitively informed response)? Does the music therapist accept this change of focus and move fluidly into a musical encounter with the young people on the new instruments (a humanistically informed response)? Does she/he consider how this kind of behaviour represents a rejection or affirmation of the dominant culture, either at the level of the school or the region, and respond accordingly (a culturally informed response)? Does the music therapist comment on the teenagers' need to challenge the rules, and contemplate the meaning of this refusal to remain in-chair, as well as the possible significance of the new instruments – what do these represent to each young person (a psychodynamically informed response)? Does she encourage the initiative and the creative expression that results from this action, by adopting an approach that is strengths-based (a resource-oriented perspective)? Does the music therapist investigate the interest shown in the instruments and consider how this could be used to participate in activities beyond the session (a community music therapy perspective)?

To adopt a blended eclectic approach does not suggest that all of these responses could be utilized. It would be confusing and unhelpful for young people if the music therapist responded in one way on one day and then changed his or her response on the next, and then again on the next. The Map suggests that the therapist's stance is ultimately the most useful guide for knowing *how* to do music therapy with teenagers. Although four potential approaches have been outlined, I have suggested that each therapist will feel a stronger affinity with some than others. This provides an important piece of the puzzle, alongside the myriad contextual influences operating on the adolescent and the therapist that are not always as easy to decipher. Consistent flexibility is one way to describe the creative approach adopted by the music therapist who is committed to serving teenagers in a way that best suits them and their circumstances.

Kenneth Bruscia suggests that music therapy, as a discipline, has reached a stage where we must 'discover the specific areas of advantage and disadvantage of each force of thought, and to develop the flexibility needed to apply all of them when appropriate' (Stige 2002a, p.xviii). In embracing new approaches to music therapy for adolescents, there are still some challenges to be articulated and addressed, such as preparing clients for performances (Chapter 10). The vast potential offered by a blended, eclectic approach that offers teenagers an array of creative opportunities that suit their needs in any given moment is worth striving for. As teenagers reach their peak capacity for growth, every opportunity could make a difference. Just don't expect them to thank you for it.

Chapter 3

What is Healthy Adolescence and How does Music Help?

Music fulfils many functions in the lives of teenagers, and one of them is in offering hope and friendship. The relationships between teenagers, their music and their health are not simple to unravel, however it is interesting to consider some of the most relevant concepts. This chapter provides an overview of some key ideas in relation to four elements of adolescent health – resilience, identity formation, competence and connectedness. Some suggestions are made about how, and why, music can help.

The relationship between music and teenagers is extraordinary. At no other time in life does music hold such a central role as it does during adolescence. The average teenager living in the developed world spends approximately two-and-a-half hours per day listening to music – a figure that is hard to believe for most adults, but was a common average across many studies, even before iPods came into existence and made music listening more accessible (Brooks 1989; Brown and Hendee 1989; McFerran *et al.* unpublished; North, Hargreaves and O'Neill 2000). Music is a preferred leisure time activity for teens and has been rated as the most popular unstructured activity (Fitzgerald *et al.* 1995). Although sports often rank highest in nominated leisure interests, music ranks first for indoor activity (at least, indoor activities that the average teenager has access to) (North *et al.* 2000).

So why do teenagers spend so much time engaging with music? This chapter attempts to answer this question from an adolescent health perspective in order to provide a rationale for the use of music with teenagers. The four key elements of adolescent health, as mentioned earlier, are:

- identity formation
- resilience
- competence
- connectedness.

The links between music and these elements are explained. The ways that music is typically used by young people are also described and counter-arguments about possible negative influences of music are considered.

IDENTITY FORMATION

Erik Erikson, a developmental psychologist, was the first to use the term 'identity formation' to explain the primary psychosocial task of the teenage years (Erikson 1963). From Erikson's perspective, healthy progression through adolescence can either be successful – resulting in the formation of a sense of identity – or it can fall into a state of role confusion. The formation of identity hinges upon increasing levels of self-acceptance that have been built up as each previous rite of passage is achieved – an invariant sequence of development as far as Erikson is concerned. Beginning in infancy, the young person needs to answer the questions: who are my support people? (trust vs. mistrust); what can I do on my own? (autonomy vs. shame and doubt); how valid are my ideas? (initiative vs. guilt); and what kind of contribution can I make? (industry vs. inferiority), before reaching the adolescent question: *who am I?* (identity vs. role confusion). Following adolescence, the main purpose of a healthy existence is centred upon forging relationships (intimacy vs. isolation), after which the tasks become mainly reflective: is my contribution valid? (generativity vs. stagnation); and have I really achieved anything worthwhile? (integrity vs. despair). The specific nature of the adolescent question implies an emphasis on career choice and establishing authentic friendships. The first has a futuristic focus, whereas the role of authentic friendships is more current.

Friends serve a particular role during adolescence, providing a mirror for the young person to consider 'what they appear to be in the eyes of others' (Erikson 1963, p.253). Intimate relationships further intensify this reflective property, since more private aspects of the self are shared in romantic relationships. Erikson explains that identity formation is a negotiated process, and the risk of confusion arises when other people do not see young people in the same way that they see themselves. The teenager is seeking equilibrium in these perspectives – for example: I consider myself funny and you laugh at my jokes; I think I am nice and a reasonable number of people want to be friends with me. To make matters more complex, the teenager does not project a stable picture of self. Instead, teenagers can be construed as conducting a series of experiments, manipulating the variables and gathering data. They may try on behaviours and ways of being that are associated with different idols or peer groups. They then monitor reactions, and this information influences the developing personality as it continues to emerge. Teenagers are seeking acceptance of who they are in their various guises.

Music is often utilized by teenagers in these experiments. Even Ruud describes this as the 'performance of identity' (Ruud 1997, p.3), emphasizing that musical preferences reflect the public representation of who we are, making information available to both friends and foe. He suggests that musical choices are as much an expression of what 'I want to be', as they are related to what 'I really am'. This is supported by studies of adolescents who have identified a difference in the music preferences expressed publicly and those that are confessed in private (Finnas 1987; North *et al.* 2000; Tarrant, North and Hargreaves 2000). Simon Frith (1981) explains that this is because music preferences serve a communicative function, expressing values, attitudes and opinions. A teenager who desires acceptance and popularity can easily establish what musical genres will solicit an approved response, and studies show that there is a high level of agreement in what kinds of music are positively, neutrally or negatively stereotyped (Tarrant, North and Hargreaves 2001). A teenager who wishes to stand out and be perceived as different is able to utilize this information to conduct a similar, and yet alternative, experiment. From this perspective it is not the type of preferred music that suggests good health and a successful progression towards identity formation, rather it is whether the teenager gets the reaction he or she is expecting. One study has suggested that having diversity in musical preferences, seen through eclectic tastes, is the best indicator of health precisely because it allows for this kind of flexibility (Schwartz and Fouts 2003). Role confusion is a risk only when teenagers are not satisfied with the response their performance of identity produces. This is most obvious in the case of a teenager who wants to be accepted, but plays isolating and unpopular music that is not in keeping with the trends in his or her community. An inability to alter publicly touted preferences will reinforce the conflict between personal perception and public response which, theoretically, leads to role confusion.

Another obvious use of music as a strategy for manipulating the responses of others is in the process of individuation, involving separation from the primary family unit (Jung 1956). During adolescence, the loyalty previously shown to the family is transferred to the peer group and music is used to lubricate this transfer in many ways. Music can create personal space as well as demonstrate more explicit rebellion against dominant adult ideologies. For younger teens, music listening justifies a move away from shared, patrolled time spent watching the family television. Music is used in this way to 'create walls of sound that repel adults' (Becker 1992, p.78), and provides the space to define oneself as an individual. Young people often retreat to the privacy of their bedrooms to dream of the future and play air guitar, dance and sing (Steinberg 1996, p.273). The loudness of the distorted guitars, the high pitched vocals, and the barely discernible lyrics are all designed to drive away parental interest, keeping involvement at bay and providing an opportunity for individuation.

How adults respond to this message varies significantly. While some may smile and reflect on their own associations with Elvis Presley, Bob Dylan or The Rolling Stones, others may feel inclined to try to control what they perceive to be 'negative' listening habits. Adults in this position often do not realize that it is mostly their lack of familiarity with the genre that is the cause of their concern, and that distorted guitars and screaming voices do not necessarily convey a message of evil. Heavy metal, rock and rap music have come under fire from many domains because of concerns regarding lyrics and other subconscious messages. Investigations of adolescent music preferences often identify a relationship between heavy metal music and emotional disturbance, or rap music and anti-social behaviours (Baker and Bor 2008; Bushong 2002). Yet music therapy research has shown that preferred music can be used to achieve positive shifts in affect for adolescent psychiatric inpatients (Wooten 1992). Bridget Doak (2003) insightfully compares the drug and music preferences of adolescents with mental health problems and suggests that unhappy teenagers use both for self-medicating, with music offering a strategy for managing psychological pain without physical dependency. Despite the fact that music has not been proven to cause negative responses, commentators persistently suggest that it can exacerbate negative behaviours during adolescence (Bushong 2002).

Robert Epstein (2007) challenges this controlling attitude towards teenagers, arguing that young people should be offered higher levels of trust as they negotiate their emerging identity on the way to adulthood. As a pundit on contemporary psychology, Epstein criticizes the American tendency to treat adolescents as children. He argues convincingly that disrespecting the ability of teenagers to make choices and decisions about their lives leads to a fundamental breakdown in emotional connection between parents and their children. Instead of seeing rebellious attitudes as a necessary process of identity formation, Epstein argues that a disrespectful attitude towards teenagers is actually the cause of the 'adolescent condition'. He laments the loss of strong and accepting parent–adolescent bonds during this stage of life, and suggests that the neo-Freudian influences in Erikson's concept of identity formation have not been adequately critiqued. With the onset of puberty and the increasing capacity of teenagers to take greater responsibility, he advocates for a team approach that positions parents as the young person's ally, respecting and accepting his or her choices and decisions. Epstein quotes figures to show that age has very little relationship to maturity and that many teenagers are as capable as adults of making intelligent, altruistic decisions and maintaining healthy, intimate relationships (p.147).

Gender is another important influence on identity formation and although musical aptitude tests reveal no differences between young women and men (Shuter-Dyson and Gabriel 1981), musical development during the teenage years is vastly different. Females express greater confidence and achieve more success in instrumental music throughout the school years until a gender reversal occurs, with males being a conspicuously dominant force in the adult music world (Eccles *et al.* 1993). Researchers are unclear about why this dramatic switch occurs, since a reversal does not occur in any other profession. How can girls be so successful throughout childhood and adolescence and then be almost completely dismissed from the profession in favour of men? Social psychology theorists posit that young people see music as gender stereotyped. Since it is common for adolescents who exhibit gender-inappropriate behaviour to incur negative responses from their peers (O'Neill 1997), it is not surprising that many young male musicians consider giving up their instrument because they are teased so much about musical participation during the school years (Howe and Sloboda 1991). An alternative explanation is based in the mechanics of musicianship. Instrumental activities during childhood and adolescence require more group work and relational skills – seen in choirs, orchestras and even individual lessons: the kinds of social skills that are commonly described as feminine. Recent investigations have identified a change in trajectories of musical participation and the emergence of an earlier rise of males to success, beginning when technological aspects of music are introduced into the music curriculum. At this point, a girl's sense of competence decreases dramatically, while a boy's interest and confidence soars (Comber, Hargreaves and Colley 1993). This assumedly continues into the adult years, where contemporary music is dominated by electronic influences and more traditional masculine styles. Women are more successful as vocalists, but are vastly under-represented in many instrument groups. This suggests that the relationship between teenagers, music and identity may be tied to some fairly traditional gender stereotypes that may be either helpful or unconstructive, depending on how they are experienced by the individual.

RESILIENCE

Another useful concept for considering how music can enhance adolescent health is resilience. Although some characteristics associated with resilience are established much earlier than the teenage years, others are malleable and can be fostered by the increasingly intelligent and capable young person (Frydenberg 2008). Personal disposition is a fairly stable characteristic of resilience, for example, whereas self-understanding is more open to cultivation. Generally speaking, resilience involves a combination of mood and behavioural self-management in response to adversity, as well as an active striving to find positive meanings in difficult circumstances. It is about being able to bounce back (Olsson et al. 2003) rather than avoiding stressful situations. It is also relative, since the points that people bounce to, and from, are not even. Some individuals have a happier disposition and their mood will fluctuate around a high biological set-point for happiness, where others will naturally sit at a lower point on the spectrum (Lyubomirsky 2001). Although happiness is a part of the resilient picture, there is not a fixed measure of happiness that is the same for each young person. This is clearly evidenced when young people are coping with conditions that are naturally debilitating or exhausting. The chronically ill teen may be coping extremely well under the circumstances, but his or her level of happiness cannot be compared to an adolescent who is healthy, well supported and successful at the same moment in time. Resilience is not about luck, it is about response and this involves a combination of happiness, insight and self-management.

Keith Roe has argued that teenagers use music to reflect these aspects of self, which he labels as self-perception (1987). In a study of Swedish youth, he demonstrated that the music preferred by individual teenagers was indicative of their own predictions of future success. Those teenagers who nominated easily accessible styles of music as their favourite were more likely to be academically successful in school. Those who identified with more isolating music were less successful in school and felt their chances of this improving were minimal. This perspective on the 'reflective' role that music plays during adolescence is the polar opposite of a causative influence. It suggests that musical preferences offer insight regarding the internal state of the teenager and communicate something of the young person's self-understanding. Teenagers dressed in black, wearing dark make-up and listening to emo (emotional) music are saying something about how they see themselves. It is not the act of listening that has led them to purchase the clothes and dye their hair. They perceive themselves as emo.

In contrast to Ruud's (1997) theory that music is the performance of identity, this perspective suggests that music functions as a window through to the internal state of the teenager that can be used to increase personal understanding. Many teenagers describe using music as a way of expressing their emotions, either through playing or listening, and this is an important facet of self-knowledge. Suvi Laiho (2004) identifies both enjoyment and emotion regulation as integral to the psychological function of music, linking pleasure and mood to health. In her review of the literature she highlights a range of emotional uses of music, from 'pumping up', to managing fluctuations of mood and also dealing with stress. In a further investigation of Finnish teenagers, Suvi (now Saarikallio) and Jaakko Erkkila (2007) establish that healthy teenagers use music intentionally in this way. Although the literature describes the function of music as being related to negative as well as positive emotions, the eight young people involved in the Finnish study used music to regulate and improve their mood. In-depth interviews revealed that these teenagers used music to make themselves feel better, not through a conscious process of selecting music that enhanced mood, but because they unconsciously knew what kind of music they needed to listen to in different situations.

The teenagers' preferred music was accesible in a variety of moods and was utterly individual to each participant.

In an online survey of 111 Australian teenagers, results were less consistently related to a positive trend in mood regulation (McFerran *et al.* unpublished). The 15–18-year-olds in this study (62% male and 38% female) also described an affinity with their own preferred 'good' music, but in the case of those adolescents who scored as being 'at-risk' of psychological distress, music listening did not lead to feeling better. In some cases, listening led to feeling worse. This study of Australian teenagers was designed to investigate how young people use music to manage their mood, and the results showed that the vast majority of respondents did use music to actively enhance their mood, particularly in states of boredom or happiness. Approximately half the group continued to report improvements in mood even when they were feeling sad or angry; however, the group of teenagers who were 'at-risk' consistently reported the least improvement when listening in these moods. Nineteen of these adolescents actually reported feeling worse after listening in negative moods. One way of understanding this result is through the construct of delayed hedonic gratification (Larsen 2000). For example, listening to music may lead the sad teenager to cry initially, but after a period of emotional release, he or she begins to feel better. This kind of response can be seen as resilient, where music assists in finding positive meanings through adversity. It is possible that non-resilient teenagers may not be successful in this positive meaning-making endeavour, instead using the music to confirm the negative aspects of their situation and exacerbate negative mood. This has been referred to as 'musical cutting' (Helen Shoemark, personal communication) since it is possible to draw a parallel with the physical act of cutting to induce pain.

The proposal that resilient and non-resilient people use music differently is supported by the results of a Norwegian study of iPod use. Marie Skånland (2009) asserts that MP3 players are used by healthy people as a medium for musical self care. Twenty adults participating in in-depth interviews described using music listening in the 'here and now' to regulate their mood, administer their emotions, adjust their energy levels and create boundaries around themselves in public places, similarly to the healthy Finnish teens. Tia DeNora's (2000) work helps to explain this positive use of music through her suggestion that music provides a structure for everyday experiences that contributes to self-knowledge. Her commentary highlights the ways that music promotes meaning making by individuals, particularly music preferences that are rooted in past experiences. For teenagers, this use of previous life experiences is more limited by their fewer years of experience and it is possible that their ability to reflect upon the ups and downs of various cycles of life is still emerging. This may partially explain why some teenagers struggle to use music as effectively as they might in enhancing their understandings of themselves, while others do this very successfully.

COMPETENCE

Another important area of healthy adolescent growth is in relation to skills and abilities. During adolescence, the nature of intellectual development is grounded in gaining knowledge, experience and wisdom. Jean Piaget (Piaget and Inhelder 1958) highlights this difference in capacity and explains that learning previously has been driven by gains in basic thinking capacity. From around the age of 11, young people develop a capacity for inductive reasoning that was beyond their reach until then. Instead of simply classifying what they see in front of them into known categories (deductive thinking) teenagers are able to generate new categories that are not necessarily tied to the same experience (inductive thinking). Piaget's theories on cognitive development illustrate the ways that adolescents try to understand and seek solutions, highlighting their ability to consider a range of possibilities and discuss their implications. Healthy adolescents are able to think about potentials beyond their actual experience, to generate hypotheses and to envisage multiple outcomes in response to a given scenario. Piaget notes that not all adolescents, and therefore not all people, graduate to this level of formal operational thinking and some will only achieve the egocentric thinking capacities of younger people.

Adolescence is a time of great potential, with neurological capacity peaking at around 14 or 15 years of age and then gradually declining – the human brain actually shrinks back to toddler size by the sixth decade (Raz 2006). The peak of potential during adolescence incorporates cognitive thinking, moral reasoning and memory as well as the more obvious crest of physical performance (Epstein 2007). Increased flexibility in thinking processes means that a range of other developments also become feasible. In terms of aspirations for neurological health, teenagers have better than adult levels of capacity for learning and achievement during this time of their life. A healthy adolescent is at his or her most competent.

Music adds another level of capacity to this prime time of development, with recent discoveries in neuroscience suggesting that musical participation further enhances learning and performance across a range of cognitive domains (Trainor, Shahin and Roberts 2009). Comparisons of musicians and non-musicians regularly identify differences in grey matter in the brain and this is frequently linked to improved visual-spatial, verbal and mathematical performance in musicians (Schlaug *et al.* 2006). As the field of neuroscience continues its rapid evolution, it is likely that further information will be uncovered to shed light on exactly how musical participation increases competence across a variety of domains.

The capacity of music to increase competence is usually tied to active participation; however, adolescents engage with music in diverse ways. Sometimes it involves live music, but recorded sources of music are far more accessible and commonplace. Sometimes musical experiences are shared with others, but often they are alone. In discussion with a group of 120 university students, a myriad of strategies for musical engagement were identified that could be classified into the four quadrants depicted in Figure 3.1. In exploring how frequently these older adolescents participated in the various quadrants, it became clear that receptive and solo musical participation was the most common.

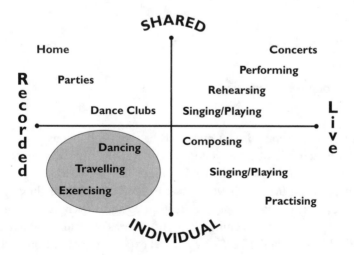

Figure 3.1: Common ways of engaging with music during adolescence

The group overwhelmingly agreed that their musical participation was most often enacted as time spent listening to MP3 players in public spaces with music serving a background function. These young people identified a number of health benefits of this individual and receptive use of music as seen in the following list:

- relaxing and escaping reality
- being in touch with oneself
- fostering creative thinking
- making meaning and connecting to personal experience
- accessing subconscious or associated material
- delivering and receiving messages
- taking communication to another level.

All of these are important, if not fundamental, to healthy living, and the group of older adolescent students argued strongly that listening to MP3 players was health enhancing, similarly to the participants in Marie Skånland's study (2009). However, when responding to an online discussion question about their most joyous experiences with music, the 120-strong group generated a set of activities where only one was receptive, as seen in the following list:

- dancing
- listening
- playing
- group performances
- live concerts.

Although there seems to be a mismatch between the joyous experiences with music identified by the young people and their most common uses of music, this does not derail the argument that music listening can be healthy. Abraham Maslow (1968) describes music as one of the triggers for peak experiences, where people are inspired and moved by an intensely ecstatic experience of listening. In light of Maslow's ideas about self-actualized ways of being, receptive musical experiences can be understood as motivational and may lead to increased self-competence without being directly related to participation.

Social competence is another example of the ways that music can facilitate development. Suvi Laiho (2004) identifies inter-personal relationships as an important psychological function of music during adolescence, including not only the use of music for identity formation as discussed earlier, but also the way that music is used as a 'social lubricator' (Roe 1999). Adolescents believe that their musical preferences are strongly related to those of their peers (Tarrant, North and Hargreaves 1999; Van Wel, Linssen and Abma 2004), and they recognize that music preferences may have positive or negative consequences for their evaluation of others (North and Hargreaves 1999). Group identities can be expressed by attachments to musical genres and Simon Frith (1981) has popularized the idea that teenagers use music as a badge of identity. Social competence is another way that music provides a resource for development and does not always require active participation.

CONNECTEDNESS

Active participation does have an important role to play in healthy adolescent development. Connectedness has been advanced as one of the '5 Cs' in the positive youth development literature, along with competence, confidence, character and caring (Roth and Brooks-Gunn 2003). There is some debate about whether connectedness is related to the action taken by adolescents in engaging with the systems available to them, or simply to their perceptions about the openness of those systems (Resnick et al. 1997). In the first case, it is the young people's response to their perceptions about whether they are welcome, cared for and acceptable. Whether they actually choose to engage then becomes an important gauge of connectedness that can be used to evaluate the effectiveness of youth development programmes (Karcher and Lindwall 2003).

Levels of connectedness have been an important focus in the study of development in context, otherwise known as bioecological systems theory (Bronfenbrenner 2005). This approach has been fundamental in social work practice as well as the field of sociology more generally and is based on the work of Urie Bronfenbrenner (Bronfenbrenner 1989) who emphasizes the importance of connectedness in the 'nature vs. nurture' debate. Often depicted as a series of concentric circles as in Figure 3.2, Bronfenbrenner's

Figure 3.2: Illustration of Brofenbrenner's ecological systems theory

ideas have been fundamental in acknowledging the reciprocal nature of development. This involves not only the immediately obvious influences on the young person such as family and friends, but also the less direct influences such as community-based resources, cultural values, customs and laws (Berk 2000).

The inclusion of culture, or macrosystems, as a significant influence on adolescent development was first highlighted by the anthropologist Margaret Mead (1973/1928). Her in-depth investigations of Samoan teenagers highlighted that the experience of adolescence was strongly influenced by cultural mores. Samoan adolescents maintained a relaxed and casual approach to adolescence, including a more liberated approach to sexual behaviour, which was in keeping with their broader community. Mead's work emphasized that teenagers both reflect their culture and are subjected to the responses of their culture. At a time when American teenagers were being labelled as delinquent, she highlighted that this notion was both culturally derived and driven.

Anthropologists have also studied the relationship between culture and music with similar outcomes. Lomax (1976) describes the ways that songs reflect core values and information about the culture in which they were created. A relevant contemporary illustration of this thesis is the rap genre. Rap music has been adopted by youth across many countries as a medium for expressing frustration and anger about local issues. This musical branch is the most well-known element of the broader hip-hop movement that originated in New York in the 1970s and also incorporates break-dancing and graffiti art. Initial adaptations of rap utilized American accents and closely imitated African American stylistic elements, particularly drawing on gangsta rap and rap battles. The adoption of this genre has gradually expanded to more closely represent local cultures, including strategies such as sampling traditional melodies and using languages and accents other than American English as the medium for expression. As a result, Andy Bennett (1999) proposes that 'the cultural role of rap and hip-hop cannot be assessed without reference to the local settings in which they are appropriated and reworked as modes of cultural expression' (p.78).

Where rap provides a useful example of the way that music depicts culture, the influence of music in defining humanity has also been examined by evolutionary theorists. At this level, music can be seen as essential in enabling connectedness. McNeill (1995) claims that the ability to move together, or connect rhythmically, has been primary in our evolutionary development and critical in separating our remote ancestors from our closest relation, the chimpanzee. Ian Cross (2008) takes this idea further and proposes that the capacity for shared and active music making is a crucial mechanism for healthy societies. In making this argument, he highlights how music enhances connectedness because of its unique capacity to overcome social and cultural barriers. This is not because music is a universal language per se, but because shared music making creates opportunities to communicate without a specific intention. Singing or working rhythmically together does not require agreement on anything but the musical elements. In this way, it underpins the ability of humankind for social capacity, without which there can be no social justice (Cross 2006). Music can therefore promote connectedness at all systemic levels and may even be essential in ensuring the ongoing evolution of humankind.

DRAWING THE THREADS TOGETHER

Perhaps it is obvious that the relationship between teenagers and music can be related to health. Music is a resource that is available in every culture across the world and teenagers take an active interest in it. They use music intuitively as a mirror of their public self and also as a window to their private selves. Their use of music is not always positive, although it seems that healthy adolescents do mostly use music for constructive outcomes. However, sometimes adolescents use music to make themselves feel worse, for experimenting with alternative facets of identity or to avoid learning and interaction with other people. What is worthy of note is that teenagers make active choices about their ways of engaging with music. Some teenagers make choices that lead to positive outcomes and some take a less healthy path. The direction of influence in this relationship does not cast music in the causative role. Music is powerful, but it is not that powerful. It supports, represents, motivates and communicates, but it does not control.

In the front of his book, Robert Epstein makes a request on behalf of his two teenage children: 'May you grow up in a world that judges you based on your abilities, not on your age.' The underlying quest of this book is similar in arguing that all teenagers should have the option of engaging with music in fruitful ways. It is my view that music is essential to healthy development and some teenagers require assistance in drawing on the potential of music. They may not have the resources, the skills, the strength of character or the natural buoyancy to intuit how music could help them. In these cases, music therapists and other youth workers can open the door of music and welcome teenagers in. Traditional music therapy practice has always used a process of assessment, design and evaluation, and this is still very important in working with teens. What is their relationship with music? How can this be used to help them achieve their full potential? What is the best way of engaging with music? And importantly, how do we know if it has worked?

Having outlined a rationale for the use of music therapy with teenagers in Part One of this book, the remainder of the book is practical, explaining *how* to engage teenagers in songs, playing and participation in music. How to do this changes for each teenager on each day and Chapters 4–7 illustrate how practice might change also, drawing on strategies from conventional music therapy practice. Chapters 8–10 are more progressive, arguing for a contemporary approach to music therapy with adolescents that is grounded in active and empowered participation and puts control firmly in the hands of the teenagers involved.

The core of the book is simple, however. Teenagers relate to music. Music plays an important role in society. Musical engagement can be health promoting. And most importantly, music can be fun. Just show me a teenager who doesn't want to be happy.

PART TWO

Song Methods and Teenagers

Introduction

The previous three chapters have provided a theoretical rationale for what now becomes a very practical book. The methods described in Part Two are based on the use of songs in music therapy with adolescents. This is the starting point for the discussion of *how* to work with adolescents because the preferred music of teenagers functions as both a mirror and a window to their life experience. Utilizing this pre-existing relationship is both potent and pleasurable, for the teenager and for the music therapist. The practicalities of working with songs have received scant attention in the music therapy literature, being considered both too simple and too challenging in relation to adolescents. This introduction will highlight some of the more general issues for consideration before Chapter 4 explores the use of existing songs in therapy and Chapter 5 discusses the composition of original songs.

THE FAMILIAR AND THE UNEXPECTED

If the preferred music of adolescents is the 'performance of identity' (Ruud 1980), then using songs as a part of therapy is a direct engagement with the process of identity formation. The use of popular (or unpopular) songs locates the therapeutic process in familiar territory: in the deeply personal terrain of feelings and meanings that teenagers have attached to their music. Michael Viega (2008) expresses deep frustration at the lack of encouragement encountered within some American institutions towards the use of preferred songs as an integral part of therapy. Adult concern about the influence of music can result in a lack of acknowledgement of the young person's identity and of youth culture in general. This response may be based on an overly literal reading of rap lyrics or a fearful reaction to the volume, distortion and energy of heavy rock and metal music, but it does not take into account the metaphoric and personal meanings being communicated. In contrast, being able to draw on the existing relationship between teenagers and their music conveys respect and interest, which can then be accompanied by the intention of enhancing *understanding*, offering *acceptance* or facilitating *development.*

Using songs in music therapy is particularly powerful when the relationship between teenagers and their music is acknowledged as a form of friendship. Kenneth Bruscia (1998b) describes the function of songs as 'keeping us company when we are alone' (p.9), and at no time in life is the friendly face of music more important than during adolescence. Although peers are more important during this stage than at any other time of life, it is also a very lonely time for most teenagers as they paradoxically establish what is the same and what is different between themselves and others. Teenagers in crisis are likely to feel extremely isolated, since whatever condition they are challenged by will be experienced as a significant difference and an obstacle to normality. This is the likely reason that teenagers turn to music more when they are unhappy (McFerran *et al.* unpublished; Roe 1987). Reliability and understanding make for powerful companions and are available in music.

When music therapists use songs as a part of therapy, they are accessing deeply personal aspects of the teenager. The song is a respected vestibule for important personal messages and teenagers honour this relationship time and time again. As a result, many teenagers will disclose information and feelings in the context of a song that they have not shared with anyone else. In some ways, the young person may not be fully conscious that his or her commitment to the song has bypassed his or her usual defences, and while this can be considered a therapeutic success, it is important that teenagers are cognisant of their decision and feel in control of it. One of the most delightful aspects of working with young people is that the tough and defensive exterior very quickly dissolves to a soft and naïve centre once trust is established and the music therapist is offering to truly listen. The delicate façade of adolescents makes it imperative that the music therapist acknowledges the unexpected potency of using songs, and seriously considers how this needs to be addressed within the relationship.

The implications of becoming a part of the deeply personal friendship between music and teenagers are twofold. Not only do teenagers frequently disclose private information in response to the creation of, or listening to, a song, but they also do not anticipate that existing songs can trigger sudden and unexpected emotional associations. In both individual and group sessions, teenagers can be overwhelmed by their responses to songs, even when they have chosen them. A song may catch a teenager's eye for a range of more or less conscious reasons as they flick through a song folder. Sometimes the young person may have simply forgotten that this was the song they cried themselves to sleep with after their first relationship break-up. Even when the teenager remembers the association, they may not be prepared for how raw it feels in the context of a warm, therapeutic relationship. An old favourite may also take on new meaning in the therapeutic context. A single line describing a feeling of being all alone, or a fear of never coming back, may suddenly connect with the vulnerable young person and, again in the context of the relationship, trigger a rush of emotion. These unexpected reactions can be embarrassing in a group situation and few teenagers are comfortable with bursting into tears in front of their peers. They may run from the group, or simply freeze in response.

It is crucial that the music therapist be aware of how common these unexpected reactions can be. It is often useful to warn group members that they may be affected by others' choices and establish a code or indicator for when this has happened so that appropriate support can be provided (*stay one step ahead*). Alternatively, the therapist can wait and allow these reactions, encouraging the group to respond in supportive ways when required and furthering the development of group cohesion (*stay calm*). The music therapist may also respond in the moment by normalizing this experience when it occurs (*go with it*). It is simple enough to comment that this has happened many times before and to ask others if they have had similar experiences upon hearing a song unexpectedly when shuffling through their playlist or listening to the radio. It is true to say that it happens a lot.

THE QUESTION OF REPERTOIRE

The vast amount of music available to teenagers can be intimidating for the music therapist. The challenge of staying abreast of relevant repertoire is never ending and constantly changing. Ideally, a music therapist working with adolescents will be interested and willing to learn songs on a regular basis. With the availability of musical material via the internet,

it is a simple process to download tablature and lyrics, as well as listen
to recordings online to familiarize oneself with a song.[1] It means a great
deal to teenagers when the music therapist arrives to the next session with
the requested song in hand. This communicates a genuine and enduring
interest and commitment to the therapeutic relationship. However, there
are also some shortcuts.

It is not necessary to know all of the Top 40 songs all of the time. In
fact, Top 40 songs may never be a part of the programme with an individual
teenager or a group. A recent survey of over 200 older adolescents in
Australia confirmed that classic hits can be identified for this generation,
just as they can for any other. The cohort sampled were asked to 'List
the Top 10 songs of your adolescence'. Most of the adolescents were 18
years old and in their first year of university, with a gender bias towards
more women than men. A range of ethnic groups were represented and it
could be assumed that at least 25 per cent of the group was not born in
Australia. The answers to the question of Top 10 songs were compiled and
the following table presents songs that were nominated by at least three of
the adolescents in the group (Table ii.1).

Table ii.1: Most frequently nominated songs of healthy older adolescents in 2009

Genre	Band/ Singer/Artist	Year of release	Song title	Number of times named
Pop	Spice Girls	1998	Stop	13
Pop	Spice Girls	1996	Wannabe	11
Pop	Hanson	1997	Mmm Bop	11
Progressive rock	Queen	1975	Bohemian Rhapsody	9
Grunge	Nirvana	1991	Smells Like Teen Spirit	8
Alternative rock	Greenday	1997	Good Riddance (Time of your Life)	8

---

1   This contrasts with my own adolescence where the process of getting a song meant listening
to the radio with a tape recorder at hand and hitting the record button when the desired song
finally came on. It could take hours and sometimes the song would not even be played!

Genre	Band/ Singer/Artist	Year of release	Song title	Number of times named
Pop punk	The Offspring	1998	Pretty Fly for a White Guy	8
Pop	Aqua	1997	Barbie Girl	7
Alternative rock	Coldplay	2000	Yellow	5
Alternative rock	Red Hot Chili Peppers	1992	Under The Bridge	5
Indie	The Cat Empire	2003	Hello, Hello	5
Pop	Backstreet Boys	1996	Everybody (Backstreet's Back)	5
Pop	Britney Spears	2000	Oops, I Did it Again	5
Dance	Eiffel 65	1999	Blue (Dab a Dee)	5
Pop	Christina Aguilera	1999	Genie in a Bottle	5
Pop	Britney Spears	1998	…Baby One More Time	5
Pop	Venga Boys	1998	We Like to Party	5
Heavy metal	Metallica	1991	Enter Sandman	4
Alternative rock	The Killers	2004	Mr Brightside	4
Pop	Smashmouth	1999	Allstar	4
Pop punk	Blink 182	1999	All the Small Things	4
Alternative rock	Jeff Buckley	1994	Hallelujah	4
Alternative rock	Ben Folds Five	1997	Brick	4
Pop rock	Third Eye Blind	1997	Semi-Charmed Life	4
Pop	Celine Dion	1997	My Heart Will Go On	4
Rock	Alanis Morrisette	1995	Ironic	4

continued

**Table ii.1: Most frequently nominated songs
of healthy older adolescents in 2009** *cont.*

Genre	Band/ Singer/Artist	Year of release	Song title	Number of times named
Dance pop	Michael Jackson	1983	Billy Jean	3
Indie rock	Electric Six	2003	Danger! High Voltage	3
Pop	Wheatus	2000	Teenage Dirtbag	3
Alternative rock	Goo Goo Dolls	1998	Iris	3
Hard rock	Aerosmith	1998	I Don't Want to Miss a Thing	3
Alternative rock	No Doubt	1995	Don't Speak	3
Heavy metal	Metallica	1991	Nothing Else Matters	3
Folk rock	Don McLean	1971	American Pie	3
Alternative rock	Coldplay	2005	Fix You	3
Rock	U2	2000	Beautiful Day	3
Pop	B-52s	1989	Love Shack	3
Pop	Nsync	2000	Bye Bye Bye	3
Pop	Backstreet Boys	1999	I Want it That Way	3
Pop	Britney Spears	1999	Sometimes	3
Alternative rock	Blur	1997	Song #2	3
Pop punk	The Mighty Mighty Bosstones	1997	Impression that I Get	3

The songs in Table ii.1 do not include all of the singles noted by individuals in the group. These formed the vast majority of contributions and confirm that it is impossible to be prepared to play all songs a teenager may suggest in a music therapy session. Each teenager presents with a unique identity and has connected with different songs for a range of reasons. It is possible to hypothesize that particular groups of young people will be more inclined towards a specific genre that represents their own culture, based on the use of music as a badge of identity (Frith 1981). This can also be true in the rejection of particular genres, and it is striking that there is a distinct lack of hip-hop or electronica in Table ii.1.

The songs in Table ii.1 contain a number of classic hits for this generation, and at least half of these are in my own song book for use with slightly younger Australian adolescents. Over 40 genres were canvassed in the total nominated songs of these older adolescents, which illustrates the vast range of music accessed by contemporary adolescents. Schapira (2002) suggests an even higher number in his discussion of music as both social representation and cultural identity, and includes a number of Latino styles that are more common in Argentinian repertoire, such as tango, bolero and Latin jazz. Table ii.2 provides my perception of the most common sub-genres in Western culture, although this list could also be further populated by increasingly specific references to styles.

Table ii.2: Common genres and sub-genres popular with adolescents

Acoustic	Adult contemporary	Alternative metal
Alternative rock	Blues rock	Classic rock
Classical	Comedy	Country
Dance	Dance pop	Electronica
Experimental rock	Folk	Folk rock
Grunge	Hard rock	Heavy metal
Hip-hop	House	Indie
Indie pop	Indie rock	Instrumental rock
Jazz	Metal	Musical theatre
Nu metal	Pop	Pop punk
Pop rock	Post punk	Progressive rock
Punk rock	R'n'B	Rap
Reggae	Religious	Rock
Soundtracks	Theme songs	Trance

To survive as a music therapist with adolescents it is necessary to be familiar with the small group of classics that is broadly relevant to each different genre and may be drawn from across a number of decades. A solid knowledge of these classics and a general ability to play in popular genres can sustain and satisfy a group of teenagers. A baseline of practical skills might include the ability (and confidence) to approximate a beat-box vocally, rock out on open chords on the guitar, pluck some folk-like passages and access electronic beats on a keyboard or computer. These skills are necessary to learn songs that are important to individual adolescents and they are also crucial for songwriting. Emma O'Brien (2005) describes an approach for songwriting that includes demonstrating different musical genres that clients can choose from in order to best represent themselves and their material. If the music therapist has only one style of guitar playing available (what Robert Krout (2009) refers to as the 'music therapy strum') then the capacity for songwriting is necessarily limited.

What is most important is that the therapist enjoys a range of contemporary music styles and holds no assumptions about the negative or positive influences they may have. Teenagers have likely had numerous experiences of people suggesting their music is too loud, too aggressive, too boring, too clichéd, or making other judgements about unfamiliar styles. A music therapist offering to step into the world of teenagers must be willing to do so with an open mind and a personal enjoyment of their music. The re-creation of these styles undoubtedly improves with practice, but it is also possible to fall into ruts that become less creatively satisfying; for example, the same song structure, the same chord progressions, the same backing beats, or the same strumming style. The music therapist can grow tired of endless rap songs with no harmony, or R'n'B songs with two chords. The teenager is not responsible for such repetition since it occurs across clients, so it is critical for music therapists to maintain familiarity with new genres and deepen their compositional skills in order to improve the options offered to teenagers and to maintain their own interest. This can be deeply satisfying as a music therapist and, one would hope, very helpful to the young people we work with.

Not every song needs to be played live, however, and the decision to use live or recorded music is an important consideration when using songs. The quality and availability of recorded music is excellent and it is sometimes difficult and unnecessary to replicate songs live, even for the artists themselves. Teenagers may know songs well enough to anticipate bass riffs, exact structures, solos and other details and it may be important for the music therapist to hear these details. There are some contemporary technical challenges involved in using recordings since the form of media has changed rapidly and CDs are no longer a common form for carrying songs. Instead, it is necessary for the music therapist to have an MP3 amplifier that teenagers can insert a variety of models into so that it is possible for the group to listen. In individual sessions, the customary sharing of headphones is a familiar strategy for young people and an appropriately intimate experience. The ability of teenagers to carry their entire library of music with them makes an incredible contribution to what resources can be utilized in music therapy. However, the value of live music is under-utilized in contemporary culture and music therapy may be an important opportunity to make music. The potential for connectedness is more powerful using a live medium compared to a connection that is established directly with the music, placing other listeners in a secondary position. The physical response to live music is also different and it opens up new possibilities for knowing a song. A decision about how to use songs needs to be made by each therapist in response to the nuance of each situation. The benefits of sharing live music mean that it should not be discarded as an option if it can possibly be achieved. Nonetheless, it is important that the music therapist does not develop a patronizing attitude towards shared music listening as being somehow less valuable.

In Chapter 4, a range of descriptions are provided of the use of existing songs in music therapy with adolescents. Beginning with illustrations of music therapists whose intention is to foster *understanding*, the idea of contributing songs for analysis and discussion in both group and individual settings is demonstrated. The emphasis changes when the music therapist intends to offer *acceptance* to the adolescent and active singing of songs is then utilized. Young men rapping and slapping to rock songs and a young woman expressing herself through selections from the song book provide anecdotal support for the use of live songs with the purpose of promoting identity formation. The final example also utilizes a live reproduction of a favoured song, but illustrates how powerful preferred songs can be in motivating young people when the music therapist's intention is to promote *development*, with the results seeing an increase in competence.

Chapter 5 covers the gamut of songwriting with adolescents. The powerful connection between teenagers and songs is captured in the descriptions of raw and expressive participation. This begins with a group of young people with life-limiting illness who use metaphor to depict their existential crisis. The music therapist is focused on fostering *understanding* and this is portrayed using a description of songwriting without words, drawing on computer software and casual conversation to solicit insight. A less demanding and more *accepting* approach is offered for teenagers who are struggling with the use of language, and a brainstorm on concrete ideas is turned into an original song by one group, while an individual documents the strength of her Christian faith through songwriting. Cognitive behavioural strategies are applied in the final example, and lyric substitution is utilized to facilitate the *development* of social skills and to emphasize positive strategies for improving their capacity to cope with mental illness.

The two chapters are divided into separate music therapy methods that illustrate *how* songs are used with teenagers. Within each chapter the music therapist's intentions are used to distinguish why the method is being used in a particular way. The 'Map of how music therapy can be with adolescents' is the basis for this division within chapters, and the links to outcomes, stance and orientation are drawn upon both explicitly and implicitly. This explanation risks making the following chapters sound technical when they are anything but. Tales of therapy form the majority of each chapter and my intention is to tell stories where the young people inspire you, as the reader, to remember *why* music therapy works with teenagers.

Chapter 4

Using Existing Songs

The use of contemporary songs in music therapy with teenagers is the most natural way for young people to engage in therapy. Even though it feels comfortable, it can also be extremely powerful because of the associations each teen has with the music, as well as the inherent messages communicated by the singers and composers. In this chapter I will outline the use of songs in five different ways, with a particular emphasis on how little teenagers need to say in order to gain great benefit from sharing songs that are important to them.

'What kind of music do you like?' is a great beginning to a relationship with teenagers. They may not find it an easy question to answer. Although some people have a strong allegiance to a particular genre or artist, others have fluctuating tastes, or even embarrassing preferences. Although it sounds like a casual question, it serves many purposes. For the music therapist who intends to facilitate *development*, this information is partially for the purposes of assessment. Once the answer has been elicited, the music therapist is able to determine whether to provide live or recorded versions of the songs. These songs will then be used to motivate the client and encourage the achievement of therapeutic goals. When the music therapist is offering *acceptance*, this question directs the focus on the teenager's interests and places a developmentally appropriate emphasis on his or her music and identity. It is also a very pleasant question to ask and to discuss the answer to – both for the client and the music therapist. Indeed, the question and the responses of both the young person and the therapist serve as an introduction to the power balance of the therapeutic relationship. The nature of the discussion or music making that ensues will reflect something of that individual and the ability of the therapist to engage the teenager. When this is to foster deeper levels of *understanding*, the answer to this question can be interpreted in different ways. The music therapist will note the ease or resistance with which the teenager responds, and the genre he or she chooses will be seen as symbolizing unconscious drives and needs. In reality, the therapist will ask the question and then wait to see which of these levels is most appropriate given the context they are working in and the challenges faced by the young person. Regardless of orientation, this introductory question means that a great deal has happened by the end of the first sentence. As far as establishing an affiliation, it will be on its way.

In group work, the dynamics are more complex. The question 'What kind of music do you like?' is followed by 'and you, and you, and you'. With each answer there is increased affinity between some and increased isolation of others. The banter and teasing will often begin with the first person who is brave enough to voice his or her choice, usually someone with a strong and loyal preference, or someone with little insight into what will necessarily ensue. The expression of diversity in musical tastes is as important and useful as it is unavoidable. The way that the difference in tastes is managed in the group is an indicator of the intention of the music therapist for the group. When fostering *understanding* is the focus, the music therapist will work with the dynamics that emerge, commenting on and interpreting the ways that group members judge one another, and encouraging reflection on why that might be. The *acceptance*-oriented therapist will playfully draw on established group norms to utilize this as an opportunity for reinforcing the importance of mutual respect and learning about different styles and people. When facilitating *developmental* goals, the therapist is likely to use a more structured approach to solicit this information in order to maintain some semblance of control within the group, and minimize the potential for inappropriate behaviour. The group will be lively when songs are involved, so this may feel like an important leadership strategy.

FOSTERING UNDERSTANDING

An approach that uses songs to enhance personal *understanding* will usually involve some form of verbal processing. The song is used as the inspiration for therapeutic work, with the discussions facilitating personal insight and growth. Because the music is used in therapy, not as therapy (Bruscia 1998a), it is more likely that the therapist will choose to use the recorded version of a song, although live reproduction by the therapist would also be potent. The recorded version is more directly linked to associations and it allows the therapist to be a part of the listening process rather than taking on a different role as performer. The music therapist's skills in verbal processing are particularly important in this model, and the skilful use of open questions about the young people's responses to the music is critical. Denise Grocke (Grocke and Wigram 2006) lists three levels of questions that can be used to this end, including questions about the song, about the associations with the teenagers, and about insights in regard to aspects of their life described in the music. This means that the adult needs to ask about the music – Why do you like it? What does it mean to you? What do you think of when you hear it? In some ways, it is not even the question that is important, it is all about listening to the answer and then asking more questions and then listening intently again. When working with adolescents, it is crucial to have a dialogue, and too much 'expectant' silence can be overwhelming and unproductive for many young people. Genuinely interested questioning is what is required.

Lyric analysis
SETTING AND PURPOSE

The residential setting where 16-year-old Ruth is receiving therapy services is psychodynamic in approach and the inter-disciplinary team works together towards the same goals. The treatment plan for this young woman is focused on personal discovery and the identification and resolution of issues from her past and her current lifestyle. She has been diagnosed with first episode psychosis and presents with a chaotic family history of violence and relocation, although her mother is supportive and loyal to her daughter. With this focus in mind, the specific aims for music therapy are as follows:

- to establish rapport using music as a point of contact

- to use the associations with music to elicit memories

- to encourage verbal processing of the issues related to the songs/ memories

- to promote emotional expression in response to the musical material.

ILLUSTRATIVE VIGNETTE

Ruth sits with the music therapist in a quiet room surrounded by instruments and stereo equipment. The two are facing one another in comfortable chairs about one metre apart, although the chairs are not positioned directly face to face. After some introductory banter, the music therapist passes the MP3 player to Ruth. 'Why don't you have a look through there? Tell me when you see any songs that are relevant for you right now.' Ruth scrolls through the iPod by artist, smiling when she sees that Britney Spears is there and pausing cautiously over Mariah Carey. She sometimes comments out loud to the therapist, particularly about the bands she doesn't like, but there are some minutes of silence as she slowly makes her way through the list, step by step. Once she has finished with artists, she moves back to the main menu and selects the playlists function. The music therapist has categorized a lot of the songs according to issues and emotions, and Ruth's face reflects a look of surprise and then interest. She looks briefly at the 'Sad Songs' playlist and then moves into the 'Tough Stuff' list. She chooses an old Toni Childs song, 'I've Got to Go Now' and passes the player back to the music therapist. The therapist plugs it in to the speakers and they sit listening together as the song plays.

While they are listening, the music therapist sits still and uses her body language to show that she is listening intently to the music. She taps her foot in time during the chorus and sways minimally to the music at other times. She unobtrusively glances at Ruth on a regular basis to make it clear that she is also focused on her. Once the song has finished, the two sit quietly for a minute. When the music therapist decides that Ruth is not going to start the discussion, she offers a question to get the ball rolling. 'So what made you choose that song?' Ruth shrugs her shoulders, but after a moment she says that her mum used to play that song a lot when she was little. The therapist wonders why and Ruth shrugs again, but says that it was just after they had run away from her father, who the therapist knows from her documented history had been physically and verbally abusive during the early years of Ruth's life. The therapist responds again, wondering if her father had problems with alcohol, like the man in the song, and Ruth begins to describe what she can remember from her own memories and from the descriptions her mother has shared at various times. It is a comfortable conversation, considering the powerful content, and it has emerged directly out of the song.

After a while, the two come to the end of the discussion and the therapist offers a new choice. 'Would you like to choose another song, or do you want to sing through that one with me while I play guitar?' She is offering the opportunity to process this part of Ruth's history further, by delving more deeply into this particular song, or another. Ruth decides to choose another song, but this time she scrolls immediately to the 'Upbeat' playlist and chooses a dance track. The music therapist bounces lightly in time to the music again, following the same process as the last listening opportunity, but altering it to fit the tone of the song. At the end of the track, Ruth is clear that the song has no personal meaning and states that she 'just likes it'. The music therapist takes this as a cue and engages in further light banter about the genre and other topics that arise about music and life in the Centre. After a while she notes that it has been 45 minutes since Ruth arrived and that it is probably time for them to finish up. She thanks her for being brave enough to select the first song and to talk about what it bought up for her. She asks Ruth if she is feeling comfortable to leave the session, or if the song has made her feel vulnerable. They process this a little to facilitate closure. The music therapist also notes that they can talk more in the next session and that she looks forward to spending more music time together.

EVALUATING EFFECTIVENESS

The most appropriate evaluation of the effectiveness of music therapy in this case will be based on whether Ruth discloses relevant aspects of her story in music therapy. Ruth's *understanding* of how her life experiences have impacted upon her current situation will help her to answer the question of 'Who am I in my first experience of psychosis?' The music therapist will encourage verbal processing of the material within sessions, as well as supporting Ruth to take these insights to other group and individual therapy sessions within the Centre. A summary of discussions will be documented in the client history and shared with other professionals in team meetings as appropriate. Evaluation of long-term outcomes such as recovery or positive and sustained community living will be considered by the team as a whole and not attributed to one specific therapeutic intervention.

KEY POINTS

- The music therapist should provide a diverse range of songs when teenagers do not have access to their own music.

- The therapist is guided by the teenager, negotiating progress and depth.

- The therapist is comfortable with waiting – for choices and for discussion – but does not put pressure on the teenager to answer questions by leaving overly long pauses.

- The therapist asks questions that are directly related to what the teenager has offered, seeking further descriptions and leading to deepening understandings.

- The teenager controls the intensity of the session – through clear song choices as well as more subtle indications about how much she wants to share.

- The therapist offers containment within the session by providing cues about timing and prompting the required closure and links for continuing.

- Part of the professional process involves documentation and participation in team discussions.

Song contributions
SETTING AND PURPOSE

This group of young people meet in their school on a weekly basis, missing alternating classes to attend the music therapy programme. Each teenager has come from a broken family and was initially approached by the welfare coordinator with the question of whether they might benefit from support in dealing with their situation. Those that responded with interest were invited by the music therapist to the weekly music group, and the vignette describes the third week of their meetings. The young people's experiences of parental divorce are diverse and the group members also represent a range of ethnic backgrounds. Some of the young people are seeing the school counsellor for regular or irregular support, while others have been considered 'at-risk' by their main homeroom teacher because of their behaviour in class or absenteeism. The aims for the group are for the young people to:

- have the opportunity to share the story of their family separation and to hear the stories of others

- forge connections with peers who have had similar experiences

- have the opportunity to express emotions related to their loss

- gain insight into unresolved feelings associated with the divorce.

ILLUSTRATIVE VIGNETTE

'Okay everyone, next week I want you all to bring in a song that is significant to you,' the music therapist requests at the end of the group. 'What do you mean?' asks one group member. 'Next week everyone is going to play a song that means something to them,' the music therapist replies. 'I've got mine here already,' says one young man, waving his mobile phone in the air, 'Will this be okay?' 'No problems,' replies the music therapist, 'iPods and CDs are okay too, but remember if the CD is home-burned, it might not work on the player. Take care and see you all next week.'

As the next week draws closer, the music therapist emails the group members to remind them to bring the songs. 'Hi to all. Looking forward to seeing you again this week. Please remember to bring along a song that is significant to you – MP3 or CD format is fine.' Despite the reminder, when the music therapist checks in at the beginning of the next group, only four of the eight young people have a song with them. After catching up on how the week has been, she asks who would like to share their song first. There is a long silence following this question, a sure sign that the group is aware of how personal this experience will be. The music therapist waits patiently, and then after a short time provides some encouragement. 'Now, we might not get a chance to listen to everyone's songs today, it just depends how long we spend talking about each one.' After a brief pause, she continues, 'Plus sometimes it's easier to get it over and done with. Waiting around for your turn can be stressful in some ways too.' One of the group members mutters and leans forward in his chair. 'Great. Ken, would you like to plug yours in first?' the music therapist responds, interpreting this as a willingness to go first. 'Oh, okay,' says the young man, and moves towards the stereo. The music therapist moves gently to his side to assist in the setting up process if necessary. When he is almost ready, she regains the focus of the chattering group. 'Alright everyone. The plan is not to talk while Ken's song is playing. Once it's finished, we'll have the chance to hear what he has to say and ask questions about the song, as well as talk about your own responses. Hey Ken, are you ready to go?' The music therapist moves back towards the young man to make sure there are no problems and then when she sees him standing uncomfortably wondering what to do, she indicates to him that it is okay to go back to his seat by gesturing with her hand and smiling.

The group sits silently for the most part, although there are some cheers when 'Good Riddance (Time of your Life)' by Greenday starts, and it is a clear favourite with some of the others in the group. In responding so quickly to Ken's initial gesture, the music therapist had been conscious that this young man was well liked by the group and that he was stable enough to withstand any banter that may result from this new experience of listening and discussing. Therefore, the enthusiastic response to his song is not entirely surprising. As the song progresses, two of the group members begin chatting among themselves. The music therapist looks over towards them, but the glance goes unnoticed. As they become more animated, she tries again by coughing and then shaking her head and gesturing to 'shhhh' when they look up. The young women roll their eyes at one another, but stop talking. The music therapist anticipates that she may have to be prepared for leadership challenges from the bolder of the two and decides to look for an opportunity to give her some control over the course of the session. Perhaps she would like to go next.

When the song concludes there is more silence until the music therapist quietly prompts, 'So Ken, tell us about that song.' Ken begins with a factual explanation about the song – who the band was, who is playing the drums, what album it is on. As he pauses, the music therapist asks about the meaning of the song for him. The young man continues to distance himself from the meaning, but does note that the song was used in the final episode of the television series *Seinfeld*. The music therapist then opens it up to the group and invites them to ask questions or make comments. 'Who would like to ask Ken something about the song and what it means to him?' After a minute, one of the talkative girls asks if he likes any other Greenday songs. They discuss this for a while and then one of the boys asks, 'Do you reckon that song's about people dying or just leaving?' Ken has a firm opinion on this, and he begins to explain that it is definitely about leaving because of the way that it was used on *Seinfeld*. 'You know, everyone acts as though my dad is dead in my family, but he's not. He still tries really hard to spend time with us and it's not his fault that he has to work so much!' The group joins the discussion immediately, taking up the topic of dads and sharing a range of opinions. 'My mum says that Dad could try harder, but he's just too lazy,' responds one of the young women. 'I reckon I'd rather be with my dad than my mum,' offers another. The pros and cons of dads are discussed at length.

As the animated discussion dies down, the therapist asks Ken if he is angry about not seeing his dad as much any more. Ken is briefly silent before saying, 'Yep. I'm angry at him. I really don't understand why they had to break up. It isn't fair coz now we have to move house and I might have to go to another school. It's just stuffed everything up.' The group is quiet again, but they all know what he is saying. The music therapist asks if anyone would like to say anything else and people shake their heads. 'Good song, Ken,' one young man says, and they nod at each other. 'Yeah, thanks Ken, that was a great beginning. Are you feeling angry right now?' asks the music therapist. 'Nah, I'm just tired,' says the young man, giving a cue that he is ready to get out of the spotlight. The music therapist obliges and asks who would like to go next, looking directly towards the ringleader of the talkative duo. 'Well, my song's not as good as that, but I don't mind going next,' says the young woman.

EVALUATING EFFECTIVENESS

The nature of this programme is essentially preventative, since the young people involved have experienced a challenging loss but are not struggling with a mental illness or behavioural disorder. The best indicators of success would therefore be related to improved coping in the classroom, and a long-term follow up on mental health status. In the busy environment of a high school, this information can sometimes be difficult to access. An alternative strategy that does not rely on soliciting feedback from school staff is to monitor the level of group cohesion that has been achieved. Group cohesion can be monitored casually by attendance and drop-out rates, but can be more formally documented through a survey of each individual's perception of the group at the beginning and the end. Irvin Yalom (1995) offers an example of this kind of evaluation, which I have adopted for closed programmes with groups of teenagers. An improvement in the level of connectedness between the survey results in the first session and the final session indicate increased cohesion, or liking for the group. This suggests positive outcomes from participation.

KEY POINTS

- Teenagers frequently forget to bring songs when requested. Reminders are helpful, but it is always good to have a back-up plan for the session in case no one brings a song.

- It is difficult to know how long it will take to listen to a song and process responses to it. This can vary from 10 minutes to 30 minutes per person.

- Too much silence is not necessarily helpful in group work with adolescents. The group leader needs to prompt participation, at least until a high level of cohesion has been achieved.

- It is more important that the group members ask questions than the group leader, although this can be challenging to facilitate. It can sometimes be difficult for the therapist to balance modelling with taking too much responsibility.

- Sitting quietly while listening to a meaningful song is very difficult for most teenagers. Some groups can do it and others cannot – this is not a sign of failure.

- Many people avoid getting to the significance of the song, but this does not mean that the process has not been powerful or helpful without being processed verbally.

OFFERING ACCEPTANCE

Adopting an *accepting* approach while using existing songs emphasizes the therapy that occurs in the music, rather than after the music. A music-centred approach (Aigen 2005) often suits adolescent clients at a practical, as well as theoretical, level. Although many teenagers are capable of processing their responses to music through a discussion, the majority do not choose to do so. Young men in particular are often uncomfortable with the expectation that they might articulate their emotional response or describe the meaningfulness of a piece of music. Yet they will happily choose a song that communicates more than words could. The music therapist is much more likely to utilize live reproductions of songs whenever possible, because the experience of musical process is the therapy (Aigen 2005) and this supports the development of the therapeutic relationship/s. The therapist trusts that the teenagers will utilize the opportunity as they need, fulfilling their inherent inclination to grow and actualize their potential, given the facilitative environment of shared music making.

Singing together
SETTING AND PURPOSE

Dorit is a 14-year-old who accesses music therapy in a paediatric palliative care setting that provides brief respite stays for young people with life-limiting illness. Dorit has a degenerative illness and each time she is admitted to the hospice she is less well and more disabled by her condition. She seems to have some associated cognitive impairment, although this is not documented and it may be that she has a flat affect because she is somewhat depressed or physically unable to be dynamic. It is common for young people to become 'regulars' at the hospice, and Dorit has visited the hospice three or four times a year for many years, staying for a few days each time. Similarly to a hospital ward, this means that a relationship is built up between the teenager and the music therapist, but it is based on a series of one-off interventions, and therefore goals need to suit a brief therapy model. Although the music therapist receives a handover on arrival each day, psychosocial information is not always clearly presented or even well understood by the eternally positive nursing staff. Mostly there is just enthusiasm and assurances that the young person 'will definitely want to do music!' The goals for Dorit are to:

- engage with the music therapist, as seen through willingness to attend the session

- identify preferred songs from the song book

- actively participate in the live music making experience, to a level appropriate to her health on that day

- select songs that may be relevant to her current life experience in order for her experience to be heard and accepted by another person.

ILLUSTRATIVE VIGNETTE

The music therapist approaches the young woman as she sits at the main table in the centre of the open-planned living space at the hospice. Dorit has been visiting the hospice for nearly five years and is familiar with the staff and the setting, so she has been comfortably chatting with a nurse. The last time she worked with the music therapist was in a group that was co-run with the physiotherapist. This colleague had seen Dorit's responsiveness to music and taken the opportunity to achieve some strong physical goals. That was six months ago and the music therapist is pleased to see Dorit again and have the opportunity to spend some one-to-one time together. She invites Dorit to the music room, promising not to make her do any exercises and they laugh together about the last group. Having manoeuvred her wheelchair through the doorway and past the drum kit, Dorit hesitates in the middle of the room, not knowing what to do. 'Did you get a chance to flick through my song book last time?' asks the music therapist. Dorit nods, but it is difficult to tell how enthusiastic she is. The music therapist follows up. 'Would you like to look through it now?' The young woman shrugs casually, but reaches up her arms as much as she can to receive the song book and place it on the tray of her wheelchair. The music therapist gives her some space and begins to rearrange the room a little to make it easier to move about. She reaches for the acoustic guitar and leans it up beside Dorit and then opens the lid of the piano. After a couple of minutes she positions herself beside the wheelchair and watches as the young woman pages through the songs. She builds rapport by engaging in a discussion of the various songs and asking trivial questions about whether Dorit knows the song, likes the artist, has the album. Once she recognizes that Dorit has found a song she knows and relates to, she maintains the light tone and also asks, 'Shall we sing it together?' The response is enthusiastic enough, but predictable. 'Yeah, cool. But I'm not singing. I can't sing.'

The music therapist smiles and reassures Dorit that everybody says they can't sing and comments, 'I reckon it's sad that people feel they're not allowed to sing unless they're some kind of superstar. Why don't I start singing, and you join in when you're ready?' she encourages. The music therapist begins to play an acoustic version of the P!nk song 'Who Knew?' She sings through the first two verses and then verbally encourages Dorit to join in singing the chorus without looking at her directly or losing the pace of the song. There is no singing response from the young woman so the music therapist continues through the song, pausing half way through the bridge. 'I never quite get this right. Help me out would you?' she asks Dorit, taking the opportunity to use her own lack of knowledge to empower the young woman. Dorit smiles and confirms, 'Yeah, that wasn't really right,' so they go back to the beginning of the previous verse to get a lead in. Dorit joins in very quietly and then continues successfully into the first line of the bridge as the music therapist drops back. They stumble together on the second line and laugh, before singing on into the chorus. This time Dorit does sing, still quietly, but with a small smile.

After they finish singing, the music therapist congratulates Dorit on her courage and her singing. 'There's no turning back now,' she laughs, 'Let's find one you know really well.' They pass over a few more songs before Avril Lavigne's 'Skater Boy' catches Dorit's attention and they sing through it together, with Dorit's voice growing in strength. A couple more rock ballads are selected in quick succession before there is a change to an old classic, Simon and Garfunkel's 'I am a Rock'. The music therapist comments on the song before they begin, 'I bet you feel like a rock sometimes.' She starts to strum the introductory chords as Dorit nods her head. The mood is more sombre by the end of the song and the music therapist offers a choice since it is clear that Dorit does not plan on discussing the meaning of her song choices. 'Do you want to find more songs that seem relevant to your life right now, or do you want to choose songs that help you escape a little?' Dorit smiles and suggests they do one more 'heavy' song before they chill out. 'I'm starting to feel tired too,' she notes, and the music therapist is reminded that Dorit's lung capacity is poor. She suggests they move to the piano for a different sound and this process allows them to take a pause of ten minutes as they move and chat casually. They sing two more songs together before Dorit signals that she is done for now. 'What time are you leaving today?' she asks, and is happy to hear that although the music therapist is leaving soon, she will be in again before Dorit leaves the hospice in three days' time.

EVALUATING EFFECTIVENESS

In a palliative care setting, it is accepted that patients will be gradually getting worse. Although all staff would like to minimize the psychological suffering that accompanies a degenerative illness, it is natural for young people to struggle with their demise. The music therapist aims to 'walk with' the young person, *accepting* their presenting needs and responding to them. A good indication of effectiveness can therefore be as simple as participation. Did the young person choose to attend music therapy and did they engage in the process while they were there, taking into account their physical capacity on that day? Sometimes participation may be receptive, and at other times may be indicated by relaxing enough to fall asleep. In the palliative care context, the use of popular songs is most appropriate when engagement and participation is a valued achievement and therefore these factors should be used to gauge effectiveness. This could be charted over numerous visits or described in narrative form in patient notes.

KEY POINTS

- Most teenagers resist the idea of live singing. This should be accepted initially.

- The music therapist needs to be persistent yet understanding about the reticence to perform. It is helpful to acknowledge that most people are nervous about performing.

- Although insight-oriented discussions may result from this active engagement in song singing, an *accepting* stance and minimal probing is more appropriate when this is not indicated as a priority for the young person.

- Participating in shared music making has inherent value. It fosters connectedness and reminds the young person of what he or she can do, rather than focusing on his or her disability.

- It is important to be able to have a reasonable range of songs available for the young person to choose from. These may be ordered in styles, alphabetically by artist, or intentionally randomized.

Group sing-a-longs
SETTING AND PURPOSE

The music therapy group takes place in a special school and is made up of four young men aged between 13 and 15 years, with attention deficit hyperactivity disorder (ADHD). Music therapy offers a middle ground for social encounters that occur between the highly structured and intellectually challenging nature of the classroom and the freedom and chaos of the school grounds. Although the music therapy literature often suggests highly structured, behavioural programmes for people with ADHD, the intention to offer *acceptance* means the programme serves a different purpose. Instead of achieving goals such as increased in-seat time or duration of focus on one activity, the goals for this group are more oriented to providing a positive experience of participation. The goals for this group are for group members to:

- express themselves through singing and playing the instruments

- feel more confident about their creative abilities

- communicate effectively with other group members including shared decision making

- treat one another with respect.

ILLUSTRATIVE VIGNETTE

The group of four young men straggle in one by one over a ten-minute period of time. They are coming from various classrooms across the school and it is time for their music therapy group session. There is constant noise, occasional shouting, and frequent laughter as they pull chairs into a circle, greeting one another and the music therapist, who is an animated participant in the event. Once most of the group are assembled, the music therapist raises her voice to get everyone's attention. 'Oi! Let's get going, shall we?' The group slowly quiets and one boy asks, 'What shall we start with?' There is a regular rhythm to the group and all of the members know the drill. Singing and rapping to begin, followed by playing on the electric instruments and then some chill out time and reflection at the end of the group. The boys feel most comfortable once they get to the rock band stage, but over the past 20 weeks they have started to establish a great sense of rapport during the vocal work as well.

'Well, what kind of mood is everyone in?' asks the music therapist. 'Shall we start with something loud or something quiet?' There is no question of starting quietly and the group all yell at once that something loud would be best. The music therapist strikes her legs twice followed by a clap on the third beat and a pause on the fourth. The young men recognize the classic Queen song 'We Will Rock You' immediately and join in, thumping their legs strongly and clapping vigorously. The music therapist begins the chorus, choosing the easiest part of the song to get the session going. 'We will, we will, rock you... We will, we will, rock you!' She repeats the phrase a number of times until everyone is striking and yelling in synchrony. 'Okay, here comes the verse everyone. Join in if you can.' There is some generalized yelling during the verse, as no one can completely remember the words, but things come back in line as the chorus re-enters. Before the next verse the music therapist calls for another group member to take the lead. 'Sanka, how about you?' she gestures. He shakes his head and points to Brian who jumps up immediately. Brian pretends he has a microphone and dances around the middle of the circle, gesturing extravagantly and screaming loudly. The music therapist waits for the duration of the verse and then re-introduces the chorus. At the end of the first refrain she steps up and smiles at Brian while taking the microphone, before gesturing to him to sit down again and then looking around for the next soloist.

After two boys have had a go and the other two have said no, the music therapist uses some conducting gestures to fade the chorus out. 'Nice one!' she exclaims, 'That was great. Shall we do Nirvana or The Beatles next?' 'Can I play an instrument?' asks Sanka. The music therapist nods and the boys leap up to grab some of the hand percussion and bring them back to their seats. Once again, they know the routine. The large instruments are saved for the jam session, but small percussion instruments are acceptable as part of the singing time. Having something in their hands makes it easier to participate, both instrumentally and also vocally. Greg suggests The Beatles and the music therapist immediately offers, 'With a little help from my friends?' They have made these choices before and she knows that the boys have established a bond that is well represented in this song. She has mentioned in previous sessions that the song is about the kind of friendships they are forming, but doesn't say it again now. It's enough for them to sing together today and she assumes that they remember the connection between their group and the song. The music therapist begins to strum and a cacophony of percussion noise begins. She makes no attempt to draw them into the rhythm of the piece with their instrument playing, focusing instead on using a strong voice to be heard over the noise and looking around while she sings to encourage those that are joining in. The chorus takes off, 'Ohhhhhh, I get by with a little help from my friends; Ohhhhhh, I get high with a little help from my friends.' The young men laugh at the drug reference, as they do every time, and then join in for the last line, 'With a little help from my friennnndddddsssss!' (Lennon and McCartney 1967). They are singing with real energy and feeling this week and the music therapist praises them at the end of the song. 'You guys are starting to sound alright! Okay, one more song before we jam. What will it be?'

EVALUATING EFFECTIVENESS

The focus on *acceptance* with this group means that measuring behaviour as a sign of clinical effectiveness would be a mistake. Although it is common for young people in music therapy groups such as these to focus for longer and exhibit greater rapport than in the classroom, it is not the focus for the evaluation. The most appropriate strategy is to gather the opinions of the group members about how effective the group has been for them and for other group members. This information can be collected through Session Rating Scales (Duncan, Miller and Sparks 2004) or through individual or focus group interviews conducted at regular intervals that include questions such as the following:

- Do you like being in the music therapy group?

- What do you like most?

- What do you like least?

- What do you think of the songs we sing?

- What is it like to actually sing with the others?

- What do you get out of being in the group?

- What do you think the other group members get out of being in the group?

- How do you feel at the end of the group, compared to the beginning?

- Would you recommend this group to other people with ADHD?

The nature of the goals means that a level of objectivity in the evaluation is less relevant than focusing on the young people's perceptions. These questions emphasize an empowering approach by the therapist, where she is focused on hearing the young person's perspective. The information gathered can be used to inform the ongoing development of the programme and the young people's opinions can be taken seriously with regard to what they think of the songs, the singing, and the group itself. It will be important for the therapist to take all group members' opinions into account, along with her own opinions based on her observations of what happens in the group.

KEY POINTS

- It may take some time for the group to get comfortable with the idea of singing, but a repetitive session structure is useful, with frequent introduction of new song repertoire.

- Classic rock songs with four-on-the-floor beats can be very popular with young men who need to express themselves physically.

- Movement (as opposed to structured dance) is an important part of music therapy sessions in this model.

- Music is naturally multi-faceted and the use of instruments with singing is both appropriate and effective.

- There is room for both shared singing and solo opportunities within a song structure.

- Young people shouldn't be pressured to participate. It must be a choice.

- The music therapist is part of the group and needs to model the kind of participation that is expected.

- It is usually helpful for active sessions such as these to be scheduled before a break so that the teenagers are not expected to return to the relatively constrained expectations of the classroom.

FACILITATING DEVELOPMENT

Using songs to achieve *developmental* outcomes is the most structured of the three approaches. Instead of using songs as the basis for projection or participation, in this approach songs provide an opportunity to reward positive behaviours and motivate the achievement of challenging goals. This intention is common when physical and communication needs dominate the young person's everyday experience. Communication may refer to the *development* of social skills when working with teenagers who have minimal cognitive deficits, or it may be more oriented to the beginning of the spectrum, focusing on basic skills such as attention and vocalization for those with profound disabilities. In either case, it is the teenager's attachment to the song that is crucial to its effectiveness in this orientation. Live renditions of songs are useful because some level of participation is often sought to reinforce the positive effects of the reward. Recorded music can be used, but this application of music can and will often be used by other professionals who do not have the ability to play the songs. If it is possible to play the song live, then the music therapist has greater flexibility and can therefore use the song more effectively.

Song requesting
SETTING AND PURPOSE

Simon is a 16-year-old who attends a special school and has spastic, quadriplegic cerebral palsy as well as a severe intellectual disability. He is highly motivated by music, and songs provide a structure that can be used to frame this passion into practice opportunities. The music therapist is part of a multidisciplinary team that is responsible for developing an Individualized Learning Plan for the young man each year, and the music therapist collaborates with his family and other professionals to decide the most useful role for music each year. Motivation is a big issue for this young man, who is beginning to lose functional skills as his behaviour becomes more rebellious and he refuses to do difficult tasks when requested. Simon's family is worried about the loss of previous independence in the wheelchair, as well as his dwindling communication. While music therapy has previously been offered with an *accepting* focus, providing opportunities for creative expression and pleasure, this year the team has agreed to use it in a more focused way. There is still some time for personal expression, but music therapy is also a time for working towards non-musical goals. To this end, Simon's treatment plan includes the broad goals from the Individualized Learning Plan and specific objectives to be achieved incrementally within music therapy.

- For Simon to move independently around the school
  - to push himself from the door of the music room to the piano
  - to push himself along the corridor to the music room
  - to push himself all the way from the classroom to the music room.

- For Simon to use his voice to communicate preferences

  ◦ to choose between two songs using the word 'yes'

  ◦ to vocalize freely within songs

  ◦ to vocalize on cue within songs.

- For Simon to indicate his choice of activities and actively participate in them

  ◦ to use smiles/laughter/vocalizations to indicate enjoyment of songs

  ◦ to indicate what songs are preferred from known and new repertoire

  ◦ for Simon to sing, play and dance as desired.

ILLUSTRATIVE VIGNETTE

'Hi there, Simon,' the music therapist calls out from the door of the music room. Simon has just rounded the corner at the end of the corridor and the teacher assistant farewells him before heading back to the classroom. 'Come on Simon, you can do it – push yourself down to the music room so we can have a sing together,' the music therapist calls, reminding the young man of the job ahead of him. Simon makes an effort and pushes down on the wheels of his chair, moving himself forward a little. The music therapist starts up a pulse on the djembe while standing at the door and begins to sing Simon's favourite song, 'All the Small Things', by Blink 182. Simon laughs and waves his hands in the air at the sound of the song. He pushes himself a little more and then stops, still laughing. The music therapist stops playing and calls out again. 'Good one, Simon, keep going. Push some more.' It takes nearly a minute and more encouragement, but soon Simon reaches down and pushes the wheels around some more. As he starts, the music therapist starts again from the beginning of the next phrase. The reaction is the same, another push and then smiles, laughter and hand waving. 'Keep coming, Simon,' the music therapist repeats. This time when he starts again, she waits until he begins to stop and provides the reward of the music after he has finished moving. That way he is able to enjoy the music and be motivated to get more of it. It takes 15 minutes, but eventually Simon reaches the door to the music room and the therapist offers some help to push him over to the piano. It has taken half the allocated session time just to get into the room.

Once at the piano, the music therapist offers two songs for Simon to sing along with. 'Would you like to sing "Hallelujah" by Leonard Cohen, or "Teenage Dirtbag" by Wheatus?' Simon laughs and waves his hands as the music therapist sings the first line of 'Teenage Dirtbag', and makes no movement when she sings the first line of 'Hallelujah'. 'Okay Simon, do you want to do "Teenage Dirtbag"?' the music therapist confirms. Simon smiles. 'Can you use your voice to say "yes", Simon?' the music therapist asks. 'Yeeesss,' replies Simon with some effort after about ten seconds. The music therapist is ready with guitar in hand and strums the opening chord immediately after the 'yes' is provided. 'His name is Simon, I had a dream about him, he rings my bell,' (Wheatus 2000) the music therapist rocks, substituting Simon's name and gender for the one in the original song. Simon smiles and makes some sounds during the first verse and the music therapist builds up the guitar strumming into the end of the bridge, building up anticipation for the arrival of the chorus. 'Coz I'm just a...' she begins, then pauses. Simon is silent and the music therapist keeps strumming the chord to encourage his singing, before dropping out. 'Hey Simon, you know the words. Can you sing for me?' She plays the last bar of the bridge then leads into the chorus again, this time moving to the next chord. Again there is silence from Simon. They repeat the pattern two more times before Simon vocalizes intentionally into the space. 'Yeah!' responds the music therapist and continues through the song. At the next chorus it only takes two repetitions to get the vocalization on cue, so the music therapist also requests the last word as well: 'Come listen to Iron Maiden baby with...' Simon vocalizes spontaneously at the right time and they both laugh and cheer before moving on to complete the song.

EVALUATING EFFECTIVENESS

The behaviours identified in the music therapy objectives should be measured regularly as a way of determining if music therapy has been effective in facilitating the *development* of Simon's physical and communication skills. A simple checklist can be made up for each session where a score is marked including how far he pushed himself, how long it took, how many songs were chosen and how frequently he vocalized both freely and on cue. Brief descriptive notes should also be maintained noting the quality of Simon's behaviour and to monitor whether the new regime is diminishing the positive nature of musical experiences previously achieved. If this occurs, the multidisciplinary team will need to discuss whether the *development* of skills is the most valuable use of music therapy. The music therapist will report on Simon's progress to the classroom teacher on a regular basis, as well as contributing to the bi-annual report that is sent home to his parents. She may have additional contact with the family to discuss emerging song preferences, and identify if any new repertoire could be included from home.

KEY POINTS

- The teenager already has an existing relationship with music and the music therapist which is used as the basis of the intervention.

- Key songs have been identified in advance and can therefore be used effectively.

- The therapist must be determined to provide practice opportunities and prepared to wait and then repeat opportunities until desired behaviours are achieved.

- This may involve less overt pleasure and more overt effort on the part of the teenager.

- New material should be offered regularly in order to assess changing preferences and reduce the monotony of sessions.

- Recorded music would be less effective in this setting because the music therapist is manipulating pacing in order to motivate participation.

- Record keeping is essential in order to document slow progress and to provide evidence of benefit or the need to consider a different focus.

CONCLUSION

The five case examples presented in this chapter have been divided quite clearly into each of the three different therapeutic intentions: fostering *understanding*, offering *acceptance* and facilitating *development*. Despite this, each one of the methods described can actually be used with a different orientation. It often requires only a small tweak of each method to change direction, which then requires a change in the strategy for evaluating effectiveness. For example, song contributions can be used to facilitate *development* by requiring each participant to produce certain behaviours before his or her song is played for the group – such as clear or polite requesting, or listening to the songs of others. Evaluation would then become linked to time taken to produce or maintain the required behaviour. Another example is the intention of using shared singing of songs in the paediatric palliative care setting, which could easily focus on fostering *understanding* if the young woman was prepared to discuss the meaning and reason for choosing the song. Such a discussion would potentially lead to a range of insights, taking time away from singing and emphasizing verbal consolidation instead. Evaluation would then be altered to focus on the content of that discussion, rather than the level of musical participation. The intention, rather than the method, has a clear impact on the most appropriate type of evaluation. With this in mind, it becomes relatively simple to select evaluation strategies and also to capture outcomes most effectively.

This flexibility in methods is well suited to blended, eclectic music therapy practice. Although the orientation of the setting where the music therapist works has a strong influence on how she works, it is not the only influence. Responding to the young person's needs and capacities on any given day can be the most powerful gift the therapist has to offer. It is also crucial to the client's achievement of successful outcomes. The music therapist may naturally 'go with it' when working with a group of young people with behavioural disorders, but then may resort to focusing on the *development* of social skills on a given day because of the volatile presentation of group members due to circumstances outside the session. This kind of flexibility means that the music therapist must be intuitive and focused, with a range of methods available to suit the situation as it occurs. It is important to have a documented treatment plan in most settings, but it is equally important to depart from the plan if the circumstances require it.

Chapter 5

Writing Original Songs

Music is an inspiration for many people and songs have become the most popular way of communicating this magic. The idea of writing a song is tantalizing for many teenagers and it is inspiring to experience the deep commitment they make to the process once they have decided to go for it. In this chapter, I will illustrate how to write songs with individuals and groups of teenagers in varying ways, depending on whether the intention is to foster understanding, offer acceptance or facilitate development. Although it is possible for the music therapist to create the song outside of the therapy session, the examples in this chapter are all grounded in song composition with the teenagers, not for them.

The idea of writing songs in music therapy can seem daunting for the music therapist. It does demand an instant blend of tremendous creativity and empathy. This is particularly apparent when working in brief encounters with young people, where songs can be written, recorded and burned to CD in a single session. When a longer process is indicated, a song can be composed with the teenager over a number of weeks or months and may sometimes result in a performance (as described more fully in Chapter 10). The level of originality in the composition can be wide-ranging, and the examples provided in this chapter vary from replacing words to existing songs and drawing inspiration from classic hits, through to completely original songs with or without words. This is a powerful use of the existing relationship between teenagers and songs. It is not a method for the faint-hearted and it requires a good deal of musical and therapeutic skill, combined with a good dose of genuine interest and compositional satisfaction.

FOSTERING UNDERSTANDING

When using songwriting to foster understanding, the focus is primarily on experiences that promote insight and contemplation. This occurs both within the lyrics that are composed, as well as through the discussion that takes place around the song. The therapist intends to assist young people in gaining a better *understanding* of their previous life experiences and unconscious influences. Simply put, the music therapist does this by encouraging the teenagers to contribute ideas or a story from their current life situation and then asking probing questions about how these relate to their previous experiences or current dynamics. The therapist then fosters *understandings* by listening carefully and seeking further knowledge. However, not all teenagers will wish to discuss these issues, important and relevant as they may be. Song composition without words provides an alternative to improvisation with these less articulate clients, by working on the development of a piece of music and incorporating some discursive elements when possible and appropriate. The musical material can be interpreted for meaning as it would be in an improvisatory context, but the process is structured and outcome-oriented rather than freely emergent.

Song creation
SETTING AND PURPOSE

The music therapy group occurs regularly as part of the programme on the adolescent unit of a metropolitan paediatric hospital, with different patients attending each time. The young people in the group on this day are all teenagers who have cystic fibrosis and many return to the hospital two or three times a year for a 'tune up'. Music therapy group work is highly valued by the hospital team of nurses, doctors, psychologists, psychiatrists and other allied health professionals because fostering connections between teenagers in the hospital environment is a priority. A sense of camaraderie is proven to enhance coping and music is one of the few activities young people are willing to gather for. Although the hospital is focused on medical care, fostering *understandings* in this context can assist young people with chronic illness to grapple with the existential challenges they face as a result of their life-threatening condition. Taking all this into account, the aims of the group are as follows:

- to provide a space where teenagers can access support and understanding in context of their shared experience of illness

- to offer creative and non-verbal avenues for connection

- to encourage the discussion of issues arising from their illness, and foster insight

- to accept differences in coping styles and acknowledge differing perspectives and needs within the group.

ILLUSTRATIVE VIGNETTE

'Who's coming to the recreation room today?' asks the music therapist as she wanders into the ward of the adolescent specific unit at the public hospital. There are a couple of mumbles, but Rejane is the only one to make any movement. 'What's happening today?' she asks as she begins to climb out of her bed. 'Music,' offers the music therapist. 'I thought we might get out the guitars and drum stuff and write a song or something.' There is a rustle of movement about the room, and Rejane slides her feet into her slippers. 'Righto, I'm coming. What about you Pei Xin?' 'Nah, my mum's coming in soon,' comes the reply. The music therapist provides reassurances that the nurse will let any visitors know where they are. 'You can come back any time you like. It's not like you're trapped there,' she jokes. 'How about you Dominic? Robert, I thought we might make it rock a bit today, so it would be great to have someone who can play guitar.' The music therapist has worked with four of the six young people in the room, so it is not so difficult to convince some people to attend. One new guy on the ward is brave enough to join in as well, and eventually four of the teenagers amble casually over to the recreation room, yelling to the nurses at the main desk to say where they will be and what they will be doing. It is never easy to get a group of tired and sick teenagers out of bed, over to the music room and in the mood to really talk, but usually somebody comes. It might be one person one day, six the next and none the day after that, but it is a lot to ask of hospitalized teens, so this needs to be accepted in context.

Once the small group reaches the recreation room where all the musical equipment is kept, the music therapist asks the young people to help her get the instruments, microphones and amplifiers out of the cupboard and set them up. There is casual banter throughout this process, with the music therapist focusing on building up a sense of engagement and anticipation. 'Some days you just wake up wanting to rock, don't ya?' Finally they are all seated around the large art table in the middle of the room. 'So what do you think we could write a song about today?' There are mumbles and general cries of 'I dunno' in response. 'Well, what do you guys have in common? Usually when musicians collaborate on writing a song, it has to be about something they all understand. What would that be for you?' she prompts. 'Well, duh, we're all in hospital,' groans one of the young men sarcastically. 'Well, that's pretty obvious,' replies the music therapist, responding in the same tone. 'But *why* are you all here?' This is a tougher question, and despite the fact that these teenagers are living on the same ward and watching one another receive treatments on a daily basis, they do not often talk about such things.

The music therapist writes the words 'Why are we here?' at the top of the big white piece of paper. Silence. The music therapist reflects on the multiple levels that are opened up by this question. She has used this phrase before in generating songs with groups of teenagers in hospital, and often it is an opportunity to compare diagnoses and symptoms and complain about the fact that they would prefer to be at home. But this particular group of young people has the same chronic illness and all of them are constantly confronted by existential questions about the meaning of life as they come to terms with the loss of their peers. The music therapist is ready to offer a comment about the complexity of the question when Rejane pipes up. 'I wrote a poem about that the other week,' she says. The group looks at her with respect. 'It's called "The Rainbow Travellers",' she continues. 'How do you know how to write poems?' one of the boys asks. 'I do it a lot,' she replies quietly, 'It helps me cope.' 'I'd love to hear it,' says the music therapist, and some of the group offer enthusiastic support. With more encouragement, Rejane goes back to the ward to get her journal. In her absence, the music therapist engages the remaining three teenagers in a discussion of the music. 'Are you good to play guitar, Robert?' she asks. He has been completely quiet until now, but at this question he nods and walks over to plug in the electric. The remaining two participants do not play instruments so the music therapist holds up some percussion instruments, one after the other, to show how they work and explain a little bit about them. 'The djembe is a drum that is often used in African music, it's great to play with your hands and really easy to do. These egg shakers look pretty simple, but you can get a nice action going on them like this. The wind chimes sound really atmospheric, but it's hard to make them shut up...' The young man chooses the djembe, and Pei Xin, the youngest of the group, grabs the wind chimes.

When Rejane returns she passes the poem to the music therapist to read out loud.

Where are we going to?

What do we bother for?

When everything we do

Won't last for that much more.

We're always chasing stars

We are the rainbow travellers

'Wow, that's intense,' mumbles Robert. Rejane looks at him angrily. 'No,' he says, 'it's good, it's just full on.' She relaxes a little, but is obviously feeling vulnerable after sharing her personal material. 'What kind of guitar would sound good with that?' asks the music therapist. Robert fiddles with the neck of the guitar, making actions over the strings, but not playing anything out loud. The group watch him and wait, knowing that he plays guitar a lot and is possibly having an important creative moment. A minute passes before he speaks. 'Maybe something like this…' He plays a poignant riff on the middle strings. It is a falling melody, and the music therapist comments on it. 'That sounds like a falling star, or the end of a rainbow or something. Did you mean to do that?' Robert nods and starts playing the riff over and over, getting annoyed at himself whenever he plays a wrong note. 'What do you guys think?' asks the music therapist. The group nods their support and Rejane seems satisfied. The music therapist grabs an acoustic guitar and tries out some chords to find something that will fit with the melody. This takes a few minutes and some discussion with the group to make sure they approve.

Once the chord sequence, riff and words have been worked out, it is time to pull the song together. The music therapist is conscious that they have been working for nearly 45 minutes and knows from experience that some of the group members will be starting to get tired or restless. There is no guarantee of getting the same group together the next day so she offers a choice. 'Does anyone need to go and get a drink or anything, or can we keep going a bit to finish this off?' The group agrees that they can go a little longer and the music therapist proposes a structure for the song and suggests when the different instruments will come in. A glissando along the wind chimes will set the scene, then the riff should be repeated four times before the drums and acoustic guitar enter in rhythm, and then the poem. Rejane is not keen to sing or rap, and no one else expresses interest. 'How about some spoken word?' suggests the music therapist. 'You can read the poem and we will pull back in volume while you do, then we'll build up again before fading out in the opposite way to the beginning.' The music therapist looks at each group member to ascertain whether they are happy with this and all look at one another and nod. The first time through is rough, but by the third time the song is complete and the group plays it through two more times. The drums are not really in time, and the key signature of the riff is unclear, but the power of the poem is captured by the ambient musical background and no one seems to notice. The music therapist notes that it is a beautiful expression of their challenging battle with chronic illness.

By this time it is clear that the group has had enough. They are satisfied and they are also hungry. 'I'm going back to the ward,' says Robert, and the other young man agrees. 'See you later guys, nice work,' says the music therapist. They wave and smile as they wander casually away. 'How are you going, Rejane?' asks the music therapist, turning to the two remaining teenagers. 'Yeah Rejane, that was really brave. Good on ya!' says Pei Xin, 'I wish I could write like that.' 'How do *you* cope with it all?' the music therapist asks Pei Xin, and they launch into a discussion of coping with being sick, and the girls focus on the important role of their families. Ten minutes later and the two young women are also ready to go. 'Do you want to do some more work on that song another time, Rejane?' asks the music therapist. Rejane smiles, 'That would be cool,' she says. 'We can practise it over the next couple of days and make a recording if you like,' offers the music therapist. As it turns out, Rejane is discharged the next day, but when she returns five months later, she reminds the music therapist of her promise, and they work with a different young man to develop and record the song, even performing it at an adolescent health conference six months later.

EVALUATING EFFECTIVENESS

The hospital fulfils many roles in the lives of teenagers with chronic illness. It provides medical services, psychological support, peer interaction and often strong relationships with caring adults such as nurses. In this context, a range of intentions are appropriate and vary on a case-by-case basis. The focus on fostering *understanding* in this group emerged from the response of the young people to the question posed. Although this involved silence and contemplation, it was clear that deeper meanings were being considered. Given this, the level of cohesion achieved in working together towards the creation of the song is an important indicator of effectiveness, and the level of participation should be included in each of the teenagers' files. The other focus for evaluation is related to the depth of information conveyed. In this case, verbal, non-verbal and metaphoric material was utilized to describe the existential challenge of facing an early death. Although not all the group members participated verbally in this level of contemplation, the profound nature of the poem and the musical response can be evaluated positively. The participation of Pei Xin in processing the poem was also significant. The less collaborative presence of the remaining young man is secondary, but still meaningful. This is the information that needs to be documented in the patient notes, stated in a general way.

KEY POINTS

- Engaging young people in a hospital setting can be challenging. Existing relationships with individuals can be helpful in gathering together a group.

- Young people in hospital are sick and therefore usually lethargic or in pain. Their medical needs must be taken into account at all times.

- Explaining songwriting by relating it to the processes used by professional musicians is both interesting and appealing to adolescents.

- Opportunities for meaningful discussion do not always present; however, when they do, it is important to foster them.

- Probes are very effective at taking a superficial discussion to a deeper level. Adolescents will only engage in a deeper level of discussion if they want to, so these probes can be presented as opportunities rather than demands.

- The song provides an opportunity to use metaphors and symbols to describe situations that are otherwise difficult to articulate.

- The music therapist may need to take a lead role in formulating the song in a brief intervention such as this. Making suggestions about how to structure the song is a particularly useful framework to offer.

- It is essential that the music therapist is able to be immediate in her creative contribution since each session should be conceptualized as a complete treatment, due to the possibility of discharge or worsening condition.

- Closure, or semi-closure, should be achieved in every session.

Musical composition
SETTING AND PURPOSE

The day programme that 15-year-old Christian attends is an alternative to school, providing programmes that seek to engage young people and provide them with a refuge and some hope. The team strives to reconnect adolescents with a range of systems in some way, working with individuals to identify strategies that might help them stay out of trouble and find something meaningful to do with their time. Music therapy, art and leisure activities are seen as central to engaging the interest of the young people, and this is then used to link them into services. The overarching aim of music therapy is therefore always the same – to engage the teenager in positive relationships with peers and adults through musical interaction.

Specific objectives are determined once the relationship with each young person has been established. Christian is involved in the programme after being expelled from four schools and being implicated in a number of criminal activities with gangs of youth. His tough demeanour is easily penetrable and the team feels that he would benefit from increased understanding of the historical experiences that may be leading him towards a life of crime. The objectives for Christian on this day can be constructed as follows:

- to develop a trusting relationship with the music therapist

- to reflect on his current lifestyle and how this might be connected to his history

- to articulate his level of satisfaction/unhappiness with his current situation.

ILLUSTRATIVE VIGNETTE

Christian is hanging out at the computers that are located in a central room of the day programme. He seems at a loose end and keeps moving from one computer to another, looking around in a self-conscious way. The music therapist walks over and sits down at a computer, going to www. chordie.com and looking for a piece of music that another teenager has suggested in a group. 'Watcha doin', Christian?' she asks casually. 'Ahhh, nothing,' comes the reply. Another minute passes. 'Wanna do something?' asks the music therapist. 'Nah,' says Christian. 'I've got this programme called ACID on my laptop,' comments the music therapist in response to his anticipated rejection. 'It's software for writing electronic tracks. I can show it to you if you like?' Pause. 'Oh, okay,' replies the young man, 'Where is it?' The music therapist goes to get the computer and comes back. 'Where do you want to sit?' she asks. 'Maybe we should use one of the break-out rooms so we can make some noise and also talk about stuff as we go.' 'Okay.' They wander into a smaller room down the hall, and the music therapist leaves the door a little open so people know where they are and what they are doing. She can always close the door if they start discussing very private material, and that may not be the case.

The programme boots up and the music therapist illustrates some of the features. She shows where the library of loops is and how they are categorized according to instrument and style. There are beats, riffs, effects and vocal lines that can be used to make up the composition. It is easy to listen through to the sounds and then drag the preferred sounds onto the score where they will be automatically synced and layered on top of one another. The music therapist moves her chair to the side and encourages Christian to sit in the centre of the computer. They talk about the sounds as he begins to listen through them, and the music therapist focuses on the music in these early stages, asking probing questions about what style the different beats belong to, what instruments Christian likes, and what kind of music he normally listens to. This gets a dialogue going and sets the scene for discussion during the creation, rather than the music therapist simply watching while the young man plays with the computer. Christian is not interested in talking non-stop, but he is happy to share the experience, and answers her questions.

As the texture of the piece begins to build up, the music therapist makes some suggestions about spreading the musical material out a little and thinking about structure. Most teenagers layer an increasing number of loops and the sound becomes very thick and murky. Christian grasps this concept and the piece soon stretches out to a spacious five-minute track, which impresses the young man. By this stage, it has been nearly an hour of focused work and the music therapist starts to make meaning of the musical composition. 'So what would be a good name for this piece, do you think?' 'What do you mean?' asks the young man. 'Well, whenever you make music, it says something about who you are and what your life experience is,' offers the music therapist. 'How does this piece of music say something about you?' The young man is hesitant. 'Think about what's been going on for you in the past 24 hours and whether or not this music is similar to that,' suggests the music therapist. 'Mum kicked me out of the house last night because I wouldn't do what she wanted, and we had a big fight,' reflects the young man sadly. 'I had to sleep in the park again.' 'Oh, that's tough, Christian,' responds the music therapist, waiting to see if he will elaborate. When he doesn't she returns the focus to metaphorical meanings in the music. 'Is there something of the park in this piece – it seems kind of spacious and spread out?' 'Yeah, I suppose, and it sounds a bit sad too, doesn't it?' Christian replies. 'Yep, it does,' replies the music therapist quietly. 'Why don't we listen again?' she suggests, and clicks the play button before probing further. 'Does your mum kick you out a lot?' 'Yep, ever since she got this new guy. He doesn't like me, so it's easier if I'm not around.' The music therapist asks more questions, and Christian is happy to talk about how things are not getting any better in his life. The music therapist enquires how long things have been like this and Christian identifies that his real dad left when he was three years old, and that he thinks that is when the chaos began. But it feels as though it has always been that way.

There are no quick answers to Christian's life, and it is clear that he has some insight into his situation and the challenges he is facing. The music therapist reflects that he seems committed to staying with his mum, even though it gets tough at home. 'Well, she's my mum. She needs me,' he says firmly. It has been 90 minutes by now, and the music therapist hesitates to start a new discussion about who needs whom. 'Do you need to be anywhere, Christian, or can we keep talking and listening to your new track?' 'What time is it?' he asks. 'Three p.m.' the music therapist replies. 'Righto. I've got to pick my brother up from school.' Christian stands up quickly. The two agree to meet again in the next couple of days and finalize the track and burn it to CD. 'We can talk more, too,' clarifies the music therapist, 'it might help.' There is no point making meeting times, since Christian's life is too chaotic to work with these kinds of schedules. But the connection has been made and the music therapist will follow up and keep an eye out for more opportunities. 'Great track, Christian – what will I save it as?' 'How about "Park at Night"?' he replies. 'Cool, I'll keep it here for you. See you soon, I hope.' 'Check ya,' replies Christian, and is out the door.

EVALUATING EFFECTIVENESS

The clarity of the team's plan for this young man makes it very simple to evaluate how effective the music therapy session was. Each of the objectives can be considered and the degree to which they are met provides the evaluation. Christian did seem to feel comfortable with the music therapist, as seen by his willingness to continue working on the track for 90 minutes and allow for discussion to take place in that context. It is worth noting that he seemed able to continue for this long even though his problems with school are likely rooted in an inability to focus in the classroom. After a lengthy introductory period of one hour, Christian was willing to discuss the challenges of the past 24 hours and also share information about his family history. He did not appear to be asking himself questions about repeating the behavioural patterns learned from his mother, or accepting responsibility for the problems this was creating for him. This suggests some material for further discussion, either with the music therapist or another team member, if the opportunity arises. Christian was able to express his emotional state by describing the composition as 'a bit sad' and this suggests that music therapy may be useful as an opportunity for emotional expression and release. The music therapist communicates this evaluation of the session to the team in the next meeting.

KEY POINTS

- Young people will usually say 'no' if they are asked directly to do something new. It is worth following up with more information so that they feel less vulnerable.

- Young men are usually very interested in music technology and it is often a useful entry point for music therapy.

- Composing songs on the computer does not have to be an isolating activity. It is helpful to maintain a level of engagement from the outset.

- It only takes a little time for most young people to decide whether they trust an available adult, so it is possible to ask probing questions in a single session.

- Young people often appreciate being asked directive questions because it can give them a new perspective. They can be trusted to refuse to discuss the topic if it is uncomfortable. If the music therapist persists in the face of resistance, they may withdraw and even leave the session.

- Fostering *understanding* does not require regularity if that does not match with the young person's capacity. Much as they try to be, teenagers are not usually in charge of their own schedules and many do not wear a watch or carry a diary, although they will likely have a phone which has the capacity for both these tasks.

- Team work is a much better approach to supporting young people with chaotic lives because it is unlikely that they will be regular participants in any one activity.

OFFERING ACCEPTANCE

Offering acceptance through songwriting is the most natural and empowering combination of values and methods for teenagers. Their natural affinity with the song genre is accepted and respected in this approach, and no further expectation is put upon the therapeutic encounter. The role of the music therapist is to facilitate the teenagers' ability to compose the song and to take a role appropriate for complementing their creative capacity. For some teenagers, this will involve the music therapist providing most of the musical material and helping them to structure their ideas into lyrics. For other teenagers, an entire composition is within their reach with the support of the music therapist. The music therapist needs to ask questions that help teenagers develop a language for the kind of music they want to create and then fill in the blanks for the levels of understanding that are not feasible. The responsibility of the teenagers is to commit to the song, and to pour themselves into it – a role they usually take up with relish. Musical engagement is central – incorporating composition, lyric development and sometimes performance and recording. It is possible to compose many songs within a therapeutic encounter; however, teenagers often find that a small number is satisfactory unless they are very musically inclined, so pacing should be considered with this in mind.

Group song composition
SETTING AND PURPOSE

A group of ambulant 14-year-olds with moderate intellectual disabilities form one class group in a special school and spend many of their days in close proximity to one another. Most of them also spend some days in conventional school settings as part of an integration programme. Although these teenagers are not capable of the curriculum requirements of the mainstream school, they attend for the opportunities for peer interaction and community building. The friendships between class members in the special school are significant, and contrast with the isolation individual teenagers often experience when trying to be a part of the community setting. The dynamics of the classroom are usually intense and the teacher has conveyed that team work is an important objective for the group this year. With this in mind, the goals and objectives for the group are as follows:

- For the group to function as a team during the process of songwriting

    ◦ to cooperate in writing the song

    ◦ to resolve disagreements in ideas about the song

    ◦ to compromise about various aspects of the song

    ◦ to choose the genre of the song collectively

    ◦ to allocate roles to group members in practising/performing the song.

- For the group to express themselves in the songwriting process

    ◦ to contribute their own ideas for lyrics

    ◦ to choose a style that reflects their preferred music

    ◦ to participate in a role that suits their self-perception

    ◦ to sing/play in an expressive way.

- For the group to have a positive and engaging experience
  - to be involved in the creation of the song
  - to join in practising and performing the song
  - to enjoy some aspect of the song creation – writing, making decisions, singing, playing or performing.

The music therapist is also conscious of the specific goals for each student according to their individual learning plan. These are incorporated into the session as appropriate.

ILLUSTRATIVE VIGNETTE

The group has just completed the Hello Rap. There are six 14-year-olds present, accompanied by one classroom assistant. They are seated in a circle facing one another and there are 45 minutes left of the session. 'Who wants to write a song today?' asks the music therapist enthusiastically, looking around at each of the group members. 'Me!' yells Leslie. 'Me too!' comes the chorus. Some students jump out of their chairs with excitement. 'Can we perform it in the Christmas concert?' asks Inge. The classroom assistant and music therapist exchange glances and raise their eyebrows then nod at one another. 'That's a great idea, Inge. Let's see if we can organize it. But first, what will we write a song about today?'.

The group members look at one another and make some suggestions. 'How about football?' suggests one young man. 'No, I want to make it about dancing,' counters a young woman. The music therapist writes both ideas on the blackboard. 'I don't want to sing,' says Leslie, 'I want to rap!' The music therapist nods at the young man and writes 'Rap' on the board, over to the side. 'What else could we write about?' she repeats. 'We'll get a bunch of ideas together and then choose.' The group continues to suggest concrete topics and the music therapist validates them all, writing each one up on the board, circling ideas that are suggested more than once. The teenagers are enthusiastic and uninhibited, so the process is fast and furious. 'You know, I can see an idea in this,' suggests the music therapist. 'Lots of these ideas are about things that you do with friends.' Many of the teenagers nod their heads vigorously, although a couple look blank. 'You see,' explains the music therapist, 'you play football with friends, dance with friends, go to the movies with friends.' 'I go to the movies with my mum,' Bella counters. 'Yeah, you're right. A lot of these things are also about families. What shall we do, write a song about friends or families?' 'Friends!' 'Family!' come the replies. 'Okay, let's vote. Who is for friends? Family?' Three raise their hands for each. Bella starts to sound distressed, 'I really want to do it about my family,' she says. 'But I *really* want to do it about friends,' replies Leslie. 'Why don't we do both?' suggests Inge, brightly. 'Yeah!' the group yells, 'Good idea, Inge'.

Having agreed on the topic, the group turns to the discussion of style. 'Leslie asked for rap,' reminds the music therapist. 'What does everyone else think?' Once again there is some disagreement and the volume increases as different students start demanding their own way. 'It's easy to do both,' says the music therapist after a minute. 'We could swap between rap and singing – like the Spice Girls do.' The music therapist launches into the first verse and chorus of the Spice Girls hit 'Wannabe': 'Yo, I'll tell you what I want, what I really really want' (Spice Girls 1996).

Some of the young people join in for parts of the song and most are jumping around in the middle of the circle by the time it ends, including the music therapist who is pretending to sing into a microphone. The group laugh and gradually sit down. 'Why don't we do a rap like that at the beginning,' suggests the music therapist, 'and then we'll make up a way to sing the rest?' The teenagers agree. They are excited now and find it difficult to stay seated. 'Why don't we practise the rap bit?' says the music therapist, deciding that it is not the right moment to try to focus on lyrics. She grabs some microphones out of the cupboards and connects them to the mixing desk. 'Who knows how the Spice Girls rap goes?' she asks. Leslie and Inge hold up their hands and are passed the microphones. 'Anyone want a tambourine or a shaker?' The two remaining girls say yes and grab something. 'I wanna play drums,' calls one young man. 'Not today,' replies the music therapist, 'but you can have a hand drum,' she offers. This is accepted. 'Jonathan, do you want anything?' 'No.' 'I think there's one more microphone?' 'Oh, okay,' he says and comes over to the cupboard to look. 'Be careful with this one,' whispers the music therapist, 'It's a really good one that I don't get out very often.' Everyone stands in the middle of the chairs and the music therapist counts them in: 'One, two, three, four. Tell me what you want,' she begins, and the group joins in the yelling.

After five minutes the group begins to tire, and after ten minutes they are more subdued. 'Okay, we have 20 minutes left,' comments the music therapist, 'Let's see if we can get some of this song written.' The group sit back in their chairs and stare up at the words on the board. Most of the group can only recognize one or two words, so the music therapist reads all the ideas out loud. Once she has finished doing this, she offers a suggestion. 'If we start with "I want to 'something' with my friends." What could go in there – instead of something?' she asks. 'Sing,' calls Inge. 'Dance,' calls another girl. 'I want to sing with my friends. I want to dance with my friends. I want to...we need one more, what do you think Leslie?' 'How about hang out?' he suggests. 'I want to hang out with my friends. My friends are... How could we end this verse?' asks the music therapist, looking around. 'Fun,' says one of the group members. The music therapist runs through the four lines again, this time singing a melody. 'Do you like how that sounded?' she asks the group. There is some response, but not much. 'What about if I sing-rap it like this?' She tries again, using a talking style but moving between two notes a major fourth apart. 'Yeah, that's better,' someone calls. 'What do you think, Inge?' asks the music therapist. 'I liked it,' she replies.

The music therapist runs through the same process again, but focusing the next verse on family rather friends. 'I want to "something" with my family.' Soon the song is partially complete. 'We've got time to run through it once before the end of the session,' the music therapist calls. 'Stand up and we'll have a go.' The music therapist leads the song with a strong voice and yells out the action word in each line before they arrive at it. It is messy but fun and the group are laughing as the bell rings. 'See you next week, everyone,' calls the music therapist as she begins to wind up the microphone cables, 'We'll see if we want to do more then.'

EVALUATING EFFECTIVENESS

Although a traditional plan with goals and objectives has been developed, the approach adopted by the music therapist means that a more subjective style of evaluation is appropriate. The objectives documented under each goal are not easily quantifiable. It is not simple to count the amount of 'involvement in the creation of the song', or measure how well a group member has 'chosen a style that reflects his or her preferred music', although it is possible. The objectives should be used as a guide to the implementation of the method, but not as the basis of evaluation. The focus of evaluation will be the way that the young people engage in the process, and the therapist will need to document the happenings of each session in a descriptive form. In particular, each teenager's participation should be documented individually so that the music therapist is able to determine who benefited from involvement and who has struggled. Documentation focused only on the group as a whole would be less insightful.

KEY POINTS

- It is helpful to sample ideas from other songs as inspiration. This does not result in any lesser experience of creativity.

- Being able to incorporate different ideas into one song assists in working with group dynamics. Collaborative song creation is a challenge for anybody, so creativity in managing group dynamics is crucial.

- Songs may not sound cohesive in the traditional sense when different styles are incorporated into one, but this is not the focus in music therapy song creation where *acceptance* is prioritized.

- Being able to work with concrete ideas is crucial for this population because of their intellectual capacity.

- Keeping lyrics simple and repetitive assists in memorizing/ learning the lyrics.

- The music therapist needs to offer clear choices between two options throughout the process. This makes it possible for the young people to drive the composition without creating expectations that are too high.

- Singing the song over and over is the best way to learn it.

- It is useful to make a rough recording of a song at the end of the session so the music therapist, as well as the group members, can remember it the following week.

Song composition
SETTING AND PURPOSE

Grace is a 15-year-old Sudanese young woman attending an English language school for newly arrived students who do not have adequate skills to enter into the mainstream school system. Students stay at the school for a maximum of 12 months and the programme aims to assist them in successfully negotiating the demands of school as well as preparing them for participation in the wider school community. Music therapy is one of a small number of creative arts programmes that the school offers in addition to classroom support. Grace was referred to music therapy because she was not making connections with other students in the school. She was silent in the classroom and was seen sitting by herself during break. She did not respond to approaches from her classroom teacher, although she seemed comfortable with him. Music therapy was seen as an opportunity for non-verbal expression that may lead to a greater engagement in school activities. With this in mind, the goals and objectives for Grace were as follows:

- For Grace to participate in music therapy

    ◦ to attend sessions willingly

    ◦ to engage in musical experiences

    ◦ to communicate either verbally or musically with the music therapist.

- For Grace to express herself in music therapy

    ◦ to make choices about preferred activities

    ◦ to use the musical opportunities to express something of her identity

    ◦ to consider how to blend the two cultural identities of her old and new countries through music

    ◦ to communicate about her level of coping either verbally or musically with the music therapist.

- For Grace to engage in the school community

    ◦ to feel more confident as a result of successful experiences in music therapy

    ◦ for this confidence to be reflected in greater levels of participation in the classroom

    ◦ to interact with others outside of the classroom situation.

ILLUSTRATIVE VIGNETTE

Grace enters the small classroom with little hesitation. This is her fourth session with the music therapist and she is beginning to feel comfortable with the expectations of music therapy. The first session was very different. She arrived looking timid and this had escalated to terror when her teacher actually left to go back to the classroom leaving her alone with the music therapist. Luckily, the music therapy programme was well established and the music therapist was able to show her some traditional instruments from her own country as a way of offering something familiar. She had engaged with the instruments a little, but not been willing to play because they were for 'the men'. The initial sessions had involved lots of listening to music together at the computer and gradually building up some rapport while talking about different pop stars. Grace was able to use language effectively once comfortable, and the music therapist had suggested that they compose an R'n'B song.

Grace smiles widely when the music therapist reminds her of this decision, saying, 'Yes, just like Beyonce!' The women grin at one another and the music therapist moves to set up a keyboard that has a good range of beats in it. 'Okay, let's start by choosing a beat. Listen to these and see which one you like.' The music therapist supports her words with hand gestures and Grace is soon scrolling her way through the list of beats in the keyboard, listening to each one for at least a minute and then saying 'yes/no/maybe'. The music therapist reaches for a piece of paper and writes down the number of each beat and the verdict. There are only ten loops in the R'n'B section, so after ten minutes it is time to make the final decision. They listen through again to the ones that were 'yes' votes and after some consideration Grace chooses the first style she heard. It is a fairly traditional representation of the genre with little embellishment. The music therapist notes that they are half way through the session and comments that this may take a few weeks to finish. 'Now, how fast do you want it to be?' She shows Grace how to alter the tempo by exaggerating the beats per minute to full speed and then back down to 80 beats per minute (BPM). Grace again makes a moderate choice after some consideration, and 110 BPM becomes the pace. At this stage the music therapist suggests they sit back and listen to the pre-programmed variations on the beat so they get a feel for the song. 'Have you thought about the words?' she asks the young woman. 'A bit.' 'Think some more during the week and when you come back next week we will start writing,' she suggests. 'Okay.' They sit and listen for another few minutes before the bell rings and it is time to end.

Grace is sick the next week but is back the following week and full of energy. 'I want to write a song for my God,' she says immediately. 'Great topic,' smiles the music therapist supportively, 'Have you written anything down?' 'No, too hard,' smiles Grace. 'Let's do it together, then. Tell me what you want to say.' The music therapist gets some pieces of coloured paper from the cupboard and a set of felt tip pens. 'What colour will we use?' she asks, and Grace selects the pink paper and blue marker. The music therapist acts as a scribe for the young woman, who has not formed her ideas into any structure at this stage. She asks questions to encourage Grace to think of more ideas. 'Loving God. Take care of me. My family are in your care. Great One. Faith.' This young woman is filled with a sense of spirituality and has learned many English words that describe her relationship with God. The music therapist asks how long she has been a Christian and Grace describes her home town and the church that she attended with all her family and friends. There are many positive associations from her past to draw on during this difficult transition. She talks about their new church and mentions that people in the congregation stare at her family. 'Does that bother you?' asks the music therapist. Grace shrugs. 'I guess it would make me feel a bit funny,' offers the music therapist, and the young girl nods. 'You are brave to keep going when people stare. Do you think it will get better?' Grace nods again. 'We are good singers,' she says, 'That will help.' 'Maybe you can take a CD of your song to the church when it is done?' suggests the music therapist, 'I can help you.' Grace looks amazed. 'If you can tell me the name of your minister, I can call him and see. But let's write the song first.' 'Okay, let's do it,' says Grace.

The music therapist puts the beat on and they stare at the words on the page. The music therapist reads through the words in rhythm, conscious that Grace may not be able to read them since they are in English. Once they are read, she prompts, 'What would be good as the chorus? The chorus is where you put the most important words in the song because you sing them so many times.' 'Oh praise thee, mighty God, you have been so good to me,' Grace offers immediately. The music therapist writes it down quickly. She turns the beat up. 'How would you sing it?' she asks. Grace barely hesitates before making up a tune that is grounded in Sudanese rhythms and runs playfully up and down. She is not quite in time and her melody line does not match with the harmony suggested in the bass line of the R'n'B beat, so the music therapist sings it back to her in a slightly altered form to make it easier for them to keep working on it together.

She retains the rhythm and pace, but synchronizes it with the Western backing beat. 'Yeah, that's it!' Grace yells. 'Let's sing it again,' says the music therapist, and they sing the adapted version together a number of times to get it into their heads. 'What next?' she asks the girl. Grace is not sure, so the music therapist reads out a couple more of the sentences she has written down that make general statements about the Lord. 'Yes, that one. "Thank you for watching over us, and taking care of our family."' The music therapist offers a complementary melody that is very similar to the first, but adding a little more vocal play to emphasize the stylistic qualities. They sing the two lines over and over until the bell rings. 'See you next week to do more.'

The verses evolve similarly over the next few weeks and the music therapist encourages Grace to tell something of her own story in some parts of the song rather than staying at the general level of praising God. The song details her personal connection to God and His role in her life. 'When everything was scary, I would pray to my Lord. When no one would talk to me, I would talk with my Lord. When my father went a long way away, I would ask my Lord to watch over him. This would bring me peace.' The music therapist makes contact with the church minister and arranges for him to speak to Grace at church and ask about the song. With Grace's permission, she explains that the song has been written in music therapy and that it is a personal expression of faith in a popular genre. The music therapist emphasizes that the recording will be of a 'demo' quality and notes that a live performance would be difficult because of the technology used. The minister is intuitive and understanding about the situation and asks a number of insightful questions to inform his approach to the young woman. Grace is very excited to report that he spoke to her and that they are talking about using the song in a service when it is complete. Grace and the music therapist make a recording over two more sessions, taking their time to get the piece just right in anticipation of the performance.

EVALUATING EFFECTIVENESS

The structured goals and objectives used in this scenario are well suited to a school environment where applied behavioural approaches tend to underpin thinking. They make communication with teachers about the purpose and outcomes of music therapy relatively simple. It is clear from the case vignette that the first goal was achieved at every level and this can easily be described in a narrative summary. Feedback can be offered to teachers about the strength of Grace's Christianity and her strong sense of connectedness with her family and with her faith. Discussion with teachers will inform the degree to which the third goal has been achieved. It is an important goal, and was the purpose of the original referral; however, the outcome of music therapy has also been to offer a different perspective on Grace's situation. Her disconnection in school is not indicative of her state in all settings. Adopting an *accepting* stance has allowed unexpected capacity to emerge, and this may now serve as a more explicit resource for this young woman.

KEY POINTS

- Songwriting is not always suitable as the first method to be offered to a teenager and song listening can provide a gentle chance to establish rapport.

- Limited language does not mean that songwriting will not be helpful. Repetition can be used to great effect in songs.

- Teenagers will often nominate the most significant thing on their mind as a topic for song composition. They are usually not defensive enough to think about this in a more complicated way.

- It can take a long time to write a song. This depends on the personality of the teenager and his or her capacity to grasp the medium.

- Ultimately, the style of the song may not bear a close resemblance to the genre it was intended to imitate. This is usually not conspicuous to the teenager.

- Songs can be a powerful medium for communicating with other people in the teenager's network if handled carefully.

FACILITATING DEVELOPMENT

The use of songwriting in order to facilitate *development* is both simple and effective. The lyrics are used to outline the desired behaviour or action, and the music functions as both motivator and inherent reward. This is varied to suit the cognitive ability of the teenagers who are involved. For those with some level of cognitive impairment, the music therapist will take a lead role in writing the song and focus it on the targeted behaviours of the individual or group. The song may outline a series of physical movements that join to create a coordinated action, for example. Alternatively, it may outline a set of behaviours that can be used in social situations or in daily living. For teenagers whose thinking is impacted by mental illness, the potential to be involved in the creation of the song is much higher. The composition also has enduring value because repeated listening creates opportunities to rehearse and links positive association to the intended action. The level of involvement should directly reflect the capacity of the teenager to think independently and creatively; however, the function remains consistent. The song provides opportunities for rehearsal of positive thoughts and behaviours.

Lyric substitution
SETTING AND PURPOSE

The music therapy group takes place in an inpatient psychiatric facility that provides early intervention services for teenagers experiencing first episode psychosis. The service aims to reduce the disruption to the young person's development by responding quickly with evidence-based therapy approaches. The facility supports short inpatient stays when required for safety reasons, as well as a more extensive community-based programme. Some of the young people stay on the ward for a number of weeks and may return two or three times, so a structured weekly programme is offered, with music therapy being one of the group programmes. The unique contribution that music therapy makes relates to the opportunities for creative expression and inter-personal skill development that are used to enhance confidence and facilitate a return to normal functioning. Taking this into account, the music therapy group aims are consistent across the weeks:

- to encourage participation at a musical and verbal level, as appropriate

- to facilitate successful experiences of creative expression through song singing, songwriting and instrument playing

- to provide opportunities for interaction between group participants

- to engage in fun and age-appropriate experiences.

ILLUSTRATIVE VIGNETTE

The music therapist greets each of the teenagers as they enter the music room. Up to ten people will arrive in the next few minutes and each one will sit on one of the chairs that are loosely arranged in a u-shape, facing a whiteboard and the therapist's chair. Most of the young people don't speak much, although one young woman is talking in a manic manner to anyone who will listen. Once the core group has arrived, the music therapist begins the session by making a more formal acknowledgement of those who are present and thanking them for coming. 'I mentioned last week that we were going to work on writing and recording a song. Does anyone remember that?' she questions. There are some nods and some blank looks. 'Rather than writing the whole song from scratch, I thought we might use a song that has been written already and change the words to suit ourselves,' she suggests. More nods and some looks. 'Does anyone have any suggestions for what song could work?' asks the music therapist, looking around the group. There is no response, which is predictable in this early stage of the group, so the music therapist does not wait a long time before following up. 'Perhaps we should use one of the songs we have been singing from the songbook. Dylan's "Knockin' on Heaven's Door" has been popular, and so has Gary Jules' version of "Mad World". Another one that comes to mind is "Everybody Hurts" by R.E.M.' The reference to these favoured songs elicits some murmurs from the group and they are beginning to warm up. 'Okay, let's vote,' begins the music therapist. 'Hands up for R.E.M.'

It takes a little encouragement and some reminders to the teenagers who are unfocused, but eventually everyone is able to indicate what song they prefer. 'Mad World' is the most popular, and the music therapist sings through the original lyrics while playing guitar, inviting the group to sing along if they choose. The song lyrics are powerful and describe a depressed child on the verge of suicide. The music is equally strong and easily reproducible on the keyboard with the open arpeggiated chords played in a melancholy way. Suicide is no stranger to this group of young people and this song has led to a number of powerful discussions in previous groups. 'Today we will change the lyrics for this song to describe the coping strategies that you use when you are feeling really down,' leads the music therapist. 'It's really important to be able to express the difficulties, but sometimes it's even harder to think about what to do. Can anyone suggest a strategy that they use to pull themselves up when they're feeling blue?' It is always a challenge to get the ball rolling, so the music therapist is directive. 'Lucy, what's your strategy?' 'I don't know what you mean,' Lucy replies. 'Well, if you're having a bad day but you really want to get out of bed to go and do something, how do you convince yourself to do it?' the music therapist asks, knowing that many people with depression find it difficult to get out of bed. 'Usually my mum makes me get up,' Lucy reflects, 'otherwise, I don't think I would.' 'Alright, thank you. So you get help from other people. That's a strategy.' The music therapist writes 'Get help from other people' on the big piece of white paper on the wall and then writes Lucy's particular situation below it in smaller letters – 'Mum makes me get out of bed'. 'Does anyone else rely on their family to help them to cope?' she asks, working to build rapport between group members. There are some murmurs and the music therapist asks one of these teenagers to expand. 'Well, my dad takes me out to play golf sometimes. That usually makes me feel better,' says Rune. The music therapist nods and writes on the board 'Playing sport – Dad takes me to golf'. She draws a line between this comment and the comment about Lucy's mum. 'Listening to music,' another teenager volunteers. The music therapist writes it on the board immediately and turns back to the group to keep the ball rolling. There is a burst of enthusiastic suggestions: 'Go out with my friends.' 'Talk to my counsellor.' 'Play on the Playstation.'

Soon the piece of white paper is covered with suggestions. Once the contributions began, the music therapist spent most of the time scribbling down every word so that all contributions were acknowledged. Now she attempts to draw out some major themes. 'Well, looking at this, I can see a few different strategies that have been repeated. "Help from Family" is a big one. And "Being Active" is another – can you yell out which ones are about being active, and I'll circle those in green. Actually, John, why don't you do the circling while I get another piece of paper?' The group makes their way through all the suggestions, and John is systematic in putting a coloured circle around each to indicate what kind of coping strategy it is. On another piece of paper the music therapist writes the list: Being Active, Help from Family, Chilling Out, Seeing Friends, Professional Support. 'Alright, let's use this to write the song. We just change the words that are in the song now to these words,' she says confidently. There is silence. 'How do you do that?' asks Rune. 'Well, you have to be a bit creative, but it's usually pretty easy once you get going. I'll show you what I mean with the first line.' The music therapist points to the words as she goes.

'When I'm feeling down I try to be active, get out and play golf, go for a walk,' she sings. 'Oh wow!' the young people mumble. 'What shall we put in next?' the music therapist asks, 'What comes naturally after being active?' 'How about seeing friends?' suggests Felicity. 'I like to see my friends...' begins the music therapist. 'They make me feel good,' responds Felicity immediately. 'I like to see my friends, they make me feel good, going out and...' offers the music therapist. 'Having fun,' Lucy offers. The music therapist sings through the two lines that have been created and then asks for suggestions for the next line. By the end of the hour they have created some verses and used up most of the ideas that had been suggested. The music therapist has written the lyrics on a third piece of paper and the group stumble through singing it together, laughing at times when they can't get the words to fit or when they all sing it differently. 'Okay, that's a great beginning,' says the music therapist, 'Next week we can keep working on it and work out some more verses, as well as get some instruments involved. Felicity, do you want me to get you the music for the piano part – you play, don't you?' Felicity nods and the music therapist makes a mental note to remember to do this and to lend the keyboard to the girl for the week. 'Can the rest of you keep an eye on yourselves during the week and think about the things that you do that help you to cope? It might surprise you to see how much you do without even thinking about it.' The teenagers are slow to disperse, some of them hanging around to chat and others to ask if they can have particular instruments when they come together next week. The energy level of the group is higher than it was when they arrived and some people are communicating.

EVALUATING EFFECTIVENESS
Effectiveness is measured directly against the programme aims. Participation is documented at the conclusion of each group and noted in each patient's records, at both verbal and musical levels. Verbal sharing is noted and any distorted thinking is documented. The music therapist's observations of interactions between group members is also documented, as well as her subjective reflections on the level of engagement and energy achieved within the group on a given week. Each teenager will respond individually within the group context and the music therapist considers the above factors against their individual goals. Group cohesion is a less useful indicator of success in this group, because it is an open group and participants will vary from week to week. In addition, the nature of psychosis may involve

a level of detachment from others that impacts on the achievement of connectedness, hence the need to compare each individual against his or her own achievements.

KEY POINTS

- The music therapist is required to take a directive role with this group because they are not expected to be highly communicative during an episode of acute psychosis.

- The topic has been chosen specifically for this group at this time in conjunction with team members.

- The music therapist does not use long silences to demand contributions because some participants may be unsettled by this.

- Clear directions and direct questions are useful in this setting, e.g. offering songs to choose between, and giving examples that clarify what the music therapist means.

- The use of lyric substitution provides a solid structure that still demands original verbal contributions from the participants.

- The pre-existing song provides a motivating framework and also allows for some level of achievement within a one session format.

- Dividing the songwriting process into sections – this week lyrics, next week instruments – means that some closure has been achieved but it is also possible to continue working.

- Asking the young people to reflect on the topic during the week increases the potential for transfer into the context outside music therapy.

CONCLUSION

Songwriting is an adaptable method that can be adjusted towards *development, acceptance* or *understanding*. Lyric substitution is particularly flexible and although it has been explained here in the context of learning coping strategies, it is also very suitable for an *accepting* orientation, because teenagers can quickly achieve success and positive reinforcement of their achievements. Instilling new meaning into old songs is more complex when *understanding* is the focus; however, the dual layers can sometimes be used to good effect and provide a lead into discussion of topics that the young person may be consciously or unconsciously avoiding. The case vignettes have also illustrated that the creation of songs does not necessarily mean the creation of lyrics, although songwriting without words can seem like an oxymoron. Composing a song stands in contrast to the free and spontaneous nature of improvisation because it relies on planning and editing. Songs also imply an audience in a way that improvisation does not. In most of the vignettes, verbal consolidation was minimal in comparison to the therapeutic work that took place within the music, either through metaphor, connection or negotiation. This is typical of my experience when working with teenagers. Some young people can use words to grapple effectively with the challenge of their condition, but most are much more comfortable with a music-centred experience. Teenagers exist on the cusp between expression and articulation, and music matches this level of experience very successfully.

PART THREE

Using Improvisation
with Teenagers

Introduction

Musical improvisation is about stepping into a free musical space. In a therapeutic context with teenagers this involves both creativity and spontaneity, vulnerability and embarrassment. The extremes of this experience are real for all clients but are particularly pertinent for an adolescent who is focused on identity-related issues. Unlike the comfortable familiarity of songs, teenagers have no idea why they would be expected to make music as a part of therapy. Luckily music therapists do.

THE THEORY BEHIND USING IMPROVISATION

Ian Cross (2009) argues that shared music making has been critical in the evolution of the complex social interactions that mark humankind. What is unique about music, in comparison to language, is that it allows a more flexible approach to communication of meaning. Cross frequently uses the idea of 'shared intentionality' to explain the sense of joint purpose that is experienced in making music with another person. This is particularly pertinent to the therapeutic encounter with teenagers, because in the moment of making music together the therapist and the young people are in agreement about the intention of the experience. The music therapist may have *understanding, acceptance* or *development* on his or her mind before and after the encounter. The teenagers may feel nervous, embarrassed or incompetent before beginning and after finishing. But the shared intentionality that is created while playing together surpasses these semantic ideas as the participants entrain to one another's rhythms or feeling states in music making (McNeill 1995). Kenneth Aigen (2005) puts it more simply, describing music as 'the connective tissue among the spirits of human beings' (p.89).

Walter Freeman (1997) takes this one step further when he attaches the concept of joy to the experience of shared music making. He suggests that although drugs can be used to imitate the feeling of happiness, true joy is experienced in sharing activities with those we trust. Improvising within the context of therapy creates such opportunities for joyous shared experiences that are not linked to the communication of specific messages. What is communicated is inevitably authentic self-expression, unattached to specific information. This means that teenagers have the opportunity to express themselves honestly without disclosing 'secret' information. What they choose to do before and after making music produces the detail of the therapeutic encounter, but it is rooted in the potentially joyous action of shared activity.

The fact that improvisation is a creative act is another crucial element in explaining why teenagers may benefit from stepping into this unfamiliar space. Abraham Maslow (1968) has described creativity as inherent to self-actualization – the process of reaching one's full potential – which is exactly what teenagers in therapy are trying to do. He does not see creativity as originality or novelty, but rather as a natural state of unselfconscious being that is gradually buried as children are indoctrinated to societal expectations. Creative expression in the musical context is therefore authentic and closely related to the 'real teenager'. Gary Ansdell (1995) explains that this is how music therapy often reveals the hidden parts of clients – the person behind the disability, the illness, the disguise.

This interpretation of the musical act as a potentially authentic self-representation is endorsed by Christopher Small's introduction of the term 'musicking' (Small 1998). Instead of seeing music as a distant object that is created by the person, musicking returns the emphasis to 'the act of' making music. Although music in this sense can be analysed later in order to enhance understanding or measure improvements, this is a separate process from the act of improvising. Lawrence Ferrara (1991) makes the same point and uses phenomenological strategies in his attempts to provide ways of understanding the music as it happened, rather than focusing on the notes.

THE ACTUAL EXPERIENCE OF USING IMPROVISATION

The division between experiencing and understanding music is not a challenge for music therapy clinicians who are present and participating in the act of music making with teenagers. Musicking is far more familiar to music therapists than the idea of a distant musical object for critique and analysis. There are other challenges in the experience of musicking for music therapists, however, not least of which is the requirement to facilitate creative, authentic and even joyous musical experiences with reluctant young people. Gary Ansdell (in Skewes 2001, p.193) suggests four playing rules to discuss with adult groups before beginning to improvise, which are as follows:

1. It's a free improvisation group which means there's no right and wrong.

2. Listening is more important than playing.

3. You don't need to play all the time.

4. You can change instruments if you feel moved to.

For the teenage population, less is more. Before commencing the first improvisation it can be useful to offer something along the lines of the following:

1. Okay, prepare yourself, coz this could sound a little weird but trust me.

2. No matter what you play, you can't get this wrong.

3. Let's go. Tap tap bang!

The music therapist should then launch into a confident rhythm and appear focused.

After the first improvisation with adolescents it is possible to be more collaborative. Once teenagers have heard it, seen it, felt it and done it, they are free to make their own decisions. But the first time you make music with a group of teenagers, it is best to just do it. This is much easier with adolescents because they are more likely to follow instructions, trained as they are for the classroom. You say 'join in' and more often than not, they will. Adults are less likely to find such a determined tone convincing and may not join in at all, but teenagers usually do and it is important to avoid the opportunity for the young person to say, 'I just don't want to.' This would be the most likely outcome if the teenager was given the opportunity to comment on the concept before beginning. 'I don't want to' is an irrefutable statement in most approaches to therapy, and with adolescents it is a stalemate. It may be time to move on to something different for a while.

In reflecting specifically on group improvisations, bereaved teenagers have made some very powerful statements about its unique contribution to the therapeutic process. From the mouths of babes, they claim that improvisation offers opportunities for fun, freedom and control, but they say it in typically adolescent ways (McFerran-Skewes 2000).

> 'It was fun to make music together, but hard to really make anything out of it.' (16-year-old boy)

This statement encapsulates the experience of improvisation for most teenagers and is closely related to the value of music described by theorists. The action of making music with trusted others is fun and teenagers want to have fun. If too much emphasis is placed on making something that will be 'significant' on reflection, then the pressure of participation is too high. After all, most self-conscious people would want to practise for such an event and not just make it up as they go. Teenagers are no exception.

> 'Music was like a good time in a gap where we had a break from it [*discussing grief*] and then we'd go back to letting it out.' (15-year-old boy)

Even when *understanding* is the intention of the music therapist, as it was in the work with this young man, the teenagers involved may not find this the most important aspect of therapy. Improvisation is fun and it is also a chance to be both free and in control, an important dichotomy for the adolescent.

> 'In improvisations you can do whatever you want and it was your choice.' (14-year-old girl)

Identity formation is once again a useful construct for understanding why improvising may be appealing to a teenager. Making music up does not connect with something teenagers already know about themselves, rather it allows them to discover something new. This can happen both for individuals and for groups, since the music created by a group allows all of the members to speak together. The whole that is created is greater than the sum of its parts.

The sound of improvision can be surprising. In individual improvisations the music therapist contributes approximately half of the material and the overall sound is usually recognizably musical at some level. Tony Wigram

(Wigram 2004) introduces the idea of 'frameworking' to explain the music therapist's role in such cases. In a group this is not necessarily the case. In playing audio recordings of adolescent group improvisations to expert music therapists around the world, the responses were distinctly different between each individual regarding what could be heard (Skewes 2001). Where one heard the sounds of dysfunction and mental illness, another heard remnants of Indonesian Gamelan music. Where one focused on providing a description of what happened in the music, another interpreted emotions and group dynamics. Interpretations of music improvised in therapy are located as much in the listener's experience as they are in the music itself. But the sound of the music is influenced both by the expression of identity and also the resources available for this expression.

The resources that the music therapist offers to young people have a powerful impact on the kinds of sounds they can make. Susan Gardstrom (2007) provides a detailed rationale for the value of improvisation in groups and in doing so, makes useful recommendations about the music therapist's instrumentarium. The inclusion of electric guitars has a significant impact for example, or a lack of melodic instruments can limit what is expressed. When providing teenagers with instruments it is important to remember that they are being encouraged to express their identity. A bag of old and battered percussion instruments does not 'convey an attitude of respect for one's self as a professional, for the client as a musical human being, or for the music itself' (Gardstrom 2007, p.32). The availability of resources is impacted upon both by the nature of the programme and the capacity of the teenagers to physically access instruments. My own preferred instrumentarium for improvisations is documented in Table iii.1.

Table iii.1: An adolescent-friendly instrumentarium

Electronic keyboard with range of contemporary beats, plus case and stand

Electric keyboard (touch sensitive) with range of keyboard sounds, plus case, stand and pedal

Acoustic guitar (steel string) with pick up, hard case and strap

Acoustic guitar (nylon string)

Electric guitar with leads, strap and case

Bass guitar with leads, strap and case

Assortment of picks

Microphones with leads   *continued*

Table iii.1: An adolescent-friendly instrumentarium *cont.*

Powered speakers

Drum kit including crash, hi-hats, two toms, snare, bass, stool and sticks

MP3 recorder with good quality condenser microphone, headphones and stand

Alto metallaphone

Bass metallaphone

Alto xylophone

Bass xylophone

Wooden bongo

Set of congas

Traditional African slit drum

10" djembe

Doumbek

Cow bells

Agogo bell

Wind chimes – gold aluminium with cymbal stand for independent positioning

Tambourines – half moon, headed, non-headed

Rafiki prayer drum (large)

Monkey drum (large)

Range of shakers – light, large

Triangles with beaters

Cabassa

Guiro

Tone block

Maracas

Claves

Brass finger cymbals

Range of good quality beaters – soft/hard/plastic/wool

Laptop with music software for creating beats, recording acoustic sounds and creating video clips (e.g. Garage Band for Mac or ACID for PC)

MP3 amplified speakers

Portable CD player

DV video camera

In Chapter 6, three illustrations are provided that utilize most of these instruments with groups of teenagers. Acoustic improvisations are used in the description of fostering *understandings* with a group of young men with chronic illness. In this example, thematically guided improvisation is utilized in order to pursue meaning making. Electric instruments are incorporated into the example when offering *acceptance* is the intention of the music therapist, since these are more aligned with popular genres and easily related to identity expression. The group being described emulates a rock band but could equally simulate a night club. The music is improvised and the stylistic features are distinctively adolescent. The final example illustrates how improvisations can be used to facilitate *developments* in social competence, and free improvisations are used to practise ways of interacting with others.

In Chapter 7, the focus is on individual encounters with young people using improvisation. A young woman is supported to deepen *understandings* of her own experiences through music at the beginning of the chapter. The style of this teenager's musical interaction is understood as reflecting elements of her pathology, and she is encouraged to consider this interpretation. A young man is the focus of *acceptance*-oriented improvisation work. The drum kit is used in this teenager's expression of identity as he and his father journey through the terminal phase of cancer. The final example emphasizes the inherently motivating characteristics of improvised music, where a young woman with profound and multiple disabilities works on *developing* communication skills within the reciprocal musical encounter.

Chapter 6

Group Improvisation

There is no reason to avoid group improvisations when working with adolescents. Apart from sport, there are very few other ways for groups of young people to spend time together actively participating in the creation of something bigger than themselves. Of course they will think it is weird, but they will also understand that this is music therapy. They will assume that it might make them feel better. In this chapter, three different styles of group improvisations are described in relation to the different ways making music can lead to feeling better. The musical material sounds chaotic in each, but the experience can be helpful at any of the intended levels.

Musical listening lies at the centre of group improvisations (McFerran and Wigram 2002). The music therapist is present, listening, noticing and responding to every aspect of the group. After the music therapist has created a musical environment for the young people to step into, she begins to listen to what is created and to respond to it intuitively. The listening and responding occurs at both musical and therapeutic levels. She listens to hear what is needed musically in order to progress and then balances this with consideration of how much responsibility should be taken. The intention of the music therapist influences this considerably since fostering *understanding*, offering *acceptance* or facilitating *development* each require a different emphasis. For the first, the music therapist focuses on staying calm to allow for the emergence of insight; in the second, the music therapist jumps in and is a personality within the group through the improvisation; and the third requires thoughtful direction and planning.

These plans and intentions are all left behind when the moment comes for making music, resulting in the creation of a shared intentionality that is purely musical. It is essential to engage fully in music making, both as a model for the young people and also in order to be an authentic and creative human being. Too much analysis during music making can preclude creativity. For their part, teenagers are conscious of the fact that the music therapist is focused and listening and will often respond to musical gestures, or look up if they feel her gaze. This awareness of what the music therapist does should not be underestimated. Although the only manual preparation required for the use of group improvisations is providing the instruments, it is a demanding method at a creative level. In my view, it is also the most connected and creative music therapy method for working with teenagers and can lead to unexpected and important growth.

FOSTERING UNDERSTANDING

Using group improvisations to foster *understanding* with adolescents is very different to insight-oriented work with adults. The level of verbal disclosure is lower and often only present in a limited way. The kinds of questions that young people are willing and able to engage with should be altered accordingly. The teenager may be reaching conclusions and gaining insight, but this is not necessarily articulated in the group. Where songwriting provides a direct line to verbal discussions, the therapeutic power of group music making with teenagers often takes place privately. Any spoken understandings need to be tied to concrete events and the expectations for verbal discussions need to be clearly modelled. Direct questions are more useful than open questions because they lead the teenagers more clearly to the kinds of answers that will foster deeper personal understanding.

Thematic group improvisation
SETTING AND PURPOSE

The music therapy group involves five young men with Duchenne's Muscular Dystrophy who have gathered together for a support weekend. Social workers and psychologists will involve them in a range of activities across two days that focus on forming connections between the young men, using games, discussions and other creative strategies to work through some of the issues confronting them. Music therapy is regularly included in these weekends because of its capacity to cultivate emotional engagement as part of the process – ranging from the expression of frustration to sheer pleasure.

The team finds that music therapy complements the other strategies, which are more language driven and coping oriented. The expressive capacity of music is valued and the opportunity to access feelings is intentionally utilized. With this in mind, the aims for the music therapy group on this weekend are as follows:

For the young men to:

- express their feelings on the instruments

- discuss their feelings in relation to their experience of living with a deteriorating illness

- express their identity through music making

- listen to others' musical and verbal contributions.

ILLUSTRATIVE VIGNETTE

'Hi everybody. What's happening?' begins the music therapist as she enters the room where five young men are hanging out in their wheelchairs. 'Playing Playstation,' comes the muffled reply. Computer games are a powerful competitor for the attention of young men, and the music therapist does not attempt to win this battle. 'Music group in 20 minutes,' she says, 'See you in the multi-sensory room. I'll go and get the drums and stuff organized.' 'Okay,' say one or two of the young men. The music therapist leaves the room and goes to talk to the staff, asking them to organize the boys to come to the music room when the time arrives. She actively avoids having to motivate the young men into action on these weekends, since her role in the session is usually much less directive. The music therapist explains this and expresses her appreciation to the nurses, who have no hesitation in organizing the young men to do something other than stare at a television screen.

The music therapist organizes the room so that all the instruments are on display when the young men enter. Instead of placing them on the floor as she normally would, she drags tables and chairs over to the side of the room and places the instruments where the young men can reach them from their wheelchairs. As they enter the room, they go straight to the instruments and start making noise. The room is not large and soon the volume is loud. The music therapist participates in the creation of sound, picking up instruments that have not been chosen and modelling how they can be played. She also turns on the electronic keyboard so that there is a beat playing in the background. This free experimentation goes on for ten minutes and the music therapist does not attempt to contain or control it. As the young men's interest in free experimentation begins to diminish, the music therapist offers a focus. 'Okay everyone, we're going to have a go at playing different feelings. Choose an instrument that will be good for playing "happy".' The young men look bemused. 'What do you mean?' they ask. 'Well, you know songs have different feelings that go with them. Some are sad songs, some are happy songs, and some are angry songs. Well, we're going to do that too, just with instruments, not with songs.' The young men look less confused so the music therapist gets quickly to the point. 'So choose an instrument that you think would be good for making happy music.' She walks over to the instruments and models experimenting with a few sounds before choosing one and going to sit down. The young men slowly choose their own instruments and turn around to face her.

'That's great, you guys. Now let's see what happy sounds like. One, two, go!' The young men hesitate and the music therapist begins playing in an exaggerated way, laughing at herself as an expression of happiness. 'Come on, you guys, join in,' she says. The young men do and soon the sound is loud and chaotic again. There is some laughter as they play and although the improvisation is short at around one minute, it has got the ball rolling. As the boys stop playing, the music therapist does too and she smiles at them. 'Perfect!' she says, 'Did that sound like happy music?' 'That sounded like crazy music to me,' says Jos. 'Yes,' the music therapist smiles. 'It's not like anything you've done before is it? But did it feel happy as well?' She brings their attention back to the focus question. 'Yeah, I suppose,' offers another young man. 'Yeah,' say a couple of the others. 'Alright, now go and choose a different instrument, and we'll see what happy sounds like with those,' directs the music therapist. The young men go over and choose new instruments fairly quietly. 'Do I have to change?' asks Tony, 'I like this one.' 'No problem,' replies the music therapist, walking over to choose an instrument and accepting his decision without drawing attention to it. A minute later she suggests the same thing. 'Okay, let's do happy again. Can you start this time, Tony?' Tony hesitantly hits the doumbek, the music therapist joins in immediately and soon the same cacophony emerges. 'That sounded kind of the same, didn't it?' the music therapist suggests at the end. The group confirm that it did. 'Alright, this time choose a different instrument that will be good for playing "angry" music,' she prompts. The boys are slow to move, but in less than a minute they manoeuvre their chairs over to the instruments and choose again. Most have drums now and the music therapist chooses the slide whistle to complement the sound. 'Let's see if this sounds the same or different. You can listen to one another to get ideas if you need to,' suggests the music therapist, directing their attention to one another.

The angry music is powerful. The boys thump their drums as hard as they can and the sound is thick and driving. The music therapist plays a staccato melody, punctuated with slides to add some depth to the sound. This improvisation goes on for two minutes and the young men appear to be quite focused on their playing. The texture gradually thins as the participants drop out one by one in exhaustion, while the music therapist keeps playing until the final note is struck. The group is silent after this shared expression. 'That sounded different to happy, didn't it?' begins the music therapist, 'How did you do "angry" on your instrument, Jos?' 'I just banged really hard,' says Jos. 'Is that what being angry feels like?' probes the music therapist. 'Yeah, I just want to hit things,' he replies. 'What about you, Patchi?' 'I didn't play much,' he says, 'coz I don't like to talk to people when I'm angry.' 'Interesting,' comments the music therapist, 'People do anger differently, don't they? What about you, Tony?' 'I just like this instrument,' he replies. 'Fine,' says the music therapist, 'What about you, Stuart, are you quiet or loud when you're angry?' 'Loud!' he yells with a smile, 'I always yell at my sister and then she cries.' 'Hmmmm, so you take it out on other people then,' interprets the music therapist, 'Does anyone else do that?' 'Yeah, I yell at my mum,' says Jos. 'What kinds of things do you get angry about?' expands the music therapist. The group launch into a discussion of the way that they are treated when they go to public venues. They share their frustration about the lack of access for wheelchairs. 'Sometimes they say there's disabled access around the back, so you go all the way around there and up a long ramp, and then it turns out to be locked!' vents one young man. 'Yeah, and people are always treating you like you're an idiot, just because you're in a wheelchair,' says another. There is shared frustration and the music therapist contributes little other than to ask 'Is that true for you, too?' to group members who look like they have something to say, but haven't had a chance.

The music therapist moves to the next theme as the discussion comes to an end. 'Now, let's choose another instrument, this time for playing "sad" music,' she explains. The boys move over to the instruments again, talking a little among themselves as they negotiate for the instrument of choice. 'Who wants to start this one?' asks the music therapist. 'I'll do it,' says Patchi, and the group launch right into playing. This time the music is softer and there is lots of space. The music therapist plays a repeating riff on the djembe, not enforcing a tempo, but playing an obvious pattern separated by short periods of silence. The improvisation is little over a minute and the sound gradually fades away. 'Wow. That's heavy isn't it?' starts the music therapist again. 'Yeah,' say a few group members. 'How did it feel?' she follows. 'Sad,' says Tony. 'Yeah, it sounded like it,' says the music therapist, 'Do you guys feel sad sometimes?' 'Yeah,' comes the reply again. 'How come?' follows the music therapist. 'I get tired of being sick all the time,' says Jos. 'Me too,' says Stuart. 'Sad and tired kind of go together, don't they?' offers the music therapist. 'Yep,' they say. The music therapist is quiet for about 15 seconds. The boys sit quietly. 'Alright, let's do one more,' says the music therapist, 'Do you want to do happy, angry, sad or something different?' 'Happy!' comes the chorus. 'Okay, grab an instrument,' smiles the music therapist.

The cacophony of sound is soon pounding strongly again and the boys laugh at the end. 'Ahhh, it's good to feel happy isn't it?' says the music therapist, smiling. 'Thanks for playing through those feelings. Sometimes it can help to play them out. Do you feel like it gave you some relief?' Some of the boys shrug or nod. 'What are we doing now?' they ask.

EVALUATING EFFECTIVENESS

The contribution that music therapy makes to this weekend will be evaluated by the young men's willingness to engage in the process. Motivating these teenagers to attend is more of an indication of the team's commitment than a gauge of the programme. However, their level of preparedness to express their feelings through shared music making within the session is an important indicator of success. The potential for greater self-understanding emerges when they are able to articulate their feelings and explore the experiences around them. This can lead to more resilient responses to adverse experiences. In addition, by describing their own experiences the opportunity exists to make connections with others in the group and hear about similar and diverse strategies and experiences. The depth of insight shared in the group is therefore an important measure of effectiveness, but it will vary depending on the particular young people involved and the context of the other activities over the weekend.

KEY POINTS

- It is more congruent to avoid an organizer role initially so that the intention of fostering *understanding* is not a conspicuous contrast.

- The first improvisation should be introduced quickly and implemented with minimal delay.

- The music therapist should choose her instrument last, so she can supplement the musical material and add depth to it.

- With each successive improvisation it is possible to be less directive and foster more insight-oriented discussions.

- Themes provide a useful focus and a more concrete alternative to free improvisation.

- 'Happy', 'Angry', 'Sad', 'Happy' is a useful sequence. Most young people want to feel happy and this is the best entry and exit point.

- The music therapist needs to ask direct questions that make it clear what kind of verbal discussion she is expecting.

- Not all teenagers in a group will be able to verbalize their feelings or reflect on their behaviours in response to emotions. Those young people who find it difficult benefit from hearing others discuss them.

OFFERING ACCEPTANCE

When the music therapist uses group improvisations as an expression of *acceptance*, it inevitably incorporates some aspects of deepening *understanding* and facilitating *development*. The distinguishing feature is that verbal consolidation is not a requirement and nor is any kind of 'improvement' or achievement. The musical material is nonetheless understood as being meaningful, but there is less space for interpretation, since more structure and direction are offered in order to make it comfortable. There is still tremendous freedom within the group jams; however, the music therapist often maintains a leadership role in these sessions. She may assist in negotiations about instrument choices and provide solutions rather than leaving this responsibility with group members. The music therapist does not have requirements about how to play appropriately, however, and will accept and encourage any expression. There is no attempt to improve the quality of the musical material and, as a result, it may sound chaotic and often loud.

The increase in volume is partially due to the selection of instruments made available to the young people. Adolescent-friendly instruments and stylistic influences are integral when the music therapist's intention is to offer *acceptance*. This means the inclusion of drum kits, bass guitars, electric guitars, keyboards, beat makers, microphones, effects boxes, video cameras that facilitate the making of music videos, and more. These contemporary instruments supplement the traditional sounds that are available in music therapy group improvisations. The musical influences on the improvisations may also be overt. The group might rock out like a band or pump like a DJ in a club. They might equally be interested in jazz, blues, hymns or any other musical genres. The genre of interest is often an important influence and inspiration for the jam, although the group does not work towards conquering it – just loosely imitating stylistic features. This approach is more closely related to fantasy than it is to identity and it invokes a commitment to personal expression.

Rock band jam
SETTING AND PURPOSE

The music therapy group takes place as part of a community-based day programme that offers intensive support to bridge young people back into the school system or to some kind of appropriate employment. A range of groups are offered over three weekdays and the teenagers are expected to attend regularly. Karate and self-defence, art, excursions and music therapy exist alongside cognitive behavioural programmes, daily group times and insight-oriented discussion groups. The young people who attend are struggling with a range of mental illness, from depression and anxiety through to undiagnosed conditions that have led to suicide attempts or the inability to leave the house. The music therapist participates in a team meeting prior to the beginning of her session and has the opportunity for handover from the team of social workers, psychologists and teachers. She proposes goals for each session in response to these discussions and then feeds back to the team afterwards through further discussion or documentation. On this day, the team has reported flat energy levels and a feeling of failure as two of the group members appear to have dropped out of the programme. There has been some blaming within the group for this loss and the complex dynamics have been addressed through group discussions. The team decides that music therapy may be a useful opportunity to reinstate a sense of hope and energy on this day. The aims of the programme for the day are for the group to:

- engage in musical activities
- express themselves on preferred instruments
- experience some relief following musical participation
- reconnect with one another, and the team, through a fun and creative experience.

ILLUSTRATIVE VIGNETTE

'I thought we might get out some of the electric instruments and have a jam today. It would be good to release some of this tension, don't you think?' the music therapist offers. There is no excitement in response to the proposal and the group maintains a steady silence. The music therapist convinces some of the young people to help her collect the amplifiers and guitars from a nearby storeroom. The noise level begins to rise as the instruments arrive in the room. Some of the teenagers are thrilled as parts of a drum kit are unveiled, and one young man hoots when he picks up the bass guitar and works out how to plug it in. Two of the young women remain cool and neither help with the collection of instruments nor experiment with them once they have arrived. The music therapist moves casually through the group, explaining different functions of the instruments and providing positive feedback on the attempts that are being made to play. She approaches Cheryl casually and has a quiet discussion about the different instruments, asking if she has seen them before or if she has any interest. After a minute, Cheryl reveals that she is keen to play the drum kit. The music therapist comments on the popularity of the instrument and assures her that she will have a turn, offering her a hand drum in the meantime. Cheryl accepts the djembe and places it beside her, not touching it. Next the music therapist approaches the remaining group member, with the drums crashing in the background and the keyboard and bass guitar occasionally audible in the gaps. Jinah is much more difficult to engage in this new activity. She is usually an astute contributor in the verbal processing, but this musical opportunity has left her feeling vulnerable. 'I just don't want to play,' she says. 'You know what, that's totally okay,' offers the music therapist, 'I just don't want you to feel left out, either.' 'I'm okay, just leave me alone,' comes the reply. 'No problem,' replies the music therapist, 'I'll check back in with you later.'

Once all the group members have an instrument that they are relatively pleased with, the music therapist gets their attention. 'Hey! Everyone stop playing for a minute!' she yells. There is a gradual decrescendo and eventually it is nearly quiet. 'Let's just play the instruments today without any discussion, but it's still important that we listen to one another. Musicians in bands still have to be able to hear one another. So let's all start together and see what happens. One, two, three, let's go!' The music therapist strums the lead guitar energetically, and after a pause the rest of the group start playing together. There is chaos for about ten minutes and the music therapist is a part of it, playing solos on the guitar and dancing around. She is conscious that Jinah is still looking uncomfortable, but is interested that the young woman hasn't left the room. The music therapist gradually pulls back on her playing until it is relatively inconspicuous and wanders over to Jinah again. 'Here, have a go at this,' she offers the young woman, holding out the electric guitar. Jinah shakes her head, 'No thanks,' she says. The music therapist rejoins the rest of the group and leads them into a frenzied climax by increasing her pace and volume and then draws them to a conclusion by gradually reducing her tempo.

'Let's do it again!' yells the young man on the drum kit. 'Yes, let's,' replies the music therapist, 'but it's Cheryl's turn on the drum kit. And what are you going to do, Jinah?' The music therapist has not asked the group to process the musical material, but she does amplify the group dynamics with these two directives. 'I wanna play drums again,' calls the young man. 'You can go again next if no one else wants to,' says the music therapist, 'but it's Cheryl's turn now,' she repeats. Cheryl stands up and moves over toward the drum kit, and the young man concedes. 'What am I going to do?' he asks. 'How about the doumbek?' responds the music therapist, and it is grudgingly accepted. 'Do you want the keyboard, Jinah?' asks Brynjulf. 'Nah,' she replies, but it is clear that she is touched that someone has noticed her. 'What about the metallaphone?' offers the music therapist. 'Alright!' exclaims Jinah, 'Just stop nagging me!' 'Good on you. Thanks, mate,' replies the music therapist. 'Anyone else want a swap? What about you, Brynjulf, what are you going to play?' The two remaining boys choose to keep the same instruments, and this time the music therapist asks Cheryl to get them started. 'The drummer always calls out the one, two, three, four, Cheryl,' she reinforces and Cheryl calls the numbers and starts thumping the drums. As the piece begins, the music therapist starts rapping, using a freestyling approach to make a commentary on what the group is doing. 'We got Brynjulf on the keys and his playin's set to please, there's Cheryl on the drums, what a rum, dum dum. Niels is on the bass and he's leavin' tonnes of space, while Jinah is just staring at me. Oh, Jinah just tell me what you see, plleeeeassse!' The group are laughing at the music therapist for her hysterical attempt at rapping and Jinah cannot believe her eyes or ears. 'You are mad!' she says, and the music therapist smiles and continues dancing round the room. 'I'm just having fun,' she says as she spins around, 'Can you hear me on the mike, we got...'

EVALUATING EFFECTIVENESS

The end of the music therapy group leads straight into the daily closure activity and the team members casually make their way over to the group room to join in at the end. On this day, some of the team had tapped on the window and given 'thumbs up' signs to the group to indicate that they were impressed by the cacophony they could hear. After the group of young people and professionals are assembled, the team leader starts to process the day and asks about the music therapy group experience. 'It rocked,' said Cheryl, still on a high from playing the drum kit. 'Yeah, the drum kit was good,' counters the young man. 'I liked the keyboard,' offers Brynjulf. Jinah is quiet and the leader asks her directly about her experience. 'It was totally weird,' she begins, 'they all just sounded so crap and acted as though they were having the best time!' 'But not you?' the team leader questions. 'Ahhh, it was alright, except when she started trying to rap!' she says, rolling her eyes and smiling a little.

In terms of evaluating the effectiveness of the session, this verbal feedback provides a lot of information to the team about levels of engagement in addition to the expressive playing they have already heard coming from the room. In the team meeting after the group has finished, the music therapist elaborates on her perception of the experience. 'Courageous of Cheryl to say what she wanted, then stand up to go and get it. When she played, she really smacked those drums with some force, which is quite interesting for such a timid girl. I've never seen that side of her before. Jinah seemed out of her depth without the verbal component, and I assume she is feeling bad about the missing group members. Brynjulf was really engaged, but seemed to lack some insight into the social dynamic. He was trying to buddy up with Jinah again, which she rejected, although today she was feeling so isolated that she actually seemed pleased. Niels was off in his own world on the bass guitar, very little attachment to the group, but did appear comfortable and calm. Matthew conceded the drum kit to Cheryl without too much defiance, and didn't complain again, although he got another turn later, so there was no need to. Very expressive playing, seemed to be thinking about what he was doing and trying to play what he had in his mind...' Communication with the team is central to evaluating the effectiveness of this programme, and the music therapist regularly contributes to and learns from team meetings, despite only being contracted to work for the half day it takes to run the group.

KEY POINTS

- Offering *acceptance* is particularly useful when talking is not helpful or available as an option.

- Teenagers may resist doing something that they have not done before, but exciting instruments can be a powerful lure.

- It may be necessary to raise one's voice in order to be heard over the instruments.

- Too much discussion prior to a musical activity is not always necessary.

- The music therapist should be prepared to use humour in her role as a model of participation. This will differ between each leader depending on his or her personality type.

- Rejection of participation by a teenager should be accepted, but the door should be left open for future opportunities.

- Group jams are noisy and it is helpful to have a team that understands the purpose of such a chaotic sound.

- Even if the music therapist's hours are limited, it is useful to schedule work days to be present for team meetings, or arrange informal handovers.

FACILITATING DEVELOPMENT

It is common to utilize group music making experiences to facilitate *development* in two particular ways. Playing on instruments together can be a reward to the group for the achievement of non-musical *development* goals, where the young people have completed a more challenging task and then have the opportunity to play. In this way, the group improvisation is not the therapy itself, it is the incentive for participating in less inherently pleasurable experiences. Music and movement groups offer a simple example, where strenuous physiotherapy exercises are interspersed with instrumental playing to maintain motivation and focus. Sometimes the teenager will be required to reach out to play the instrument and this is an example of how group improvisations can also facilitate the development of skills within the music making. With young people who have higher cognitive function, social skills are often rehearsed through group improvisations. Listening, waiting, taking turns, acknowledging, contributing and finishing are all important skills that are often learned through negative reinforcement in daily situations – 'don't do that' and 'stop interrupting'. Group improvisations are a more enjoyable forum for facilitating the development of skills in an authentic way, since teenagers behave in improvisations as they do in social encounters. In music making the feedback they receive is musical rather than verbal. It tends to feel less critical and more constructive. The practice opportunities available in music making can lead to sustainable change, resulting in improved relationships based on more successful communication strategies.

Free improvisation
SETTING AND PURPOSE

The music therapy group consists of young people who are struggling to cope with the social requirements of the school environment and are either victims of bullying or completely isolated at school. They have been referred to a community-based, weekly music therapy programme by professionals at an adolescent health service. The group is ongoing, with new members joining at the beginning of each term and ceasing participation at the end of one, two or three terms. Some of the long-standing members in this group are now very capable of dealing with the social requirements of the therapy group but have yet to transfer these skills successfully into the less structured setting of the school ground. Newer group members are less confident and capable of participating in the interactions of the group appropriately. All the teenagers have been interviewed by the music therapist before joining the group in order to ascertain their commitment to developing new ways of dealing with their school situation. As part of this process, the teenagers have identified their challenges and listed their goals for personal growth and greater success at school. With this in mind, the goals for the whole group are as follows and are supplemented by the individual plans:

- to gain insight into their social strengths and limitations

- to identify patterns of behaviour that impact upon their social encounters

- to utilize the opportunity to practise different ways of being with peers

- to discover that other people face similar situations in their school environments.

ILLUSTRATIVE VIGNETTE

'Thanks for sharing that song, Barbara,' says the music therapist, 'It really got a great discussion going. Now it's time to get the instruments out and have a play together.' This is the seventh week in a ten-week series for these young people. They have been working with a variety of music therapy methods over the weeks and have been participating in free group improvisations for the past two weeks. Prior to this, the music therapist had utilized songwriting to encourage connectedness and highlight the issues that group members have in common. Since then the young people have been bringing in songs that are meaningful to them and discussing them, as well as processing the issues identified by the songwriting through drawing and other creative strategies.

'You know the drill, guys. Choose an instrument that you identify with and we'll have a jam together,' directs the music therapist. Two group members are quickly on their feet so that they can get their preferred instrument before anyone else. There is no tussle for instruments this time, but there have been physical moments in previous sessions. The remaining group members move more slowly. Some walk around the collection of instruments that lie in the middle of the circle of beanbags, cushions and chairs. They pick instruments up, give them a play and put them down again before finally deciding on one. A couple of group members reach out and grab the instrument closest to them and then put them down by their side. It takes some minutes and the music therapist waits quietly and then selects an instrument from what remains.

Once everyone is seated they look at the music therapist. 'Okay,' she comments, and then begins to play. Today she plays a gentle African rhythm on the tone block. After about ten seconds, the group members begin to join in. One player rubs his egg shaker on the floor, contributing a gentle swooshing sound that continues for the whole improvisation. One of the young women begins experimenting on the alto metallaphone, playing small melodic fragments that she repeats a number of times before variations appear and it merges into the next shape. The other metallaphone player joins by hitting each note three times before moving to the next, moving steadily up and down the instrument. The overall tone is subdued but consistent. No one sound stands out and there is little dynamic or rhythmic variation throughout the improvisation, which lasts around six minutes. The music therapist steadily maintains her rhythmic contribution, reflecting the way that group members are playing simply by altering volume or emphasis. She looks around while she plays, focusing on the players' hands and instruments more than their eyes. When she senses someone looking towards her she looks up and smiles at that person and then refocuses her eyes down. The music therapist ends with the rest of the group, who drop out one instrument at a time during a coda that lasts about 20 seconds.

'So, what did that sound like?' she asks after a short silence. 'A bubbling brook,' suggests one of the young women. 'Peaceful,' says another group member. 'Mmmm,' comments the music therapist, 'Was anyone listening to any of the other people in the group?' This had been the outcome from the playing last week when the group had played in a disconnected way and then discussed listening as a part of playing. 'Not really,' comes the general reply. 'Try and think of one other person and what their music sounded like,' suggests the music therapist. 'Gary, who could you hear?' Gary looks startled. 'Ummm, I guess I heard Matthew,' he says, looking at the young man beside him. 'Great. What was he playing?' prompts the music therapist. 'The drum,' replies Gary. 'Yep. And how was he playing it? What did it sound like?' 'Ummm. I dunno,' says Gary. 'How would you describe it, Matthew?' asks the music therapist, taking the pressure off the first young man. 'Uhhh, I was just playing quietly with my fingers. You told us this was a Middle Eastern drum and that's what they do, so I was trying to do that.' 'Yeah, it sounded cool,' responds the music therapist, 'Did you notice what anyone else was doing?' 'No. Not really. I was concentrating,' he replies. The music therapist asks if anyone noticed another player and Ulla responds in the affirmative. 'Yeah, I really liked your rhythm. It gave me something to play with,' she says. 'Okay,' replies the music therapist neutrally, smiling at the girl. 'Remember how I said that when we play together it's like having a group conversation, but everyone plays at the same time? Well, this time I want you to try and listen to the conversation and talk to people with your instruments. Grab something different and we'll get ready to play again. It might sound quite different this time.'

'Someone else can start,' suggests the music therapist once the group is seated again. She waits for a minute and when no one begins she decreases the tension. 'Ulla, how about you?' Ulla starts shaking the cabassa and the rest of the group join in right away. This time there is no shared rhythm and greater variation. The improvisation doesn't seem to have a forward momentum, instead it is punctuated and sporadic. Diego thumps the doumbek repeatedly, growing louder and louder. After a minute one of the group yells at him to quieten down, but he ignores them. Another minute and a number of the group are yelling together, trying to get his attention. The music therapist stops playing and the other group members also cease. A short time later the young man does too. The yelling group members don't stop straight away and the music therapist stands up to get their attention. 'He's stopped already, you guys. Why are you still yelling?' 'Because he was annoying,' says Barbara. 'He wouldn't listen to us,' says Gary. 'Hmmm, so what is a good way to get people's attention?' questions the music therapist, 'Yell at them? Did that work, do you think?' 'He should have listened,' says Barbara. 'You shouldn't have yelled at me,' replies Diego. 'But you were too loud. It was hurting my ears.' 'I don't care,' he responds again. 'That's interesting, Diego,' interjects the music therapist, 'Do you really mean that – you don't care if what you did hurt somebody?' 'No,' he replies quickly. 'Think about it,' suggests the music therapist. 'What did you think, Gary?' she asks another group member. 'It didn't bother me,' says Gary, 'They shouldn't have yelled at him like that.' 'Okay, and you, Ulla?' 'I don't care,' she replies. 'I was having fun. HanneMette and I were playing the same thing.' She smiles at her friend in the group and the girls giggle. 'Great. Did anybody else play along with another person?' asks the music therapist, accepting the change in direction. 'I was listening to other people,' says Scott. 'Me too,' says Barbara, 'until Diego started playing so loud!' The group is quiet.

'Is this what happens at school, you guys?' the music therapist asks. 'We don't play instruments at school,' replies Scott. 'No, you don't,' says the music therapist and smiles. 'I mean, do things get out of hand so quickly? If someone does something you don't like, is it hard to deal with?' The group ponder the question and the music therapist makes it more concrete by directing the question to Barbara. 'Do you yell at people at school?' she asks. 'Yeah,' Barbara replies quietly. The music therapist asks some more specific questions, drawing a description from Barbara about what happens in the classroom. 'And what about you, Diego, do people get annoyed at you a lot?' Again, the reply is in the affirmative and a similar discussion ensues. The music therapist doesn't offer advice, but highlights how these are patterns of response. 'Why don't we choose a different instrument this time and while we're playing, think about how other people respond to us?' The group members are a little confused, but they move to get instruments. 'We'll take a break after this one,' says the music therapist, 'It's been more than an hour and you guys must need a drink.'

EVALUATING EFFECTIVENESS

Although some individual group members may appear to be more successful in this setting, each group member has entered with a different baseline and needs to be compared individually to it. The individual goals for each young person provide a template for this, and the therapist's capacity to help shape realistic goals at the outset will be tested through this process.

The ultimate measure of effectiveness will be an improved capacity to cope with the social requirements of school, whether this is the ability to make friends or avoid being targeted for bullying. These achievements are monitored by ongoing conversations with the young person, both in the group and in private conversations by phone or during individual interviews that are scheduled before or after the group. The young person's reports are supplemented by regular contact with school professionals and family members, who sometimes agree and sometimes have a different perception to the young person. This ongoing communication is explained to the teenager at the beginning of the group and any contradictions are therefore easily bought up for discussion with them.

Group cohesion is the most useful indicator of likely therapeutic success within the group itself. Yalom's (1995) cohesion questionnaire is used for this purpose and the young people spend ten minutes filling this out at the end of the first session and at the end of the penultimate session. The results of this survey are regularly calculated and provide a form of evaluation of the programme. This is considered more effective as programme evaluation because the individual achievements will vary depending on the nature of those being referred. Good levels of cohesion indicate that the programme has the potential to be helpful for the young people involved.

KEY POINTS

- Preparation interviews are essential for establishing a collaborative approach towards *developmental* gains.

- Within a group there will be various levels of ability to engage with the abstract level of thinking required to comprehend the relationship to behaviours in other settings.

- Free improvisations do not require any directions other than asking group members to play. Themes can be distracting when authentic self-representation is sought.

- Music making can be a more effective way for teenagers to understand social interactions than ungrounded discussions that reflect on these dynamics.

- Tension can arise in free improvisations with groups of people whose social skills are poor. This is to be expected and accepted as the crux of therapy.

- The music therapist may need to ask a number of questions in order to elicit the material she is looking for. If teenagers do not grasp the intention, it is important to let it go as either irrelevant or too complex.

- Silence is an important part of therapeutic work, but the length of silence adolescents can tolerate is less than many adult groups.

CONCLUSION

The results of group improvisations can vary a great deal depending on the intention of the music therapist. Although what each person plays within the improvisation is entirely up to the individual, the music therapist shapes all of the elements around the improvisation. When the music therapist is fostering *understanding* of unconscious drives and experiences, it is helpful to direct the improvisation to this material using themes or imagery, as in the first example. Although teenagers do not usually articulate the insights they have gained, group improvisations ensure that they will have experienced them. When *acceptance* is offered for the purpose of fostering a sense of community or encouraging individuals to be truly present in the moment, it is essential that adolescent-suitable instruments are available. It is difficult to build a sense of identity when the tools are substandard. When *development* of skills is the focus, the music therapist must be one step ahead, ready to ensure that the focus area is being addressed. In this case, she highlights what social skills are being developed through the verbal dialogue between improvisations. The therapy happens outside of the music time, but is grounded in the social interaction of music making.

The music therapist's intention should vary on a regular basis depending on the capacity and needs of the group on a given day. Her approach can be altered within the session by working through the familiar towards the unfamiliar, or the focus can be steady and development can occur over time. It would be unusual to rely on only one method, used with the same intention, over an extended period of time with adolescents. Working with teenagers is usually more dynamic and the music therapist may blend methods, using group improvisations in any of these orientations to move away from a reliance on words. Although it may not appeal to teenagers when explained, making music with other people is a powerful experience that most young people enjoy. It is also a strong method that may invoke intense levels of joy, fear, connectedness and insight, depending upon how it is used. The music therapist needs to be prepared for anything. After all, improvisation is about stepping into the unknown (Rothenberg 1996).

Chapter 7

Individual Improvisations

Music therapists love to make music and there is nothing more intimate and meaningful than playing with another person and really being there. In this chapter, three examples of individual improvisation are offered with a specific focus on how to engage adolescents in this method. Overall, it is more casual in appearances and more meaningful in action than you might expect. Since improvisation involves expressing oneself, the nature of the improvisation is often related to the challenging condition being faced by the young person. Escaping via fantasy, representing pathology, and expressing one's true inner nature are just three of the possibilities.

Individual improvisation is a favoured method of music therapists. Creating music in the moment with a teenager is the purest way of working towards *understanding, acceptance* and *development*. As a music therapist, it is extremely rewarding because it provides opportunity for the most exciting musical material, both harmonically and rhythmically. Tony Wigram (2004) has comprehensively described musical techniques to assist the music therapist in developing skills that support this intimate interaction. He explains how to convey empathy through mirroring and matching the music made by the client; how to develop frameworks that support clients to express themselves; and also how to challenge clients to move beyond ritualized patterns of playing. All of the descriptions of the music therapist's music in this chapter draw heavily on these ideas. What is unique here is the way that individual improvisations can be used to foster identity formation with adolescent clients in a range of settings.

Although improvisation is thoroughly documented as a music therapy method for working with people who have disabilities and mental illness, it is rarely considered in relation to teenagers. Adolescents are protective of their psychic safety, and stepping into the unknown of spontaneous musical interaction with a therapist either requires a strong faith in the therapeutic relationship or a lack of insight. The music therapist needs to be skilled in providing a firm framework for the encounter, encouraging freedom of expression through modelling and a swift provision of resources. Opportunities for improvisation arise more casually in encounters with adolescents within the disability sector and the spontaneity begins as the music therapist grasps the opportunity to make music freely with the young person. Introducing individual improvisation to the verbal teenager requires therapists to trust their method because without a deep commitment to individual improvisation, it is unlikely that any teenager will be convinced to 'have a go'.

FOSTERING UNDERSTANDING

Individual improvisations draw on the full power of music and the connection to emotions and associations that often exist beneath conscious control. For most teenagers, conscious control is a newly emerging ability that is closely linked with identity formation and increased self-awareness. Prior to this stage of development, concrete thought has dominated the intellectual state of play and only with the onset of abstract thought does the possibility for deeper levels of understanding emerge. For this reason, adolescence is often seen as a transitional period between concrete and abstract understandings, expressed as a movement between behaviour and contemplation. The potential of individual improvisations to help the young person understand the influence of life experiences on his or her current state is suddenly available. As a result, these kinds of musical experiences can be either incredibly rewarding or overwhelming for the cognitively able adolescent. In many cases, verbal consolidation of how the music reflects the psyche may prove too much for the young person to bear, although there are exceptions – usually the extremely intelligent teenager grappling with mental illness. But even without verbal processing, a great deal of understanding can be gained experientially through this process. The music therapist may offer gentle interpretations and use probing questions to develop the improvised material. The teenager may not respond or may not participate in a detailed dialogue, but these interpretations are often heard and contemplated at a later time, particularly if they match with other experiences that occur outside of therapy.

Reflective improvisation
SETTING AND PURPOSE

Mercédès is a 15-year-old woman who participates in music therapy through an outpatient mental health programme. The programme is closely associated with a local paediatric hospital, and a medical orientation dominates the team. Paediatricians, psychiatrists, psychologists, occupational therapists, social workers and teachers are also involved in the programme. Music therapy is utilized for gathering information about the challenges perceived by each teenager and is equally valued for its capacity to solicit information about the healthy aspects of the teenager. The music therapist has worked with Mercédès for more than two years as the young woman has grappled with a pervasive eating disorder, and the treatment goals have gradually moved from a focus on offering *acceptance*, towards a more demanding intention of fostering *understanding*. At this time, the goals and objectives for this young woman are as follows:

- For Mercédès to gain greater insight into the disordered nature of her thinking about food

    ◦ to consider interpretations offered by the music therapist in relation to her musical material

    ◦ to challenge or agree with suggestions made by the music therapist about what the musical material might mean

    ◦ to offer interpretations of her own musical material.

- For Mercédès to feel comfortable in her relationship with the music therapist

    ◦ to engage willingly in music therapy sessions

    ◦ to feel comfortable to question/challenge the music therapist

    ◦ to verbalize any paranoid or self-conscious thoughts that are triggered by music therapy experiences.

ILLUSTRATIVE VIGNETTE

Mercédès has participated in more than 40 music therapy sessions, and until now this has mostly been focused on songwriting in both group and individual sessions. Time spent making music is supplemented by plenty of talking, and Mercédès utilizes the music therapist to send information to the multidisciplinary team as well as for more personal, insight-oriented discussions. There is a strong sense of connection between this young woman and the music therapist and it is clear that a trusting relationship has been established. In fact, in 12 months' time, Mercédès will exit the programme and will credit music therapy as providing her with the necessary tools for her recovery. But at this moment, the actual benefits of music therapy are far less clear and Mercédès is locked in a vicious cycle of starvation and enforced recovery in hospital, with outpatient support in between.

On this day, the music therapist meets with Mercédès following an inpatient stay at the local hospital where she has been drip-fed in order to re-establish metabolic stability. She is still in a malnourished state, but has been discharged in order to attend the outpatient programme, since her psychological state is seen as a priority. Mercédès is not talkative, although she says that she is pleased to see the music therapist. After some initial attempts at casual dialogue, the music therapist decides to offer a different musical experience. Although shared song listening may be one way to further their established relationship without putting too much pressure on the young woman, the music therapist intuits that this is an important opportunity for increasing Mercédès's self-understanding. The increasingly frequent hospitalizations suggest that supportive work is not strong enough to help her conquer the disorder at this time, and the fact that she has been discharged from hospital suggests that she is well enough for insight-oriented work. 'How do you feel about playing a drum to express yourself today?' asks the music therapist, holding out a metal doumbek and placing it in Mercédès's hands. 'You play that and I'll play along on the guitar,' she directs, as Mercédès dubiously accepts the drum.

'I don't know how to play!' comes the predictable response from the young woman. 'It doesn't matter,' responds the music therapist immediately, 'It's about expressing yourself, not art!' As soon as the young woman taps the top of the drum in a casual and slightly sarcastic way, the music therapist begins strumming the guitar. Mercédès had alternated her tapping between both hands at a quick speed, and the music therapist is inspired to offer a flamenco-style accompaniment. She estimates a tempo that would match the playing if it did continue, and provides a musical framework for the young woman. Instead of refusing, Mercédès looks relieved and settles back in her chair as she begins to play the hand drum. The two women lock into a tempo and the music therapist notices that Mercédès has a well-developed sense of rhythm. She leans back in her own chair and repeats the three-chord pattern with a Spanish flavour. Each time Mercédès alters her playing, so does the music therapist, echoing and mirroring her modifications. She wants Mercédès to know that she is listening closely and her responses are dramatic and conspicuous.

After ten minutes, the music therapist begins to wonder about how creative Mercédès's playing is. Her style has not changed for at least five minutes and the music therapist feels trapped in a repeating cycle that is going nowhere; she wonders if it will ever end. She changes the order of her harmonic framework, but Mercédès seems oblivious to the change. This confirms to the music therapist that the improvised material is no longer expressive of the dynamic aspects of this young woman. Instead, it seems to be reflecting her disorder and her rigid, self-perpetuating thinking. The music therapist decides to alter the tempo, and attempts to gradually decrease the pace of the rhythmic patterns. Mercédès responds intuitively, but the change is not registered in her facial expression or her body posture and the music therapist is still not satisfied with the level of inter-personal engagement. She speeds up the tempo, smiling at Mercédès to indicate that it is a game, but this time Mercédès does not concede, and after some time the music therapist returns to Mercédès's pace. Over the next 15 minutes, the music therapist continues to make small gestures towards more dynamic interaction. Sometimes Mercédès moves with her and sometimes she does not. The music therapist eventually initiates a close after nearly 30 minutes of playing.

Mercédès sits quietly, having accepted the musical cues towards closure – an overt rallentando followed by a dramatic and prestissimo coda. After some silence, the music therapist comments, 'Wow! We played for a long time, didn't we?' Mercédès nods. 'Yeah, I suppose so.' 'What was it like for you?' probes the music therapist. 'Good,' replies the young woman. 'Hmmmm.' The music therapist considers whether it is a suitable time to push towards understanding and decides to use one more probe before withdrawing and accepting that Mercédès is not prepared to analyse the experience. 'You sounded as though you were just going round and round in circles,' she offers, 'you must feel like that sometimes when you end up in hospital again, being forced to eat?' Mercédès looks at the music therapist. 'What do you mean?' she asks. 'Well, you seem to be locked into a pattern of starving yourself, followed by recovery and then returning to starving yourself. That's a cycle. And after the first bit of playing together, your music started to sound locked in as well. It's just my opinion. What did you think?' Mercédès stares at the music therapist again. 'Yeah, maybe,' she offers. 'Do you want to try playing again, but avoid getting too repetitive?' asks the music therapist. 'Your playing actually sounds great, and musically, repetition is really important, but I'm more interested in how your music reflects who you are, which is much more than just harmful cycles. Let's see what else is there.'

Mercédès does not protest and joins in as the music therapist initiates a different style. The tendency towards rigid playing is still present, but the music therapist is more directive this time and talks to Mercédès during the improvisation if she feels her drifting off. She knows that Mercédès often hears voices in her head, telling her how useless she is, and she is watching carefully for moments when this appears to be the case. At the end of the session, Mercédès is not sure of how to process the experience. Conscious of the tendency towards vicious self-criticism that accompanies this disorder, the music therapist repeats her positive interpretations of the musical nature of the young woman's playing. 'What do you think of what we did today?' she then asks. 'It was weird,' Mercédès replies. 'How do you feel about it now?' follows up the music therapist. 'Okay,' responds Mercédès, 'but I'm not sure if I agree with you about being in a cycle.' 'Well, it's just a guess,' the music therapist offers, 'Do you want to talk about it some more?' 'Nuh,' comes the reply, 'I'm bored. I think I might go check my email.' 'Cool. I'll catch you tomorrow and see where you're at,' the music therapist agrees, smiling. Bored is such an important word. It could mean anything. And she will definitely follow up tomorrow to process this experience further.

EVALUATING EFFECTIVENESS

The goals that have been set for Mercédès are closely related to the content of this session and the music therapist is clear in her intentions. She uses reflective improvisation techniques (Pavlicevic 1997) initially, and incorporates more challenging techniques in order to re-establish interaction with the young woman. The use of individual improvisation has provided an opportunity to contemplate the cyclical nature of disordered thinking, and although Mercédès does not suggest her own interpretations, she has achieved the previous two objectives of contemplating meaning and challenging the music therapist. She listens to the interpretations offered by the music therapist and is willing to explain her own response to them. The music therapist considers Mercédès's level of comfort throughout the session and does not push her to engage in the session, but she does lead strongly – both into the shared playing and then with multiple probes at the conclusion. This decision is based on her faith in the strength of their existing relationship and the perceived importance of helping Mercédès to move beyond her current coping strategies. Mercédès does not articulate any particular thoughts at the end of the session, and the music therapist immediately recognizes that this may mean that she is holding back. The opportunity to follow up the next day is critical, particularly in the context of the high level of self-critical thinking that is common among people with eating disorders.

KEY POINTS

- Individual improvisation is a strong method and should be used with discretion.

- A safe and strong therapeutic relationship provides a solid basis for fostering *understanding* through insights related to the musical experience.

- The music therapist should not be hesitant in offering improvisation experiences – any lack of confidence on her behalf will undoubtedly lead to rejection by the teenager.

- Teenagers do not easily participate in activities that they have not experienced before.

- An adolescent is unlikely to sit at an instrument, take a deep breath, and launch seriously into an improvisation. Any sound offered should be used as a starting point.

- The music therapist should join in quickly, and immediately reflect any musical contribution made by the teenager.

- If a teenager does not engage in the first attempt at verbal dialogue about the individual improvisation, it is not fruitless – he or she may just need more time.

- The teenager may process ideas suggested by the music therapist outside the session. Failure to participate in verbal discussion at the time does not indicate lack of consideration.

- Teenagers often use the word 'bored'. It should not be taken as a personal insult. It is an effective means of communicating something for which they have no words.

OFFERING ACCEPTANCE

Making music with another person is a powerful experience in its own right. It does not always require interpretation, or a drive towards the achievement of developmental objectives. Individual improvisations are an intimate way of communicating respect and *acceptance*. The music therapist tunes in to the teenager's interests and preferences. She listens carefully to the ways that the young person interacts on a chosen instrument. She responds with empathy and care. *Acceptance* is conveyed through each of these deeds and is felt by the young person during the music making experience. For a teenager who feels isolated, excluded, unsatisfactory or uncertain, individual improvisations provide an opportunity to alter these negative perceptions by replacing them with creativity and joy. Spontaneity and *acceptance* work freely together and improvisations are usually pleasurable for all involved.

Grounding improvisation
SETTING AND PURPOSE

Thirteen-year-old Tony and his family visit the children's hospice initially for a tour. The purpose-built facility for young people who have life-limiting illness caters for a combination of children with terminal diseases such as cancer, and those who have more long-standing chronic illness and disabilities that will ultimately result in an early death. Tony has a brain tumour and his family is clearly struggling with the implications of his fast-progressing illness. Where he has previously been involved in a constant stream of sporting and social commitments, there is now very little that he can participate in, especially with the onset of winter and the fear of catching a cold. When introduced to the music therapist, the family expressed enthusiasm about the programme and an interest in regular sessions. In addition to servicing young people who are staying at the hospice, the music therapist provides an outpatient programme where children visit the hospice for family-centred music therapy. Tony and his father have a long-standing shared interest in music and their participation in regular music therapy sessions would also provide some space for Tony's mother to spend quality time with his sister. The following goals are constructed with the priorities being for Tony to:

- choose to attend music therapy sessions
- indicate his preferences for musical participation
- engage in music making at a level that is suitable for his progressing illness
- have fun with his father during sessions
- have opportunities for self-expression
- be distracted from the limitations of his illness.

ILLUSTRATIVE VIGNETTE
The first thing Tony says to the music therapist is, 'Do you watch professional wrestling?' He then pushes himself up and out of the wheelchair and walks with assistance from the door of the music room to a comfortable chair. He has the swollen look that results from high doses of steroids and yet photographs of this young man only 12 months earlier depict a healthy 12-year-old boy in football attire. Wrestling is to become one of the inspirations for shared music making in the coming months, as will his favourite football team. Everything about this young man speaks of energy and a yearning to be active, although his body is already not able to fulfil these desires.

'Cool drum kit!' Tony exclaims, looking over to the corner of the room. Although the kit looks a little battered, it does have the full set of toms, cymbals and black shiny shells that represent rock 'n' roll. 'You wanna play?' asks the music therapist, walking over to pick up some drum sticks and holding them out to Tony. 'Me too. That drum kit looks awesome!' exclaims Tony's dad, who has walked in behind his son. 'Too late,' laughs the music therapist, 'First in, best dressed.' They all laugh and Tony looks over to his dad to request help in getting out of the comfortable chair. Together they struggle around to the back of the drum kit, with the music therapist subtly moving drums and cymbals out of the way to make the journey a little easier. A few minutes later Tony is poised with sticks in hand. The music therapist grabs a guitar and plectrum and sits on a piano stool right next to the drums. 'One, two, three, GO!' she calls and without a second of hesitation Tony is smashing the drum kit vigorously. He makes moves that look like drum rolls and leans on the cymbal to keep the texture thick and full, and most importantly, the volume fortissimo. The music therapist joins in with equal enthusiasm. She strums a basic series of open chords in a rock style. The pacing is relentless and there are no moments of space to punctuate the improvisation. From beginning to end the two play with gusto – nearly three minutes of raw energy reminiscent of speed metal.

When they finally finish playing, all three burst into laughter. 'Wow. Great work, Tony,' his dad comments, 'You must be exhausted.' 'Nah, let's do it again,' comes the response. 'Do you want to join in?' the music therapist offers. 'Oh no, I can't really play,' Tony's dad begins. 'Come on Dad. Play guitar,' Tony yells. 'Do you play?' the music therapist asks. 'Just a little.' Within seconds the guitar is in the father's hands and the music therapist is sitting at the piano with her back to him, looking at Tony. 'I won't even watch,' she calls, 'You count us in this time, Tony.' 'One, two, three, smackdown!' Tony yells and launches into the drums for the second time. This time the music therapist plays dissonant clusters on the piano, picking up rhythmical ideas from Tony's playing and allowing a little more space than in the previous improvisation. Tony is more tired, too, and pauses occasionally to listen to his dad and catch his breath. Each time he rejoins the pandemonium he yells, 'One, two, three, smackdown!' again.

As the improvisation finally fades out, the music therapist asks what he has been yelling. 'That's what they call in the wrestling,' he responds, 'when the fight begins.' 'Ahhhhh,' nods the music therapist, smiling, 'I should have known.' Tony is clearly tired by the playing, but does not want to move from behind the drums, so the three talk about football and rock music. The music therapist is conscious that Tony's dad had tears in his eyes at the end of the second improvisation, and after she has given him time to recover, she begins to encourage him to play for Tony at home. 'It's easy to lose the music in your life at times like this, isn't it?' she comments empathically, and both of the men nod. 'And it's something you can do when Tony is tired, huh Tony? Dad can just play for you to pass some time.' The discussion turns more seriously to songs, and the music therapist offers to source chords for pieces if that helps, but this never eventuates.

Tony returns to music therapy sessions regularly over the coming months, and even as his illness progresses, the 'smackdown' phrase becomes a dominant theme in sessions. After a while, Tony can no longer sit behind the drum kit, and the music therapist brings a cymbal and tom over to him so that he can strike them from his wheelchair. She continues to play in the style that he parodied in the first session, reinforcing the aspects of his identity that he is no longer able to actualize. Tony's dad joins in when he can, but he finds the emotional connectedness overpowering at times, and the music therapist leaves the decision to him once he knows that his participation is welcomed. Tony's participation gradually lessens to the point that the music therapist will mostly play for him, and his dad reports that he does the same at home, sometimes copying what the music therapist has done in the previous session. Despite his diminishing abilities, Tony will always smile at the call of 'One, two, three, smackdown!' A recording of one of the early improvisations is played at Tony's funeral some months later, and the congregation smile as they recall the energy and enthusiasm of this irreplaceable young man.

EVALUATING EFFECTIVENESS

The nature of palliative care is such that the child's health will diminish over time. The focus of services across the board is therefore on quality of life. An accepting attitude that conveys empathy and support does not lead to objective evaluation. In this case, evaluation is as simple as the acknowledgement of Tony's sustained engagement in music therapy, fostered by his father, and is evidence of a perceived benefit in terms of quality of life. Tony's musical preferences direct session content and his level of engagement is in keeping with his physical capacity, but he has the opportunity to express himself regularly – both his identity and his emotions. The transfer of these experiences into the family home is a significant additional benefit, since it is common for family members to feel unsure how to engage with a child of diminishing capacity. While participation in a funeral should not be an indicator of success, it does provide an opportunity to share the successful experiences Tony had in music therapy and to represent the well parts of his life. The experience is significant for all involved.

KEY POINTS

- Individual improvisations do not always sound beautiful.

- Each individual teenager should have a unique style and this should be clear in the improvisations that emerge. If many improvisations sound the same, it is probably the sound of the music therapist.

- Musical acceptance is easily conveyed through an enthusiastic joining of the teenager in his or her preferred musical style.

- A broad knowledge of contemporary music genres can provide a useful platform for improvisation.

- Playing in a familiar style, such as speed metal, immediately makes an improvisation comfortable and non-threatening for the young person.

- Parents may wish to be involved in sessions and this should be encouraged whenever possible.

- Parents should not be expected to be professional in this encounter, however, and it may also address their own therapeutic needs.

- Working with dying clients is a powerful process and professional supervision is required in order to work with feelings of grief and loss in an appropriate way.

FACILITATING DEVELOPMENT

Using individual improvisations to facilitate *development* incorporates the opportunity to practise skills in a spontaneous way. Instead of music working as a reward that is achieved after a required act, the reward of the music is intrinsic to the experience. Physical, communication or social skills are the most common targets, with music providing the motivation for continuing participation and commitment. Motor skills are inherent in the act of accessing an instrument, and parent–infant interaction theory (Stern *et al.* 1985) suggests that the same is true of non-verbal communication. Learning and practising social skills is also easily encompassed within the individual improvisation framework. Games of stop and go, copying, as well as turn-taking are concrete examples of how social skills can be improved through shared music making. This approach is common in special school settings and is the bread and butter of music therapy in a *developmental* approach.

Empathic improvisation
SETTING AND GOALS

So Jeong is a 17-year-old young woman with cerebral palsy and a profound intellectual disability. She has participated in individual music therapy on a weekly basis as part of her special education programme for the past three years. So Jeong experiences regular epileptic seizures and is frequently sick with colds owing to her compromised lung function. Although some changes have occurred across the three years, the nature of the work is repetitive and preferences have remained fairly static. So Jeong is still at a pre-intentional stage of communication and it is unlikely that she will develop any further. Nonetheless, communication goals are a priority, as are motor skills. The following goals and objectives reflect this.

- For So Jeong to use her voice in a communicative way

    ○ to use her voice on cue in the 'Hello Song'

    ○ to use her voice in response to preferred musical sounds

    ○ to use her voice within a musical interaction.

- For So Jeong to indicate her preferences

    ○ to use eye gaze to nominate preferred instruments

    ○ to use facial expression to convey emotional preferences

    ○ to use her body to access preferred instruments.

- For So Jeong to maintain her current level of head control

    ○ to maintain an upright posture during the music therapy session

    ○ to use her head to access the wind chimes

    ○ to move her head in order to gaze at objects of interest.

ILLUSTRATIVE VIGNETTE

The session has been running for ten minutes and So Jeong has now moved into an alert state. During the 'Hello Song' she had been restless, moving her body in the wheelchair and opening and shutting her eyes. The music therapist had followed the 'Hello Song' with 'Lean on Me' (by Bill Withers), So Jeong's favourite song. As the music therapist sings, So Jeong begins to move her mouth and her tongue moves in and out on a number of occasions. She appears to swallow and her head position stabilizes. This increasing level of engagement alternates with a vacant look and a lethargic posture, but by the end of the song it is becoming consistent.

'Are you ready to play an instrument, So Jeong?' the music therapist asks after a moment of silence. She reaches over to her side and picks up two of So Jeong's known favourite instruments. The music therapist moves the wind chimes in the air so that the tones sound. 'Would you like to play the chimes, So Jeong?' She observes the young woman and notices that her eyes flicker towards the chimes, but that So Jeong does not look back towards the music therapist after this. To gaze at the chimes and then the music therapist would be understood as an intentional choice according to speech development guidelines. The music therapist then shakes the tambourine gently about 50 centimetres in front of So Jeong's face. 'Or would you prefer to play the tambourine today?' she asks. This time So Jeong is more physical in her response, moving her head and her tongue, which suggests an attempt to vocalize. The music therapist offers the choice again, but this time it is the wind chimes that elicit the stronger reaction, with So Jeong gazing towards the sound source, using tongue movement and a smile. The music therapist interprets So Jeong's behaviour as choosing the wind chimes.

The next few minutes are spent placing the wind chimes in the custom-built stand and adjusting the height so that the chimes hang just above So Jeong's forehead. So Jeong is able to move her head from side to side and usually reacts positively to this musical and physical experience. Today is no exception, and a huge smile appears on her face as she moves her head and the wind chimes sound in response. The music therapist returns to the piano to begin improvising. Positioning is crucial, not just for the teenager but also for the music therapist, who twists at the piano to face towards So Jeong. In this position she is able to see So Jeong's facial expression and body movements, as well as hear her sounds and glance towards the piano keys as necessary. The posture is a little awkward, but if she holds her spine straight at 45 degrees between her two knees it only involves occasional gross motor movement. Similarly to So Jeong, the music therapist uses her head movements to ensure the intimacy of the musical communication.

The music therapist waits for So Jeong to move her head again. The excited physical response of the young woman to the first success has moved her position a little and the chimes are no longer in a perfect position. After about one minute, the music therapist considers standing up to reposition the chimes but in that moment So Jeong has further success and uses another head movement to produce a larger shimmer from her instrument. The music therapist matches her immediately with a string of arpeggios flowing up the keyboard with both hands. The volume is initially forte in response to So Jeong's sound, but there is a gradual diminuendo as she reaches the high notes of the keyboard. This time the music therapist plays a rocking octave in the left hand while she waits for So Jeong to play again. Another minute passes and the music therapist uses her voice to add interest to the musical texture. 'Will you play, will you play, will you play, So Jeong?' she improvises encouragingly. Soon there is another sound and another smile and the music therapist mirrors in the same way, using her voice to complete the phrase once the arpeggios have finished.

So Jeong's mouth is moving again now and although some saliva spills onto her top, the music therapist does not stop playing to wipe it away. She is sure that So Jeong is working on a vocalization and wants to be present and attentive so that she does not miss it. Another head movement from So Jeong results in more mirroring arpeggios on the piano and then the sound emerges from the young woman's chest. 'Ahhhh, ahhh.' The two tones are almost a fourth apart and the music therapist matches with a Debussy-inspired siren sound that captures some of the tonal inflections. For the next two minutes, both music therapist and teenager interact musically, staying with the atonal framework, siren sounds and cascading chimes. So Jeong appears to be working hard, moving her head backwards and forwards and punctuating her playing with the vocal sounds. The music therapist does not move her gaze away from the teenager and works equally hard to respond to each attempt at sound production, reflecting each one.

After this, So Jeong stops vocalizing and the number of head movements gradually reduces over the next five minutes. The music therapist pulls back in volume and texture, both so that she can hear any sounds that are made, and also to respond empathically to the slow journey towards closure. As the gaps between actions increase, the music therapist reintroduces words into her singing, using So Jeong's name and providing a commentary on what they have achieved. There is one more smile from So Jeong and then very little movement. The chimes suddenly look beyond reach and the music therapist simply moves into a slower song, with a conventional harmonic framework. She will wait and see if there is another indication of energy and offer another choice of instrument if possible. But it is more likely that the session has peaked and the two will now move slowly towards singing goodbye.

EVALUATING EFFECTIVENESS

Within special education it is typical to develop goals and objectives that are observable and therefore measurable. This is also true in the case of an adolescent who has profound and multiple disabilities; however, some interpretation is usually necessary. So Jeong's use of her voice within the session appears to be communicative. It is accompanied by smiles on some occasions and paired with motor actions at other times. All of these behaviours together suggest an intentionality to her playing, although it is impossible to be entirely sure. Similarly, the head movements seem more frequent when the chimes are positioned above her but it is possible that these movements are not under So Jeong's control. It is commonplace for all professionals working with young people who have profound and multiple disabilities to adopt a positive approach. Even if the behaviour is not intentional now, it may become intentional within the interaction. This is in keeping with parent–infant interactions, where the parent will assist babies to learn how to communicate by interpreting their behaviours and teaching them about the power of communication. So Jeong's parents and teachers believe that she is displaying some intentionality in her playing and that she gains pleasure from the musical encounter. The music therapist agrees. They all hope it is so.

KEY POINTS

- Working towards *development* does not always mean that it will be achieved. It is simply the intention.

- Expectations of improvement need to be developed that are feasible and attainable for the teenager in question. Setting impossible goals does not help anybody.

- Positioning is crucial in working with people who have physical disabilities. It is extremely important to spend time placing an instrument so that it is accessible.

- Appropriate instrument choices need to be contemplated in terms of feasibility to produce a quality sound. The wind chimes are ideal because a small movement results in a series of sounds.

- A subtle musical accompaniment can cover a silence and provide a framework for communication without demanding immediate response.

- Teenagers with multiple and profound disabilities grow tired easily and sessions should be structured to work towards a peak moment and then towards closure. Sometimes the child will have another energetic patch, but this should not be expected.

CONCLUSION

The experience for teenagers of participating in individual improvisations does not vary much according to the different intentions of the therapist. When the focus is on *understanding*, young people are encouraged to play and express themselves. When the therapist is offering *acceptance* the experience is essentially the same, and in the final example of working towards improvements it is again repeated. What happens around the improvisation is quite distinct, however, and the degree to which the music therapist will strive to achieve something beyond the immediate musical experience will vary. As with every method, it is likely that the therapist will not strictly adhere to only one of these approaches. If an opportunity for meaning making or skill building arises, it will be grasped by the music therapist. Similarly, if these intentions are not actuated by the teenager, the music therapist will be satisfied with musical participation as a building block of the relationship.

In some ways, making individual improvisations with teenagers is a greater challenge for the therapist than for the young person. As professionals, we are sometimes more locked into verbal ways of being with other people than are young people, who are still transitioning into the world of abstract thought. Being able to let go and enjoy the experience of making music with another person is intimate and deeply touching. Our desire as therapists might be to consolidate the meaning of the experience verbally, or to prove the benefits of music therapy through visible improvements, but the actual moment of making music simply is. Although individual improvisation encompasses the performance of identity, it is more significant as what Brynjulf Stige calls the 'performance of relationship' (2002a).

PART FOUR

Contemporary Approaches

Introduction

Conventional models of music therapy practice have been the focus of previous chapters, and the use of songs and improvisation has been described with individuals and groups of teenagers. These methods represent current practice, but they do not represent more contemporary approaches to music therapy that are gaining both prominence and popularity. The strength of conventional practice is the diligent attention to each individual teenager, even within a group. What distinguishes contemporary approaches is the broader view of the young person not only as an individual, but also as being located in context. Contemporary approaches place a greater emphasis on the transfer of *developmental* achievements to situations outside of music therapy. The teenager's capacity both to lead the therapeutic journey within the session and also to take it beyond the bounds of the therapy room through the creation of musical products is *accepted*. The young person is *understood* as being influenced not only by unconscious motives rooted in childhood experiences, but also by cultural and societal expectations. The 'Map of how music therapy can be with adolescents' (Figure iv.1) depicts these conventional approaches side-by-side and inserts an ecological approach as a fourth strand. However, it is equally true to suggest that contemporary approaches exist across and expand those perspectives already proposed, rather than being seen separately, as will be illustrated in the remaining chapters.

COMMUNITY MUSIC THERAPY

Community music therapy is one framework that can be used for seeing contemporary approaches as a fourth force[1] within the discipline and is a

---

1   What Kenneth Bruscia (in Stige 2002 p.xv) describes as the fifth force in music therapy, including spirituality as the fourth dimension.

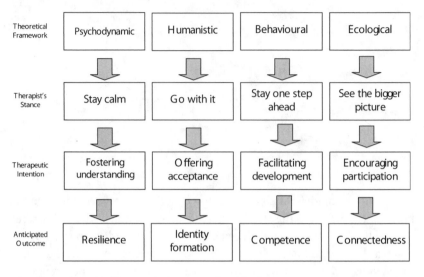

Theoretical Framework	Psychodynamic	Humanistic	Behavioural	Ecological
Therapist's Stance	Stay calm	Go with it	Stay one step ahead	See the bigger picture
Therapeutic Intention	Fostering understanding	Offering acceptance	Facilitating development	Encouraging participation
Anticipated Outcome	Resilience	Identity formation	Competence	Connectedness

Figure iv.1: The Map of how music therapy can be with adolescents

powerful influence in each of the following three chapters. Although it is only one of the models that can be aligned with an intention of encouraging *participation* (see Chapter 2, Table 2.1), the discourse on community music therapy has been rich with both theoretical and practical perspectives. Historically, the term 'community music therapy' is usually credited to Florence Tyson (as outlined in McGuire 2004) in proposing alternative approaches to institutional practice with psychiatric patients. A range of other philosophical and practice-driven influences are outlined by Brynjulf Stige (2002b), and in Australia the work of Catherine Threlfall (Threlfall 1999, 2007) has been an inspirational influence. Theoretically, community music therapy appears to have merged together a range of relevant models such as culture-centered music therapy (Stige 2002a), context-sensitive practice (Pavlicevic 1997), community-based music therapy (Bunt 1994), as well as some feminist perspectives on music therapy (Hadley 2006). In addition, the practicalities of community music therapy appear to overlap with contemporary interpretations of Creative Music Therapy, as espoused by Gary Ansdell (1995) and Kenneth Aigen (2005).

The discourse on community music therapy gained traction with the publication of Gary Ansdell's (2002) discussion paper 'Community music therapy and the winds of change' just prior to the 10th World Congress of

Music Therapy in Oxford. The debate that ensued from this contribution has subsequently driven the development of a theoretical rationale for community music therapy. Some music therapists argued that there was no need to 'add a word' to music therapy in order to label an already existing, context-sensitive approach to practice (Edwards 2002). Others of us expressed relief that the restraints of conventional practice could be loosened, and existing but unconventional approaches to practice be given credibility as truly 'music therapy' (McFerran-Skewes 2003). Public recognition of music therapy practice that did not sit easily in the three conventional therapeutic intentions of fostering *understanding, acceptance* and *development* found a more comfortable resting place in a *participatory* approach. Initial elaborations were permissive, embracing all music therapy practice that did not focus only on the individual client and group. The first *Community Music Therapy* textbook (Pavlicevic and Ansdell 2004) presented a diverse array of practice examples, situated mostly in community settings and challenging conventional thinking on power dynamics and the potential of including performances in music therapy. The web-based 'World Forum for Music Therapy' (www.voices.no) became a primary site for the publication of clinical exemplars of *participatory* practice. Instead of emphasizing outcomes and interpretations based on scientific rationales, articles began to focus on context and empowerment through a range of novel therapeutic and musical strategies.

Within this book, ideas inspired by community music therapy discourse are combined with practical experiences and mostly encompassed within an eclectic and blended approach to practice. Chapter 8 provides the most compatible case study with current community music therapy theory, where a group of disenfranchised youth use music therapy as an opportunity to have their voices heard. A different perspective on encouraging *participation* is to focus on access to music, challenging the traditional emphasis on the provision of professional music therapy services by a trained and registered clinician. Cheryl Dileo (Dileo and Bradt 2009) has been a proponent of an expanded role for music therapists, offering consultation to other artists working with vulnerable populations in order to improve the quality of services being offered and increase the potential benefit for a wider group of people. This strategy is encouraged as one of the approaches to grief and loss in Chapter 9, where workshops for other professionals are outlined in order to encourage a greater inclusion of music in the support of teenagers. The model proposed encourages the choice of different approaches to grief work depending on the severity of the adolescent's response to grief. An emphasis on encouraging *participation* is suggested as appropriate for those teenagers who appear to be coping best and for whom a preventative approach is adopted. *Acceptance, understanding* and *development* are each highlighted as more or less dominant where different levels of coping are apparent. This is aligned with Gary Ansdell's (2002) suggestion about an 'Individual–Communal Continuum', where a less polarized approach to either conventional or community music therapy practice is required. Chapter 10 concludes the discussion of contemporary approaches with an extended reflection on performance as an important method that should be approached in a considered way. The role of performance has been contentious within the discipline and Even Ruud suggests that community music therapy gives 'credibility to a performance-based approach' (2004). This proposal is regarded as overly simplistic by the proponents of community music therapy (e.g. Ansdell 2005b; Stige 2004); however, at a practical level this is the characteristic of the approach that has the greatest implications for what methods the music therapist employs.

WHAT CHANGES FOR THE MUSIC THERAPIST IN CONTEMPORARY APPROACHES?

Everything and nothing. Everything, because the therapist is no longer focused on the teenager's experience only within the music therapy session. The increased focus on *participation* begins in sessions but extends beyond them. Participation in music therapy is one step towards active participation in a range of other systems that impact upon the young person. Connecting the teenager to these networks is a priority for the music therapist whose intention is to encourage *participation*.

Nothing has changed because music therapists have always understood this to a certain degree. There is an underlying assumption that changes within music therapy sessions will lead to changes beyond sessions. But unless this assumption is specifically targeted, the actual likelihood of this occurring is probably less than the music therapist expects. An ecologically informed stance therefore alters the emphasis, which can have a significant impact upon how methods are introduced and evaluated.

WHAT IS DIFFERENT FOR THE TEENAGER?

More responsibility is assumed by the teenager in contemporary models of music therapy. In conventional music therapy, the therapist takes responsibility for gathering information, undertaking assessments and designing treatment plans and strategies for evaluation. In contemporary models, the music therapist looks to the teenager for guidance regarding direction and acts as a resource for the young person in the journey towards better health. This can be challenging for the young person to adapt to since it contrasts markedly with the expectations of the school system in which young people spend the vast majority of their time. Supplementing the increased responsibility and faith in the young person's capacity is an emphasis on musical *participation*. There is a convergence of the musical and personal aspects of the encounter rather than a split between music and therapy (Aigen 2005, p.110). Music is not a tool to achieve extra-musical goals, such as improved social skills, self-esteem or self-knowledge; it is sufficient to develop within the music. When connectedness is the anticipated outcome, the young person is both more responsible and under less pressure to achieve goals. In reality, it can be difficult to know if they notice the difference.

WHEN IS PARTICIPATION A PRIORITY FOR TEENAGERS?

Is every teenager ready for the responsibility implied by a participatory approach? Lucy O'Grady (O'Grady and McFerran 2007) suggests that the location of the teenager on the health care continuum may provide the answer to this question. This model describes how each of us moves along a continuum of health at different times, from being in good physical and mental health at one end, to being acutely unwell at the other, and everywhere in between. The adolescent with profound and multiple disabilities might be physically healthy and psychologically stable one week for example, and then hospitalized with a chest infection the next week. This would represent the whole spectrum of the continuum for that young person. O'Grady's grounded theory analysis of interviews with community musicians and community music therapists suggested that more participatory models are better suited to young people who are healthy and less suited to those who are acutely unwell. When clients are unwell, the therapist is required to take more responsibility for decision making and musical participation. Empowerment is an inappropriate concept for an adolescent in a coma, for example, and receptive, familiar musical experiences provided by a music therapist are suitable. When teenagers are relatively well, they are capable of greater responsibility and will likely benefit from directing the therapeutic encounter.

It is my view that the adoption of a blended, eclectic approach to practice is responsive to the knowledge that every teenager changes in capacity, willingness and energy on a regular basis. It is not realistic to assume that one approach is always, or even mostly, appropriate for any particular teenager. It is more useful to recognize that a *participatory* approach may be relevant for any teenager at the right moment. Contemporary approaches to music therapy do not exclude the use of conventional music therapy methods. Rather, they expand on the application of methods considered available to the music therapist and infuse previous practice with new intentions. Community music therapy has been promoted as 'different things for different people in different places', for example (Pavlicevic and Ansdell 2004, p.17). A focus on *participation* reduces the emphasis on diagnosis and condition and highlights the importance of music making as inherently valuable. It becomes more important to know what clients can do musically, in a range of situations, than what degree of disability or disorder they have. This change of emphasis does not exclude the traditional use of music in therapy, it supplements it.

CONCLUSION

Contemporary approaches to music therapy with adolescents expand upon current practice. While avoiding a prescriptive tendency, a number of key criteria can be identified that suggest the appropriateness of focusing on *participation*. These include the following:

- a need for connection with the wider community
- a desire to be heard beyond the music therapy room
- a capacity to influence societal expectations and understandings
- a musical potential that can be shared.

When any of these criteria are present, the potential for encouraging *participation* should be considered. This may mean blending, sequencing or prioritizing different therapeutic intentions at different times. In any of these cases, the inclusion of a fourth force in professional practice may be an important and distinguishing feature that makes music therapy even more relevant to the life of a teenager.

Chapter 8

Community Music Therapy

Rap artists such as the Aussie hip-hop mob The Hilltop Hoods have played a significant role in promoting the voice of youth culture. In this chapter, rap presents itself as a potential medium for empowerment with a group of disenfranchised youth. The way that this passion is used as a resource within music therapy provides a framework for presenting the extended illustrative vignettes. The descriptions emphasize the role of the young people in determining the direction and outcome of the project that is framed within community music therapy theory.

In the most definitive explanation of community music therapy to date, the main proponents have outlined and illustrated key elements of their approach (Stige *et al.* 2010), understood in this book as encouraging *participation* in order to enhance connectedness. British and Norwegian perspectives are combined within a framework of action and reflection to identify, in retrospect, what the authors consider to be indicative of community music therapy practice. Despite moving closer to definition than previous texts, the commitment to music therapy practice that reflects local culture and responds to unique contextual influences is maintained. This includes using conventional approaches to music therapy where suitable, and some of the examples grow organically out of such situations. In the main, however, the projects are ground-breaking and illustrate just how music therapy can expand its boundaries to follow the interests of participants, wherever they lead.

The five key features identified by the community music therapy school of theorists are expressed as follows:

- Ecological:
  Alluding to Yurie Bronfrenbrenner's bioecological systems theory (2005), as discussed in Chapter 3 of this book.

- Participatory:
  In the sense of being highly collaborative and values driven, encompassing mutual respect at a face to face level, as well as justice in responding to the client's circumstances.

- Actively reflective:
  Which draws heavily on the concept of reflexivity, seen in this case as being constantly attentive to the potential needs and directions that are emerging in the music therapy process.

- Resource oriented:
  Similarly to Randi Rolvsjord's model (Rolvsjord *et al.* 2005), this incorporates focusing on the client's strengths rather than deficits, including pre-existing musical interests as the basis of the therapy process.

- Performative:
  Not only in relation to audience-driven performances in music therapy (as discussed further in Chapter 10), but also in terms of the authentic performance of each individual.

The structure of this chapter draws heavily on these key features, using them as a framework for retrospectively explaining a community music therapy group that grapples with ideas of bridging and bonding (Stige 2008). It is intended to address Mercédès Pavlicevic's (2005) plea that theory on community music therapy should not stray too far from practice. Although the authors have resisted dictating a theory of what community music therapy is and is not, the application of these key features does lead to a fairly consistent route, marked by social activism and collaborations, both within and outside the group. This chapter illustrates my experience of working in this way and the picture contrasts markedly with the conventional music therapy vignettes offered in previous chapters. It is not just working in community settings and using performance as a way of communicating beyond the bounds of the group. Each one of the five key features elucidated by the community music therapy school leads to new territory that must be navigated afresh. Each project seeks to be original because it is responsive to the unique circumstances that it takes place in, both at the level of the individual adolescents and the place where we meet. Once again, the 'Map of how music therapy can be with adolescents' is the only foothold as the adventure with adolescents continues with the dictum in this case being – see the bigger picture!

A COMMUNITY-BASED PROGRAMME

This group was formed as a part of a community-based programme for young men with emotional and behavioural problems. Participants in the programme are not labelled with diagnoses, but they are hindered by a lack of success in the school system. Each young man has been removed from a number of schools and is considered to be at risk of criminal behaviour that will lead him into the justice system. The overarching programme is particularly focused on averting this progression by providing support and fostering positive reengagement with the available systems of support. The young men are all aged between 13 and 17 years when they enter the programme.

Ecological orientation

One of the functions of a *participatory* music therapy programme is bridging the many systems that a young person is negotiating. By maintaining an ecological orientation, the music therapist strives to be actively conscious of the most relevant systems. Although it may be beyond the capacity of one individual to change the systems that shackle a teenager, it is feasible for the music therapist to assist in fostering important partnerships through music therapy. Important bridges may be built between the chaos of home life and the structure of school. In addition, assistance is often required to passage between the freedom of youth culture and the responsibility of adulthood. Successful experiences in music therapy can be one way of assisting in these transitions, and conventional music therapy approaches would hold this perspective. However, a *participatory* approach strives to connect more actively with these systems rather than to assume a transfer of increased confidence from the private experience of therapy into the public sphere of life. In order to do this, the music therapist must first be aware of these systems and then look for opportunities to engage.

ILLUSTRATIVE VIGNETTE

'So what are you up to this weekend, Simon?' the music therapist asks as the other boys disappear from the room on some urgent mission. 'Uhhh, I've just gotta make a phone call,' Simon responds, pulling out his mobile phone and beginning to look through it. 'No worries,' replies the music therapist, standing up to reorganize the equipment. Intimate face to face attention is often too strong for these young men, who quickly feel awkward without their peers around. She knows that he is more likely to talk if the situation is casual.

'My foster mum has kicked me out of the house for tonight because she's got a man coming over,' Simon explains, 'I've gotta find somewhere to stay.' 'Really?' enquires the music therapist, 'That seems a bit harsh.' 'That's nothin',' says Simon. 'She is so strict; we have to be home by 6p.m. or there's no dinner, and if we get back after 7p.m., the door is locked and we have to stay somewhere else. I went to see my dad last weekend and I got caught up helping him to fix a car and I got into massive trouble when I got back.' 'Oh, your dad. I thought you didn't see him any more?' enquires the music therapist, as she quietly packs the keyboard into the case. Simon replies solemnly. 'Well, we've been trying to put things back together over the last couple of months. In fact, I'm hoping that he'll let me move back in with him next month. I've asked them to bring my case back to the court to look at it, and I'm gonna try and change out of this programme at the same time. There's a better one in Smithstown where they have a full apprenticeship programme. I've got a diploma in cabinet making and I want to get my full qualifications.' 'I thought your dad was pretty rough with you in the past?' the music therapist persists, genuinely concerned about the risk of the home environment. 'Yeah well, he has put me in hospital a few times, well nearly every time I see him actually, and my brothers too, even my sister gets it sometimes. But he's trying, and I'm trying too. I put my brother in hospital a few times myself.' Simon is not proud of his behaviour and there is a complete lack of judgement attached to his tone. It is more of a statement of fact.

'Gosh, you tell that story in such a matter-of-fact way, Simon. It's pretty strong. Do you have a counsellor you can talk to about that stuff?' The music therapist is not avoiding analysing Simon's situation, she is simply more interested in the fact that he seems so skilled at telling such a story. Most young people in his situation do not articulate their family situation so openly, so this seems more salient than the tale of abusive family life, which is sadly common. This is not the first time he has shared details of his life and she is intrigued by his desire to do so. 'Yeah, I've got tonnes of counsellors – through the courts, through the schools, they've got people here too, you know. I've had plenty of counsellors.' 'Is that why you're so good at it? You explain your situation really well,' the music therapist asks, following up on her instinct that telling the story is more important than the content of it.

'Well you know, I had to learn how to tell it from when I was young because I had to explain why I behaved like I did at school. My mum was on "the gear" [*heroin*] and so I had to bring up my brothers and my sister, and I had to help her score her drugs. I was always tired and I couldn't concentrate in class coz I was worried about what was happening at home. And then eventually I had to go and steal stuff so we could buy more gear and then sell it and then make some money. You know, I got into a lot of trouble with doing all that stuff, but I had to do it. So I had to explain it to people so that I wouldn't get sent to "juvey" [*juvenile justice*].' 'But why was that your responsibility?' the music therapist enquires, reflecting on how loyal this young man is. 'Coz it was my fault. She was never on the gear until my dad left and then I was messing up at school and she just couldn't cope and that's how it all got started, you know?' 'Hmmm, I'm not sure I agree with that, Simon. Isn't she responsible in some way too?' the music therapist offers gently, 'You must have had a pretty intense childhood.' 'Yeah, I know. And you know what? I thought everyone grew up like that. I didn't even question it. Coz my mum and dad said that we were heaps luckier than those kids in Africa who didn't have any food on the table. So I just believed them. I didn't know it could be any different.'

BRIDGING BETWEEN FAMILY AND SCHOOL
In this brief discussion it is clear that a number of factors have contributed to Simon's failure in the school system – exhaustion, distraction, frustration, lack of support. It is easy to imagine this young man in the classroom, staring out the window and wondering what was happening at home; attempting tasks without sufficient focus and therefore not experiencing the rewards of success; not being able to relate to the childish interests of his peers in the playground; resorting to violence when his family was criticized, or he was tormented for his dirty clothes or poor hygiene. In addition, since each academic achievement is systematically built on the one before, failure breeds further failure in the school system. Even if Simon was striving to succeed with school tasks, his family responsibilities

take more and more energy as he grows older. His story is typical of an oldest sibling who slowly assumes the parental role in the dysfunctional family unit: making sure his brothers and sisters go to school, sticking up for them in the school ground and ultimately even taking responsibility for providing for them.

In order to bridge successfully between the chaos of home life and the structure of a training programme, he will need to overcome the hurdles of learning problems and poverty (Solley 2005). Success in the education system is based on attendance, completion of tasks and connectedness to peers. Family loyalty is a far greater imperative than work or education, so it is likely that he will not receive support for leaving the house each day to work towards a more successful future. Participation in the music therapy programme can assist by providing flexible and responsive experiences that help to mediate the difference between home and school. Simon's presence in the programme shows that he has the capacity to succeed. He does not have indications of a mental illness. He may be struggling with a learning disability, but he has not lost hope and is regularly attending the programme and engaging with people in it. Simon can see a way through the cycle of poverty in which he is caught, with the idea of a training programme to develop his interest in woodwork. Music therapy may be able to provide him with enjoyable experiences that connect him into networks of peers who are also striving to move beyond their failure with the school system. Making music with other people may not directly build a bridge between family and school, but it can offer an experience of bridging that fans the flames of Simon's intentions.

BRIDGING BETWEEN YOUTH CULTURE AND ADULTHOOD

Crossing over from the freedom of youth culture to the responsibility of adulthood is a much more difficult journey. Life on the street is an intense mixture of joy and sorrow, pleasure and pain. On the one hand, there is a strong sense of connection with friends and the intensely pleasurable sharing of drugs, sex and thrill-seeking adventures that are difficult to counter with the reality of responsible adult life. However, the flip side of this culture is the dark side of life on the streets. Enemies are a frequent threat and violence and abuse lay around every corner. Criminal behaviour is usually required to sustain habits, whether this is the simple act of purchasing illegal substances or the more complex act of finding the funding to do so.

Being arrested for criminal behaviour will lead the young person into a series of punitive responses that establish barriers to the transition between youth and adulthood. Incarceration means limited contact with family and friends. A criminal record means that the teenager will not be welcome in schools or taken seriously by employers. The new friendships that are developed in this system will often establish ongoing links with further criminal behaviour. The juvenile justice system represents a final attempt to avert young people from a life of crime, and can be a safe haven for some, but there are many ramifications of this experience that are best avoided.

The positives associated with a healthy adulthood are not obvious to young men like Simon, who have witnessed persistent dysfunction in the adults of their everyday world. From the violent outbursts of Simon's father to the avoidant strategies of his mother, adulthood does not appear very different to street life. Although loyalty will likely be a dominant influence in their lives, home does not provide the solid base from which to establish career aspirations. Music therapy can address this lack of vision through encouraging a focus on ambitions. There is a natural connection between musical expression and hope which can be used to foster dreams. This may be overtly fostered through the creation of rap songs or other lyric material that detail such plans. It might be fostered implicitly through successful performances or conquering new musical skills. Being prepared to strive for the future will be critical in walking the tightrope between street life and adulthood without falling into the pit of the juvenile justice system. It will also involve some luck.

KEY POINTS

- The music therapist needs to understand the particular networks impacting on the teenager at that time, as well as previously and in the future.

- Listening beyond individual experience is one way to understand the multiple systems the young person is engaged in.

- Family loyalty is a priority for teenagers who live in poverty. It should not be underestimated.

- The young person is committed to the systems he or she is familiar with – family and street life. No amount of talking will convince him or her that these systems are shackles.

- The bridging role of music therapy is to show how other partnerships might also be rewarding.

Participatory orientation

The structure of sessions with a truly *participatory* orientation is unlikely to be under the control of the music therapist. If the teenagers are to find the process empowering, it is critical that they own it and take responsibility for it. One way of offering that is to focus on the provision of resources and support, and then allow the direction of the therapeutic process to emerge. This involves more than an *accepting* stance from the music therapist, and the process of being actively reflective (described below) is critically linked to this *participatory* orientation. Young people experience this as an invitation to engage in music in an original and individual way; to participate in a creative and connected experience; to be in control.

ILLUSTRATIVE VIGNETTE

The music therapist arrives at the Centre at midday, which is just as the compulsory morning education programme finishes. The music programme is voluntary and some risks are inherent in this, since it is the last programme of the week, but attendance is a challenge for this group of young people regardless of the rules. A small group of teenagers are standing in front of the building, talking and smoking cigarettes as the music therapist parks her car. The music therapist draws a deep breath of courage and then crosses the road to engage casually. It is like being at high school again, approaching a group and not knowing whether they will talk or not. 'What's going on?' she smiles. 'Ahhh, they've got lunch upstairs,' one of the young men replies, 'and there's a few people hanging around waiting for you to come. Did you bring the bass drum this week?' 'Yep, I got it. I hope we don't scare everyone away with our noise!'

After a brief chat and an enthusiastic reminder to come back up once they're finished smoking, the music therapist ascends the stairs. Sure enough, there are five or six young people hanging around, as well as three professionals. The walls are lined with computers and half of the teenagers are watching videos or chatting online. After some more enthusiastic greeting of individuals, the music therapist begins to drag drums, electric guitars and keyboards out from various cupboards and she moves them into the room they will use. Different young men help at various stages, politely offering to carry drums and amplifiers. As the music therapist rearranges furniture, individuals drift into the room and more greetings are shared. Wai Man picks up a doumbek and starts tapping it. Hearing the first musical offering, the music therapist immediately crosses the room, picks up a guitar and sits down to the side of the young man. She waits for him to play an idea for her to framework, but as he continues to tap the drum casually she starts to strum a rhythmic pattern on an open E chord. She uses open rock chords to improvise, making eye contact with Wai Man and indicating that she is expecting him to play. 'Nah, play that one,' he says, pointing towards a large djembe, 'like you did last time.' 'Oh. Okay,' responds the music therapist, as she puts the guitar down and moves over to the djembe. She thinks back to previous weeks and remembers writing in her notes about turn taking with Wai Man.

As she settles back into her chair, the music therapist hears Wai Man play a rhythmic pattern and she repeats it back to him. His posture straightens and he plays the same pattern again. The music therapist echoes his rhythm and they make eye contact at the end of the phrase and smile widely at one another. The game continues for a while before they merge into synchronous playing that includes echoed elements. There is smiling and laughing at each phrase and it is mutually enjoyable. The tempo doesn't stay constant for long, but the music therapist adapts to the changing pace, only sometimes encouraging Wai Man to try to hold the pattern for longer. She knows that thinking too much about what is being played is often less successful that just jamming and it can be more rewarding to play together without offering verbal guidance, even if the tempo shifts around.

Another young man is sitting nearby and the music therapist stops playing for a moment to pass him the guitar she had picked up initially. 'Why don't you join in?' she says, and begins to play again. Wai Man engages again and there is more shared music making, with the music therapist also looking frequently towards Even and smiling at his noodling sounds on the guitar. Two more young men enter the room and grab drums. They play frenetically, laughing and dancing around the room before beginning to wrestle. The music therapist matches their energy also, trying to maintain a sense of tempo from the improvisation with Wai Man, looking over to Even on a number of occasions and now also laughing at the antics of Jason and Jaako. For the next ten minutes there is chaos. A loud, multi-rhythmic cacophony ensues. Different musical agendas are played out and the music therapist simply works her way around, attending to different sounds at different times.

After a while the young men lose interest and the music therapist suggests a change of instruments. They concede and there is some more playing, but the natural togetherness of the first moments has passed. It is more tiring now, and the young men are much less interested. Even is working hard to conquer some chords that the music therapist taught him the previous week. She moves over beside him and provides encouragement and direction as he slowly moves from one chord to the next. The movement between group and individual focus has become a part of the session. The young men are only able to play together for short periods of time before they lose interest or grow frustrated by the noise. The music therapist often tries to encourage shared playing on the beat but it is perpetually difficult for the group. The freedom of improvisation is most suitable at this stage, and the young men do not mind the lack of synchronicity. The music therapist feels as though she is in a constant state of attentive listening, waiting for the small windows of opportunity that arise for connectedness. There are plenty of months ahead and it is not clear how these young men are going to use this opportunity yet.

Four of the young men spend nearly 90 minutes in the room. There is plenty of banter, rough and tumble play fighting, quite a bit of noise, some serious attempts at group playing and laughter. The music therapist moves between individual and group focus fluidly and welcomes other young men into the music making as they make more sporadic appearances. Some of them are working on projects in the other room and just enter the room when it sounds interesting. Others arrive to draw group members away – for cigarettes, or to start preparing for the adventures that evening. The music therapist does not try to control the process, although she does occasionally raise her voice to draw attention to different opportunities or to ask the whole group a question. She sits with the chaos and waits for direction, trusting that it is leading somewhere. After a couple of hours the four main players have left and two different participants are still playing casually on the instruments. The music therapist signals the end of the music time and starts to pack up. It will be another hour before this process finishes, with more chatting, last minute playing and discussions with these two young men, as well as the other adults who are in the main room. There is also the music studio to explore and she knows that some of the young men have been laying down hip-hop tracks that she wants to go and hear. The time flies by in this chaotic way every week.

WHAT DOES A PARTICIPATORY ORIENTATION LOOK LIKE?
A participatory orientation looks like the people who are participating. This music therapy group is a direct reflection of the young people in it. At this early stage in the process, this group is much more closely linked to street life and family life than it is to the structure and responsibility of school and adulthood. The chaos that marks the group is comfortable for the young people and for the music therapist who is willing to sit with it. Nobody is giving directions and nobody is being told what to do. Moments of joy and laughter mark the sessions, as do moments of confusion and frustration. The instruments are provided and a warm welcome is offered. The invitation to participate does not come with any qualifications; it simply is.

The volume that accompanies this chaos is the most salient feature of the group. These dynamics move up and down depending mostly on the number of participants. There is movement to accompany the noise, and often there is some tussling as popular drums are put down and grabbed by someone who has been poised to play, or one teenager needs the one available plectrum but somebody else has it. Distortion may be suddenly switched on in an amplifier, or alternatively the plug may be pulled from the wall. The electronic beats from the keyboard may be at full volume, but the young man who pumped it up may have moved on to another instrument and left it playing.

The moments of bonding that occur in this chaos are important. There are no drugs here, and the joy that is experienced is pure creativity. Although these moments are transient now, they may grow into something more sustained as the group progresses. The connectedness that Wai Man experiences with the music therapist is profound, although it is not discussed or used as the basis to achieve something more. Wai Man asks for this again when he refers to the previous week and it is clear that he is getting something from the experience. Even's persistence on the guitar is another example of pleasure, and when the moment arrives that he can play the song along with other group members, he will experience an increased connectedness that is built on his own creative expression.

The role of the music therapist is therefore both simple and challenging. To trust these young men to make something of this opportunity is not as easy as it sounds. The urge to help (*develop*), to solve (*understand*), or to attend to the individual (*accept*) is strong. It is an adult inclination; a response to the lack of parenting that can be intuited in these young people. Instead, the music therapist chooses to let them lead the way. It is not possible to empower other people, and since respect and empowerment are the primary values of this work it is essential to pass over the power. Surviving the chaos and attending to the small moments in an optimistic and creative way is essential.

KEY POINTS

- Voluntary participation is preferred to compulsory attendance.

- There is no formal beginning or end to this group.

- Music therapy does not always involve young people sitting around facing one another in a circle.

- A participatory music therapy group looks like the lives of the group members.

- Chaos is not always something to be avoided and some teenagers are more comfortable freestyling than being structured.

- Coping with loud volume is critical in working with groups of young men in this approach.

- Listening, waiting and attending is as critical in this work as in other approaches, but what the music therapist is waiting for is initiative and potential.

- Resources provide a platform for creativity and achievement.

Actively reflective with a resource orientation

Working as a music therapist without a plan has consequences. In conventional music therapy, the most strenuous period is during the process of assessment and treatment design. Time is spent early on striving to know the young people, determine their needs and generate goals and objectives that match those needs. Music therapy methods are selected and session plans are generated. In a *participatory* model this active reflection is constant and ongoing. The music therapist is focused on recognizing the resources within the group and considering how these might best be utilized. The question of 'Where could these young people go from here?' drives the reflection process as she considers possibilities for action. This combines with an active consciousness regarding the systems the group operates within and the emphasis on participation. The music therapist does not have to answer the question alone. It is a question for everyone to answer together, in collaboration.

ILLUSTRATIVE VIGNETTE

The three young men turn towards the door of the studio as the music therapist taps gently on the window next to it. They smile and gesture for her to come in and she enters into the dark space. Although there is no cigarette smoke or empty bottles of alcohol, the vibe inside the studio is one of late nights. It is dark and the sound is cushioned with insulation. The computer screen is the brightest thing in the room and the young men are peering at it. Each one has headphones on and a suspended microphone in front of them, so it looks as though they have been recording. 'Watcha been working on?' asks the music therapist quietly. 'Have a listen to this,' responds Lars Ole enthusiastically, 'We've done tonnes of stuff!'

For the next few minutes the young men are searching through the computer to try to find the recordings they have made. They open up a couple of files, listen for a moment and then close them down. 'Nah, nah, those ones aren't any good,' they agree. Finally they settle upon one to be played. Rolando hits the play button on the computer software and a beat starts pumping through the speakers. It is one of the pre-programmed backing tracks that the music therapist has heard them rap to before. It has some nice melodic loops in it and is the usual 100 BPM. The young men like the bass, which is a little distorted and quite prominent in the mix. The voices start and the fast pace of a freestyling rap artist races over the top of the beat. Wai Man looks towards the music therapist as she listens intently. 'Is that you, Wai Man?' she asks. He nods. 'Great rhymes!'

He is talking about life on the street and making the point that he and his friends are tougher than anyone else, since they can rap harder and faster and longer and better.

You think you know me but you don't
All you do is choke
Don't speak a word, it ain't your turn
I'm just spinning in this dangerous world

You don't know me
You're just a !*&@?! phony
Sitting home listening to your Sony

We give you a fright when you enter the Heights
You don't know who you're talking to
Walking through
The Heights station
We're not hesitatin'

Come to teach us
Comin' through now they preach us
Passed out at the station
I don't know what I'm saying
All comin' out fraying [*laughter*]

The rap is passed to Rolando and now he can be heard proclaiming his lack of fear and his brilliant rapping skills. The influence of American gangsta rap can be heard in the focus of the lyrics, and the music therapist comments that it seems to be offering a commentary on their nightly lives. The Aussie hip-hop that the young men enjoy usually offers reflection as well as description and she has tried to encourage them in that direction, so the comment is familiar. 'But it's a battle, miss,' they reply, as though she must be stupid not to realize this already. 'It's all about taking the other person down!' They laugh at one another and then refocus on the end of the track. 'Ohhh, listen to this. This bit was really good!'

As the track ends the music therapist stays mostly quiet, understanding her role as an observer who has been allowed to enter the studio world. This is their space and they know the technology better than she does. They begin to try to set up for another recording but they can't alter the levels, and the previous recording was distorting during playback. The music therapist leans over the mixing desk and tries to adjust some of the channels, but she is no more capable than they are and the most obvious strategies aren't working. 'Wouldn't it be cool if you guys could create those backing beats yourselves and make them sound original?' the music therapist suggests as the group continue to fiddle and chat. 'Yeah. That would be alright,' they agree. 'Do you know how to do that with this programme?' she asks. 'Nah, this is just a simple one, you can't make new beats, you just record over the top,' Rolando replies. 'You know, Jaako can play drums. He could lay down a live beat and then someone else could add a bass line, and you could work out all the other parts as well,' the music therapist offers. 'Really?' says Lars Ole, turning towards the music therapist and pulling the headphones off his ears. 'Really,' she replies.

Over the next weeks the music therapist continues to lead into this conversation and to draw attention to the required skills that are held within the group. 'Go on, Jaako, play it now,' she says when there is a significant group of young men in the music room. After a couple of stumbles, Jaako does lay down a beat on the drum kit and the rest of the group cheers. The music therapist also continues to highlight what they would need in the studio. 'We can't multi-track here,' she says, 'We need a new programme so we can record more than one line.' 'Yeah,' says Wai Man, 'and we could use the scratching sound off your keyboard if we do it that way, couldn't we?' 'I think so,' says the music therapist, realizing that she is getting out of her depth. 'Let me make some phone calls.' During the week she calls and organizes a trip to the local ArtHouse where they run workshops on different music programmes. The young men are casual but excited when she asks if they would be interested in going with her the following week. 'Yeah, that sounds alright. I'll come.' Things are moving.

THE EXISTING RESOURCES WITHIN THE GROUP

In her constant attention to the resources that are present in the group, the music therapist is beginning to perceive a new potential. The individual group members come and go and the sporadic attendance makes it difficult to rely on attributes of specific participants. Yet overall there are a number of key features that have become an identifiable pattern. There is a capacity for *storytelling* in the group. For Simon this is a verbal discussion of his history. For others, these stories flow most easily in rap. Some of the young men spend time identifying rhymes and writing out sequences of words. This lyricism is an additional resource that is connected to the storytelling. Freestyling is more highly valued by the group however, and this capacity for improvising lyrics on the spot is also an asset. The topics have varied in the different tales that have been woven across the weeks. Sometimes it has been history and sometimes reflections of life right now, but there is little representation of hopes and dreams. Aspirations have been a dominant feature in work with other teenagers (McFerran *et al.* 2006), yet they have not been present in this group.

Another important resource available to this group is *energy*. The young men do not sit still for a moment. There is constant action, continuous noise and unbroken vitality. Some of the young men are conscious that this is not always an asset and that it impacts upon their ability to focus, yet it is also a necessary strength. These young men are survivors who have so far evaded both mental illness and the juvenile justice system. They play drums and guitars and rap into microphones with vigour. The frenetic nature of this energy means that it is difficult to connect with others, except in peak moments of excitement, and so they seek these experiences. Many of the young men play dangerous games at night, leaping between trains and chasing cars on the freeway when they are high on substances. These risk-taking behaviours are not ideal, but within the music therapy sessions the energy can be used: shared drum improvisations, jumping around the room to different electronic beats, bouncing up and down to a hip-hop track. Energy is a resource that could be well utilized to achieve something from this group.

THE REQUIRED RESOURCES FOR THIS GROUP

Aspirations are a crucial element of growing up. Without dreams, it is difficult to work productively towards any kind of future. These young men have energy and storytelling skills, and rap provides the perfect platform for achievement. These young men intuit this potential already and have independently gravitated towards the medium. Their time in the studio is separate to the 'official' music programme and the music therapist is not the only professional to engage with the young people in that setting. What a participatory approach can offer is the resources to take this further. This will require drawing on the two types of resources that music therapy has to offer: the musical and the inter-personal.

Musically, these young men are limited by the basic software they are using to compose new material. If they are going to take control of the music they create, they will need to have more capacity for creating original beats in order to feel ownership of the songs. The teenagers have made this observation themselves. The music therapist could teach them how to use another programme, but she could also link them in to other systems where they could learn these skills. This opens up their links to resources rather than remaining reliant on a partnership that is already available to them.

The ArtHouse programme is provided to many school-aged participants, and the teachers are skilled at teaching a range of software. Travelling to the ArtHouse will require the young men to enter the cultural hub of their city, visiting a venue that they may perceive as limited to a 'different' type of person to themselves. If this kind of programme was not available, it may have been feasible to contract in a local musician to teach these skills in the comfort of their own studio. But it is a great opportunity to mix with elite culture in the city.

It is important that the aspirations being developed by the young people are not for them all to become famous hip-hop artists. The purpose of the music therapy programme is bridging between the existing possibilities for these young people, not creating a new fantasy. While this outcome would be extraordinary for anyone who achieved it, bridging to something more closely related to their daily lives is more helpful. To envisage any kind of positive but realistic future is more than most of these young men will be able to do, but they will be familiar with fantasy. The resource that the music therapist can offer is grounded in reality. Simon is already expressing his capacity to do this when he describes the apprenticeship, and the music therapist can draw on his dreams to guide the other teenagers. Lars Ole has previously shared a love song from his journal with the music therapist, and this capacity for relationship might also be a good basis for hope. The group will need to continue to collaborate and agree on a direction and the music therapist will be one voice in this discussion.

KEY POINTS

- Music therapy doesn't just happen in sessions; it happens anywhere.

- The music therapist does not determine the needs based on what is missing – an understanding of needs emerges from focusing on what potential exists.

- The music therapist is only one of the contributors in answering the question 'Where could these young people go from here?'

- The sense of uncertainty that accompanies a collaborative search for this answer can be unsettling at times. It is usually uncomfortable to feel out of control.

- Other professionals who observe the programme may find the lack of direction disturbing. It is important to communicate the intention of the approach for this reason.

- The role of the music therapist is to provide resources of an inter-personal and material nature – this may involve 'thinking outside the square'.

- The music therapist does not want to be the centre of the programme, and therefore linking to other programmes is actively sought. There is a focus on establishing connections.

- By outsourcing skill development, the music therapist is freed to maintain her role as collaborator and participant, and avoids the role of instructor.

- At no point is the music therapist sure of what will happen next. Instead she is constantly attentive to what might happen.

Performative approach

Building on the resources identified through active reflection, the best part of six months has been spent working towards the creation of an original CD containing work by all the young men in the programme. The recognition of the need for new software and skills in using it was an important step. Acknowledging the existing ability in the group to contribute original musical lines was also a revelation for members, even though it came from within the group. Working on group and individual tracks was as sporadic and chaotic as the rest of the group and the music therapist drew deeply on her own resources of patience in allowing the group to lead the pace of the project. As a result, most of the actual work has not happened until the last few weeks leading up to the date of recording. This has been an intense process, blending creativity and organization, joy and frustration. A number of weeks have been spent in a community studio as the final stage, drawing on the resources of local musicians to bring the ideas of the young men together. Seven tumultuous months have now passed since the idea formed, and not all the young men are still in the programme. Those who are feel ownership for it and it would not occur to them to credit the music therapist in the journey towards the creation of the CD. This is as it should be.

ILLUSTRATIVE VIGNETTE

The day has finally arrived and the young men sit together around the computer. On screen is the homepage of a local community radio station, PumpFM, and they are due to play at least one of the tracks from their album in the coming hour. 'It's hard to believe that people are actually going to hear it,' initiates the music therapist. The young men grunt in response, focused on what the DJ is saying and waiting intently for some reference to their work. The music therapist takes the cue and doesn't instigate any further conversation. Another five minutes pass and Simon is getting restless. 'Ahhh, I don't know. Maybe I'll go down for a cigarette,' he says out loud. The other teenagers look at him as though he is a freak. 'Are you joking?' says Wai Man, 'They might play your song, you know.' Simon smiles at the thought and says no more. The DJ puts on a track, but it isn't from their album and the boys yell in frustration. 'Right, I'll be back in five,' says Even, and moments later they have all disappeared down the stairs for a smoke.

The music therapist smiles at her co-worker, a teacher in the programme, and they chat about how the group is going to cope with whatever song is chosen. 'I don't know if Even will cope if it's not his,' says the teacher, 'He's had so much positive feedback about that song. It's an inspiration!' The music therapist nods in agreement. It is the best track on the album in her opinion. It radiates hope at the same time as offering a poignant reflection on street life in the city. Of all the songs, this was the one that everyone was drawn into and made a contribution towards. The slow groove built up by Jaako on the drums and Lars Ole on the bass lent itself to a clear monologue. Other teenagers contributed melodic riffs and effects that punctuate the story and provide space for enjoyment. Even used the rhyming dictionary with aplomb and the resultant lyrics blend humour with insight.

> Yo yo, listen up everyone
> Coz I know you're havin' fun
> But I'm the new phenomenon
> And I want your attention
> We gotta talk
>
> That's right, we gotta talk
> Coz I know, coz I know, coz I know what's goin' on

Got no hope for the future
Been acting like a loser
Your girl is up the duff and you been
Treatin' her real rough
But there's another dimension
That I really need to mention
It don't need too much aggression
Just a little more intention
We gotta talk
That's right we gotta talk
Coz I know, coz I know, coz I know what's goin' on

You got a big erection
But it's led to an infection
It's worse than some detention
That you'll get for possession
But what I'm seein' is suspension
From reality, you're flippin'
You just want some protection
From the people you've been tricken
We gotta talk
That's right we gotta talk
Coz I know, coz I know, coz I know what's goin' on

Can you picture a future
Where you're not just some loser
You can walk with your head high
Maybe even touch the sky
You got a job that you're into
And a chick who really likes you
You gonna feel euphoria
Start singin' the Gloria

It could be you
But there are things you gotta do
Don't let them tell you it ain't true
We gotta talk
That's right we gotta talk
Coz I know, coz I know, coz I know what's goin' on

The teenagers return to the room and their ears prick up as their CD is mentioned. 'Now I'm holding a new CD in my hand here, it's a pre-release copy made by some young blokes down in the Heights. There's a few good tracks here, but today I wanna play you a pumpin' little mix, a song that just drives it home – Electric Rodeo.' It is the electronic dance track put together by Rolando and Wai Man and the young men are delighted. 'Wow. Can you believe this?' Rolando says out loud as the music starts pumping through the speakers. 'That sounds awesome,' Even responds immediately. All the young men stand up and start jumping around the room, turning the speakers up to full volume. The track is full of energy and enthusiasm and the effects are catchy. These young men had been really interested in the technical detail of the software and it has resulted in a good quality track. The music therapist cannot stop herself from acknowledging those who had not been played. 'That is such a great track you two. And so were the rest. We really made an awesome album everyone. Well done, huh!' There is a spontaneous cheer, followed by embarrassed laughter. It really is a great album.

CREATING THE CD

The journey of working towards this achievement has been arduous and chaotic. When incorporating performance into music therapy, the focus is often on the production and other non-musical achievements. Within a *participatory* approach it is often important that the product is of a good quality. This is not to underestimate the importance of the inter-personal and creative process. Nor is it to detract from the purpose of the product, which is to foster the creation of bonds within the group and bridges beyond the group. However, a pointed focus on performative elements necessarily demands that attention is paid to the performed elements, not as a by-product, but as central. Identifying the right computer programmes, learning how to manipulate the software, deciding what blend of acoustic and electronic sounds to use, practising musical skills, creating musical loops, writing lyrics, recording sounds, mixing multi-levels of recorded tracks, finalizing the sounds. This is an extraordinarily complex process for any group of artists and it is important that each decision to step forward is taken by the group. The music therapist has an important role to play in making resources available at every stage of this process. The attentive listening to the present moment is continued in order to hear whether this is best provided by bridging to the community and accessing the skills of others, or by providing patient support and basic information to the group members in each session. The music therapist also has her own ideas that she feeds into the process, some of which are accepted and some which are not. A focus on dreaming the future is constantly offered, and some of the young men incorporate these discussions into their creative output. Others do not.

PRIDE IN ACHIEVEMENT

The result of this particular process is impressive, and the young men are conscious of this and extremely proud of the CD. They have played it to the other staff on the programme and they have played it to their friends and their families. They have ripped it to their iPods and have no doubt played it to strangers on trains. The local community radio station is supportive of youth-oriented ventures and did not require a lot of convincing to incorporate the CD into their playlist. The CD is of a good enough quality that this is not a sympathetic gesture, it is simply supportive. These teenagers can be proud that their product is near professional in sound. They are responsible for every part of it, from their creative input to their continued focus. They have worked as a group, both together and individually. The bonds that have been built up in this process are not to be underestimated and the loss of some group members is a potent reminder of that. What is striking about this process is that their pride is not based on feedback from the therapist and the other members of the group, it is valid beyond the walls of music therapy.

Playing the song on the local radio station is one achievement and there may yet be more that emanate from this project. An upcoming art exhibition provides an opportunity for a live performance that will require another set of skills if the young men choose to participate. The audience for the CD is potentially unknown, and with 100 copies available to the young men, any number of people may yet listen to it. Currently unforeseen situations may arise for this CD, or for another one to follow it. Once again, there are few limitations on how this impact may be extended.

CONNECTEDNESS

Bridging beyond the walls of music therapy is inherent in a participatory approach. Playing this song on the radio takes the music therapy experience to an audience beyond the control of the group and beyond their horizons. This is a concrete example of bridging between street and home life to the more structured world of adulthood. Unknown people are playing their song and other unknown people will hear it. The possibilities of the unknown world are therefore less distant than previously. The young men have now had the experience of engaging with this world successfully.

The performative elements of this approach are not strictly tied to performance. In addition to this more concrete interpretation is the importance of revealing different layers of one's self through the performance of music. These performative functions were already being achieved before the decision to undertake a CD project. The project has extended these experiences, however, partly by expanding the range of performance but also by providing a focus for deepening the nature of what is expressed. As the young men worked towards the date of the recordings, some of them managed to work on their lyrics and music to perfect them. In this process they were ensuring a more authentic representation of themselves, performing themselves through music. The combination of this depth and breadth of influence is a significant achievement.

KEY POINTS

- Performative does not mean performance, but performance is a clear way of ensuring performative elements.

- Working towards a performance involves a tremendous amount of work and commitment. This will only be possible if the group is truly behind the idea.

- The quality of the product is important in this approach and it needs to be matched to the intended audience.

- Teenagers will almost invariably leave the vast majority of the work until the very last moments. This can be very stressful for the music therapist, who has a strong sense of what is involved and what timeline would work best.

- Having access to resources is essential and the music therapist should always be realistic in what she can offer and what may not be possible.

- The ripples of influence are beyond the control of the group and also of the music therapist.

- The experience of being heard beyond the group is often new for teenagers. They may have mixed reactions.

- There will inevitably be different group members who shine more than others. It will be important to prepare the group for this but they cannot be protected from it.

- Different people will perform their contribution in different ways and this is critical to the success of the group as a whole.

- A successful performance is one that connects the group to their community and results in a feeling of pride.

CONCLUSION

Community music therapy with adolescents is destined to be even more chaotic and out of control than conventional music therapy. Having clarity about intentions can be a life jacket during the inevitable weeks where nothing is emerging and the music therapist questions whether she should take control. The work that happens outside the music therapy sessions is also crucial and this can assist in keeping the group process on track during difficult weeks. What systems are relevant and how can we connect with them – either metaphorically or in reality? Is there a need for new resources, inspiration, or just deeper listening? Where is this going and what resources can be drawn upon to get there? The actively reflective nature of this work is stimulating, but it does require that time is set aside and, ideally, that a team approach is offered, thus making support available for the music therapist as well as for the young people.

While it can be easy for the music therapist to envisage what a group of teenagers may be able to achieve, this is not usually so simple for young people who have experienced multiple failures. Realistic encouragement and persistence is required in order to tend to the potential of the teenagers without offering to take responsibility for it. The music therapist's aspirations should be kept to a minimum so that unfair expectations are not created, leading to disappointment. If this is achieved, young people sense the support, and as they develop trust, begin also to use the resources that are made available. For many the experience is empowering. For some young people who may be better suited to a more conventional approach, the duty can be too much and they would prefer the music therapist to take more responsibility. As with the other approaches, the reality is usually a blended approach. The overall orientation may be *participatory*, but within that, individual work may take place that fosters *understandings*. *Acceptance* may be offered without either agenda or awareness, and *development* may be constantly facilitated and achieved. There is no reason to think that a *participatory* intention rules out the timely and effective use of other approaches. It is in the eclectic blend that the most beautiful possibilities are discovered.

Chapter 9

Four Brief Approaches to Grief

The relationship between music and emotions is never clearer than when it comes to working with grief and loss. The capacity of music to express sorrow and mourning, as well as to capture stories and memories, makes music therapy a very relevant resource for young people. In this chapter, four variations on the theme of brief interventions for teenagers struggling with loss-related issues will be broached. The differences between each are significant but the subtlety of the difference points, once again, to the value of a blended, eclectic approach to music therapy with teenagers.

Brief models of intervention play an important role in contemporary therapeutic approaches. Understandably, clients want outcomes in the shortest possible timeframes, and a brief intervention can be offered in a single session. There is an overlap of values with *participatory* models, since both emphasize the existing resources of the client and focus on context rather than on historical cause. *Understanding* of unconscious influences is therefore supplemented by an analysis of current situation. *Acceptance* and unconditional positive regard is offered, but less time is spent emphasizing this intention and instead the focus is on normalizing the young person's experience. *Development* is usually emphasized within a cognitive behavioural framework, linking in closely with the consciousness about context. The solution-focused nature of brief interventions tends to mean that issues are often targeted in a direct way. In the examples below, grief is clearly identified as the area for growth using a range of brief strategies. Music therapy is utilized to access and express emotions, foster connectedness between grieving teenagers and their networks, and normalize young people's experiences of grief. A different emphasis is employed depending on the context for the work, and the potential role of music in working with grief is expanded beyond the bounds of conventional music therapy, with a consultancy role being advocated in some contexts.

A BRIEF INTRODUCTION TO GRIEF

Grief and loss are a part of the experience of most adolescents who engage in music therapy. They may be grieving shattered hopes and dreams of the future due to physical or mental illness. Their grief may be for the childhood they never experienced due to the challenging conditions in their home lives. It may be the loss of control of their destiny as they struggle to succeed but seem to fail constantly. For some, it may be an actual bereavement through the death of one or many family members. Loss of cultural identity. Lost love. Loss of attention due to sibling needs. For teenagers who are suffering the most, these losses may be multiple and diverse. There is usually some kind of loss associated with any challenging situation.

Grief is therefore a very natural and normal experience. Bereavement experts point out that everyone loses friends and family over the course of a lifetime, until it is their own turn. Statistics suggest that around 75 per cent of teenagers experience the loss of a first or second degree relative or close friend (Harrison and Harrington 2001). Grief alone does not mean that therapy is required, as many teenagers will cope successfully with their loss. Recent meta-analyses have suggested that up to 50 per cent of people grapple quickly and easily with a significant bereavement, returning to near normal levels of stress within weeks of the loss (Bonanno 2008). The same analyses also show that between 30 and 50 per cent of people will grieve substantially, while also maintaining their capacity to function normally. Only a small percentage will be seriously impacted by a significant bereavement, and this is usually people with pre-existing propensity to such a response – such as those with existing mental illness or other significant challenges. So in theory, grief is both common and not so bad. Yet many grieving people don't seem to experience it that way.

A dual process model (Stroebe and Schut 2008) has been popularized in the field of grief and loss to explain the way that people grieve. This model suggests that teenagers oscillate between being overwhelmed by their grief to being completely distracted from it. This movement between extremes, and everything in between (as depicted in Figure 9.1), is typical rather than abnormal, and therefore the provision of bereavement services needs to take this into account. Entering into long-term therapeutic

relationships in order to address loss and grief is only sometimes required
(Neimeyer and Currier 2008); however, it is likely that there will be a need
for some kind of support and this will vary across the grief trajectory. The
level of support required by teenagers will also depend on their context
– it will be influenced by what else is going on for them. With regards to
music therapy, brief interventions may often be suitable and this should be
expected to be the norm, with the usual deviations around it.

When offering grief specific services to teenagers, each of the four
approaches described below may be appropriate at different times. If no
'symptoms' of grief have pre-empted participation, but the teenager has
volunteered or self-nominated for grief support, the purpose is preventative
and therefore an empowering *participatory* intent is most suitable. If family
or supportive professionals think that the young person may benefit from
music therapy because they see changes in behaviour or a persistent
attachment to grieving, a more traditional therapeutic approach is suitable,
but with an *accepting* intent, since the young person is still 'coping'. If the
grief programme is being offered to teenagers who are already receiving
services for other needs such as addictions or poor mental health, then
a focus on *understanding* the impact of grief on their broader experience
may be enlightening and helpful. Cognitive behavioural music therapy
bereavement support programmes have proven to be very effective in working
with grieving young children, and are often attached to palliative care

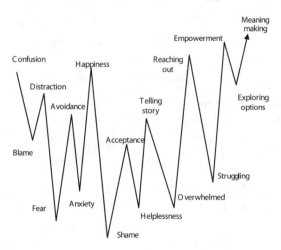

Figure 9.1: The journey of grief

programmes (Hilliard 2001). However, if the up and down pattern of grief is accepted as normal, and the young person is not struggling in other ways, the most effective way of making music accessible to young people as a support strategy may be through consultancy work. Teaching other professionals about the ways that teenagers use music and how it may be helpful in processing the grief-related aspects of their situation may lead to *development* and growth for a far greater number of teenagers than it would be possible to employ music therapists for. A train-the-trainer model can be helpful and enlightening.

Each of these orientations to practice will have a different emphasis in terms of goals; however, all will result in programmes that address core goals to music therapy grief work. The four main goals of all music therapy and grief programmes are included in the table below, attached to different orientations to indicate emphasis, not exclusivity.

In this chapter, four different methods will be outlined that match the combination of therapeutic orientation and its suitability to the adolescent's grieving status. The first two are directly related to loss in response to bereavement, while the second two are focused on the role of music in addressing grief-related issues in a broader context.

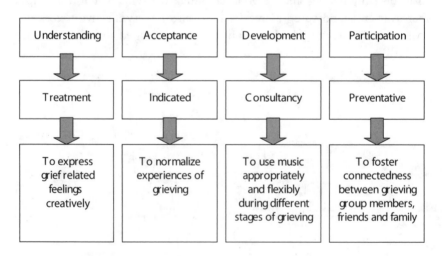

Figure 9.2: Linking the Map to brief grief approaches for teenagers

A school-based music and grief group
SETTING AND PURPOSE

This programme takes place in a secondary college in a major metropolitan city. The music therapist has been contracted in by the school in response to an identified need in their younger students. The school counsellor has noticed that around 20 of the students aged between 13 and 15 have experienced a significant bereavement and is keen to provide a programme for interested participants. Information about the Music and Grief programme is circulated and the school counsellor follows up the teenagers she knows to see if they want to attend. A group of 14 young people agree to come along to the programme, which will run during class time in acknowledgement of the fact that grief can impact upon learning and therefore is a valid use of school time. The time of the programme alternates each week so that students do not miss the same class each time. The group will run for one school term initially, with an option for extending if necessary.

The music therapist is conscious of the fact that these young people have volunteered themselves as grieving and are interested in receiving support. After speaking with the school counsellor and heads of each year group, the music therapist identifies that a core group of the teenagers are coping with the demands of school work while grieving a recent loss, although some are not performing quite as well. There are also a small number of teens in the group who were bereaved many years ago but who have nominated themselves for participation. Given the high level of coping in the group, the music therapist adopts a preventative focus, with the intention of encouraging *participation*. These young people should be capable of using the opportunity and the music therapist plans to offer a range of resources and opportunities and then encourage them to utilize them. She sees her role as bringing the focus back to grief on a regular basis, but also allowing for the oscillation between engaging with grief and distracting from it. She uses all four goals to describe her intentions for the group, emphasizing connectedness as the priority.

- To foster connectedness between grieving group members, friends and family.

- To normalize experiences of grieving.

- To express grief-related feelings creatively.

- To use music appropriately and flexibly during different stages of grieving.

Both school and family are seen as the dominant systems that are impacting upon these teenagers and therefore an approach that will potentially engage with these is sought. Songwriting provides a forum for this because it is performative in its self-revealing nature, and in addition it establishes a possibility for performance, either recorded or live, to family and/or friends. Music listening is also introduced by the music therapist because it allows for an informal engagement with grief that is suitable to the level of support required. It encourages dialogue that is both structured by the music therapist and completely under the control of the teenagers because they choose what songs to bring and whether to bring any at all. They may choose to focus on identity, bereavement or other types of grief through these songs and resultant discussions. The music therapist will ensure that each person provides the group with some detail about their loss so that the level of connection within the group can be fostered. After that is established, anything could happen. They may just want to have fun with people who understand.

ILLUSTRATIVE VIGNETTE

There is chaos in the room. 'Welcome to the Black Parade' by My Chemical Romance is playing on the CD player and the group is listening and chatting. 'MCR is so old school,' torments one of the young men, teasing the contributor of the song. 'They are not!' Denise replies, taking the bait. 'I saw them in concert last year,' peeps up another young man named Tony, 'They totally rocked!' 'Huh, you would say that,' responds Kenny, the instigator. 'Waddayamean?' replies Tony, standing up tall. 'Okay, that's enough,' interjects the music therapist, laughing, 'Are you looking for some attention, Kenny?' The banter continues, but Tony sits back down and the song peaks before coming to the conclusion. Cymbals are crashing, a guitar solo is being played high and fast, and the bass pulsates through the mix. This is called 'emo' music, short for emotional, and is a genre associated with black clothes and eye make-up, and other observable markers previously associated with similar genres such as punk and heavy metal. 'Alright,' calls the music therapist as the song ends, 'What does that song have to do with grief?'

Far from settling into a thoughtful and reflective conversation, some teenagers call 'Nothing!' and most do not respond. 'It's about how memories carry on,' says Cochavit quietly. 'What makes you say that?' the music therapist enquires. 'Well, there's the line that goes "When you're dead and gone believe me, your memory will carry on" for a start,' replies Cochavit a little sarcastically. 'Yeah, once you put it that way, it seems pretty obvious,' the music therapist replies, smiling at Cochavit, who smirks briefly. She turns back to the group, 'Do you guys have lots of memories of the person who has died in your life?' It's a direct question and the mention of the word 'died' has quieted the group momentarily. 'I like to wear my dad's jacket when I'm at home alone,' confesses Tony, 'Is that what you mean?' 'Yep, exactly,' replies the music therapist, 'how about other people?' 'Ummm, I have a photo of my sister in my wallet,' says Denise. 'My mum threw everything out,' Cochavit comments, 'I've got nothin'.'

The music therapist moves over to the whiteboard at the front of the classroom. 'You know what guys? I'm hearing a song here.' She begins to write down the different strategies used by the teenagers for maintaining their connection with the person who has died. She hopes this will draw the conversation out longer and be structured enough so that everyone makes a contribution. 'What about you, Kenny?' she asks, drawing the energetic young man into the conversation, 'Do you have any way of staying connected?' 'I thought we were talking about memories,' he responds. 'Yeah, well, memories can be of things that you did, or the way that you feel, or ways that you stay connected. It's all okay,' replies the music therapist encouragingly. 'What do you do?' The group stays on track for nearly ten minutes and soon the whiteboard is covered with the ideas that have been suggested. 'Now how are we going to turn this into a song?' the music therapist asks.

The group is struggling to maintain focus now and people are starting to talk and move around. 'Let's have a snack and come back to it,' suggests the music therapist, and the teenagers sound immediately relieved. Crisps and fruit are dragged down off the bench and juice is passed around. The music therapist puts on a song that was mentioned in the group the previous week and then mingles with the young people, talking casually and catching up on how the week has been. After a while she calls out for attention again. 'What kind of music is good for memories?' she asks, 'Rock, rap, pop, a metal ballad, blues?' The group gradually come to an agreement about the style but there are lots of distractions and the end of the session arrives before the lyrics have been constructed. 'We'll get back to this next week,' she calls as they head out the door. 'Sure, okay,' some of them mumble, 'See you,' and they are gone.

EVALUATING EFFECTIVENESS

This group is preventative in focus and therefore there is no way to measure whether it has been helpful except to ask the young people themselves. Individual interviews or focus groups should be used to solicit opinions about the group, whether it was helpful, what might be improved and what benefits were gained through participation. As discussed in Chapter 3, it is usually surprising to learn how much young people have benefited from their participation, and comments such as 'it made me feel better', 'it's taken a huge weight off my shoulders', or 'it was really good fun' are common. When the music therapist has participatory intentions, she hands over control to the group members, which is often chaotic. The teenagers may not seem to be sharing a lot of material verbally and staying with grief-related issues is usually challenging, so the music therapist may feel that nothing has been achieved. Yet improvement is nearly always described by teenagers if they are asked. They appreciate the opportunity to express their feelings. They are amazed that other people have been through a similar thing to themselves. They are proud of their songs.

Ideally, the young people will take home any CDs that are made and share them with their family. This will foster a suitable level of inter-systemic connections as emphasized by a *participatory* orientation. The group may also be willing to perform their song to the school or different class groups and in doing so have the opportunity to impact upon broader understandings of adolescent grieving. Teenagers do not always want to do this, however, and may prefer to have a loose focus within the group, but that they describe as profound. Grieving teenagers are not always willing to prioritize the time to work towards a performance and therefore the level of inter-connectedness between the individuals in the group and their various systems will be variable, depending on whether they actually play the CD to family and friends, and also, on whether anyone actually listens.

KEY POINTS

- It is often the responsibility of the music therapist to keep returning to the topic of grief.

- The teenagers in this group have come to do grief work, but they will not want to appear too enthusiastic in the group.

- Chaos needs to be accepted in this orientation, since too much controlling by the music therapist will lead the group members to feel that she is in control, not them.

- It is important that the group members take responsibility for the creation of the song, but they will need guidance in the process (see Chapter 5).

- If young people do share the song written in the group with family and friends, this may change the listener's impression of the teenager's grief, which is an important outcome.

A monthly creative support programme
SETTING AND PURPOSE

The monthly creative support programme emerged in response to a need for bereavement support for young people in the community. It is attached to a large hospital and well linked to local palliative care programmes. Young people are referred to the programme by carers or professionals who feel that the young person is struggling with his or her grief. The group runs on a monthly basis and teenagers attend as many sessions as they choose. Parent support groups and groups for younger children run at the same time in the same venue, making efficient use of the evening time slot. The adolescent group is co-led by a music therapist and a young person who has 'graduated' from the programme. This teenager has usually spent at least a year in the programme, and is invited to take up a responsible role and work with the music therapist in planning and administering the group along with the other professionals and volunteers that run the simultaneous groups.

The structure of the group is recurring and a phenomenological process is used for the first half of every session. This four-step process involves using a medley of art forms to process the individual issues bought to the group by each young person. The process moves from first selecting a symbolic photograph, to musical expression, then to expressive drawing, and finally to the articulation of the issue through story or poetry, it encourages the teenagers to explore their experiences from multiple perspectives. In addition to the personal process, sharing of reflections is encouraged at each stage. This promotes normalization since many teenagers often mistake natural grieving for 'being mental'. After a break for refreshments, the group then re-gathers and uses one art form to address chosen topics such as memories, feelings or friends.

The main goal of this ongoing creative support group is to normalize experiences of grieving, but the other goals of connectedness, expression and variable coping strategies are also addressed.

ILLUSTRATIVE VIGNETTE

The group of teenagers is sitting in a circle, and the floor in the middle is covered with pictorial cards. Photographs of waterfalls, mountains, houses and people are lying face up and the young people are looking over them. 'Choose one that seems to be related to how you're feeling today,' one of the teenagers suggests. Ju Young is co-leading the group with the music therapist and likes to be the one to begin the group process after so many years of being involved. Some of the other teenagers look confused and the music therapist supplements the instruction, 'Sometimes you just pick a card that you like the look of and then work out something to say about it,' she adds. The members who have been in the group for longest stand up and start walking around the cards to select their preference. Some swoop in quickly to get the one they want. Others take a few minutes to look at them all before selecting. Once all the teenagers have returned to their seats, Ju Young starts the dialogue. 'I chose this card because of the clouds in the background,' she says, holding up the card. 'That's how I feel about my mum's death at the moment; it's always there, but it's not in the front any more.' She looks to the person next to her and invites him to explain his choice. It takes a while to go around everyone in the group and some people tell longer stories, while others have nothing to say and just hold up their cards. There is no pressure to have to explain.

'Alright everyone, grab an instrument that seems to go with the picture you chose,' the music therapist directs the group once everyone has had a turn. The instruments are spread out on one side of the room and the various teenagers move quietly to select one. The music therapist and Ju Young move around to the new people and show them how some of the instruments work. 'Just choose anything that takes your fancy,' each suggests to the newcomers. Within a couple of minutes all of the young people are seated in a circle again and there is a quiet murmur of people talking and experimenting with their instruments. 'Okay, everyone, let's start playing,' the music therapist calls gently and begins. She plays a repeating pattern on the large metallaphone, moving simply between the tonic (C), dominant (G) and submediant (A). She plays in a straight up rhythm that invites the group to play together, in contrast to a less stable beginning which might have suggested more dramatically expressive playing. The material shared through the pictures was mostly stories and no particular emotion had dominated, so the music therapist's intuitive response was to offer something secure and familiar.

Most of the group join in quickly, tapping their instruments in time and focusing on their own playing. The most salient feature of the improvisation is this shared rhythm and as the group grows more confident the music therapist gradually reduces her volume and Ju Young continues to hold the beat. The large hand drums maintain the pace successfully and only a couple of the young people notice the change. The improvisation is stable and all of the teenagers are committed to the underlying pulse, although there is variation in the ways they play with it. Some differentiation is heard in the way the tambourines and shakers provide a backdrop to the drumming, and the melodic instruments supplement the pulse with quicker patterns that circle around repetitively. Overall, the improvisation sounds calm and centred around the pulse that continues to be provided by Ju Young who is partnered by most of the percussive instruments.

The music lasts for more than five minutes in this way before gradually reducing in volume and fading away. After a moment of silence, the music therapist speaks up. 'Thanks, everyone. Now I'd like you to choose coloured paper and crayons and take some time to draw something in response to that.' The co-leader moves around the room with a selection of these resources and the music therapist gathers the instruments up out of the way. The group members are quiet and spend 15 minutes lying on the floor drawing before they are called back into the circle. Once again they go around the circle, this time explaining the picture they have drawn, sometimes relating it to the meaning of the music or the picture card, but sometimes just describing the picture. The group is respectful, and there is only occasional talking while each person tells his or her story. 'I know it's getting late, but there's one more stage to go,' says the music therapist at the end. 'Turn the page over and write a short story or a poem about the picture that you have drawn. Then after we've shared that, we'll go and have something to eat and drink.'

EVALUATING EFFECTIVENESS

The young people participating in this programme have been indicated as suitable for bereavement support by their carers or professionals who are involved with them, often with the agreement of the young person him or herself. This suggests that when they join the programme they are not coping as well as they would like. It is therefore relevant to compare how young people feel they are coping at the beginning with the way they feel at the end. If they feel better, the programme has been effective. This information may be gathered by questionnaires, interviews or more formal measures of coping such as the grief process scale (Dalton and Krout 2005), the loss response list (Wheeler and Austin 2001) or a generalist measure such as the Adolescent Coping Scale (Frydenberg and Lewis 1993).

KEY POINTS

- The teenagers who attend this programme are coping but unhappy. They do not need an intervention; they need acceptance and support so that they can feel better.

- Normalization is an important part of bereavement support for teenagers.

- Combining art forms is a powerful way of viewing an experience through multiple lenses.

- The level of talking required is minimal, although it can be expanded by the very articulate teenager.

- Each teenager will likely have a preference for one mode of expression and this will be captured in this approach.

- The role of co-leader is well designed for a teenager who wants to keep attending the group but is actually no longer in need of support.

Music and grief workshops

Many adolescents are grappling with grief-related issues as a part of a more severe problem. Young people may be receiving regular support from programmes because of mental health problems, substance misuse, chronic illness or other family-related losses, and being supported by professionals who are experts in these areas. Music therapy is not always a regular part of these programmes, but music therapists are frequently asked to facilitate workshops or weekend programmes with these young people. This request may be motivated by many agendas, but the relationship between teenagers, music, emotions and grief can often be a relevant and potent contribution that the music therapist is able to make. Very few other professionals are as comfortable with eliciting and containing emotional expression, and even fewer have the means to increase *understandings* of the impact of grief through reflecting on emotional material aroused by loss. Grief and loss workshops can be a powerful experience for those involved, and when regular staff are engaged in following up material identified in these programmes, it has the potential to make a difference in the lives of young people.

SETTING AND PURPOSE

The music therapist has been asked to facilitate a one day programme with a group of eight young people who are struggling with loss and grief in the context of substance misuse and are interested in using music as a part of their support plan. They have been told that the day is about music and grief, although the degree to which this has been conveyed will have varied depending on how comfortable their worker is with discussing the topic of grief. Many people worry that mentioning grief may send a teenager into a spiral of depression, which is why loss is often sidelined as an add-on event. Other professionals will have emphasized the opportunity for making music in order to encourage the young person to attend and only briefly mentioned the grief and loss focus. In this case, eight young people attend a one day workshop run on a weekend. The music therapist works together with a community artist who runs a drop-in studio at the organization, and has liaised closely with the manager and some key workers in the meetings leading up to the workshop. The session plan for the day is shown in Table 9.1. All goals are to be addressed across the day with an emphasis on expressing grief-related feelings in creative and non-verbal ways.

Table 9.1: Session plan for music and grief workshop

10:00a.m.	Breakfast	
10:30a.m.	Ice breakers	Guess my favourite performer Selecting photographic cards
11:00a.m.	Group improvisations	Introduction to instruments Free improvisation with rhythmic ground Emotion-based themes
12noon	Lunch	
1:00p.m.	Songwriting	Identify song Improvise Brainstorm words and stories
2:30p.m.	Break	
3:00p.m.	Song creation and recording	Fill in lyrics Practise song and record
4:00p.m.	Jam session	Rhythm-based and free improvisations
4:30p.m.	Close	

ILLUSTRATIVE VIGNETTE

Once the warm-ups are completed, the music therapist starts to work seriously towards the focus for the day. 'Now, I've brought along a whole bunch of instruments today. Some of them you will have seen before, and others you won't. Let me introduce you to my collection.' The music therapist pulls open the drum case and draws each instrument out, naming it and explaining a little about its traditional use. 'This is a guiro. Even though this one is made of metal, they are usually made out of wood. You can imagine that tribal people would have carved lines in the wood and then dragged a stick over it to make a different percussive sound for dancing and singing. We tend to use beaters to do that, and you can use backwards and forwards motions like this, with taps to emphasize different rhythms. This is a bodhrán. It is an Irish drum that you hold behind like this...' The music therapist is not in a rush and it is important to give credibility to these instruments so that the act of music making is not mistaken for a primary school activity.

Once introductions are complete, the music therapist asks people to choose an instrument which appeals to them and leads them through a rhythmically based, free improvisation. With this final warm-up completed, it is time to start talking about emotions. 'I'm sure you guys know that music and feelings often go together. Music is a good way of expressing emotions, and some people even feel better afterwards. Right now we are going to work through a few different types of emotions and listen to how different they sound. Let's start with "happy", since that's usually the easiest.' The group look at the music therapist as though she is from another planet. 'Just choose anything that you think will sound happy,' she encourages, and moves into the centre of the room to consider the different instruments, modelling what she expects the group to do. Colin is the first to follow her lead and stands up to choose a conga drum on a stand that he missed playing in the free improvisation. This gives the other teenagers courage to move, and one by one the young people select their instrument. As soon as the last person has an instrument, the music therapist begins playing a cheerful, four-on-the-floor beat and calls 'Join in!' A brief improvisation ensues that is loud and chaotic, and the teenagers are trying to retain some sense of being cool by making fun of the music making. The music therapist laughs along, understanding that this is a natural reaction to being asked to do something that makes them feel vulnerable.

'Alright. That was fun. This time we're going to do "sad", though. That's usually a bit more intense, so try and choose an instrument that will suit.' There is less hesitation to engage this time, but a sombre mood has already descended. The teenagers sit down slowly and there is very little eye contact. 'Righto. Let's begin.' The music therapist offers a slow rhythmic ground on the cabassa, keeping her eyes down and waiting patiently for people to join. They do after a short time, and the most salient features of the improvisation are the slow tempo and a quiet volume. A level of tension is prominent in the playing, communicated through the body language of the players as well as the lack of variability within the improvisation. The sounds are incongruent at the level of rhythm and harmony, but there is a strong sense of partnership in portraying the slow and steady representation of sadness. The music therapist is quiet once the sounds have all drifted away and she then comments. 'Well, I know you guys all have experiences with grief, and we could really hear it in that, huh? Thank you for playing so honestly. Does anyone have anything they'd like to say?' 'That was full on,' says Thomas immediately. 'Yeah, I didn't like it,' adds Barb. 'It's usually pretty hard to play sadness,' the music therapist offers. The group is not ready to process the experience any further at a verbal level, so the music therapist suggests they wrap up with something more energetic before breaking for lunch. 'Choose an instrument that you think would be fun,' she suggests and leads into a steady beat for the next improvisation.

They break for lunch after the playing and then dribble back to the room an hour later for the afternoon session. 'So, that was pretty intense playing that sad improvisation before lunch,' the music therapist begins. 'But it can be very helpful to actually recognize and express your grief rather than always trying to run away from it. What I want to do now is for us to write a song where we try and put words to that feeling.' The group is quiet but they remain. 'Since we only have a few hours, I was thinking we might change the words to a song that we all know. Does anyone have any ideas of songs that go with the grief theme?' In response to the silence that follows, the music therapist offers more structure. 'Do you know any songs that actually talk about sadness or loss?' 'How about that Metallica song, "Nothing Else Matters"?' suggests Thomas. 'Or "See the Sun" by Dido,' responds Barb. '"Eulogy" by Tool is great, too,' adds Colin. 'They're all great suggestions,' responds the music therapist, 'and I can play the first two, but I've never been able to do Tool songs well enough. They are such awesome players.' Colin seems satisfied by this response, since Tool fans are usually pretty proud of the technical skills of their band. The group then sets about reaching a compromise on the song to use, ultimately choosing the classic Metallica song.

'Before we start brainstorming ideas, I think we need to play another sad improvisation,' says the music therapist. 'It will help us remember what we really feel, rather than just making stuff up that we think is right.' The group agree and move to select instruments. This improvisation has a little more energy but still maintains the intensity and lack of harmonic and rhythmic congruence. Once it is finished, the music therapist asks Sue to be the scribe and write everyone's ideas on a large piece of paper. She is the quietest group member and seems unlikely to make suggestions herself, so it gives her an important role. 'So try and put words to the feelings we just played then,' starts the music therapist. 'Sad,' says Barb, cheekily. 'Yep, good. Can you write that down Sue? Now, what else?' By accepting this joke and taking it seriously, the music therapist is letting the group know that she is willing to hear any suggestions they have. The group brainstorm a lot of words that describe different emotions related to grief, and the music therapist then asks about the kinds of experiences that cause grief. Everyone is warmed up now and the ideas flow thick and fast, from stories of watching friends die of overdoses, to being banned from seeing boyfriends, and losing pets. Soon pages are covered and the task of substituting the lyrics of the Metallica songs looms large. 'Let's have a break and then get back to it,' suggests the music therapist, amazed at how long they have been willing to stay with this difficult material.

By the time the break is done there are only 90 minutes left before the workshop concludes. The music therapist is conscious that she wants to wrap up on a high and does not want to send these teenagers back on to the street feeling vulnerable and raw. Closure will be crucial, so that means they have 60 minutes to write and record the song and 30 minutes to jam on the instruments without any agenda apart from connectedness and positivity. 'Okay, so far we've got a page of emotional material and a page of experiences to draw on. What about if we use some kind of repeating framework where we paint a picture of each experience in the verse, and then outline the emotions that it triggers in the bridge? For the repeating chorus we could have some kind of message about grief that we think it's important to say. You've mentioned that it can eat you up inside if you hold it in, so what's a better way of dealing with grief?'

A six-verse version of 'Nothing Else Matters' is drawn from the original ideas in the next 30 minutes and all of the participants have a story in the song. The chorus is finally agreed to, after much debate. The final line is a reference to the bigger solution they have identified, which is that it is really important to have the chance to grieve losses and to hold onto dreams of the things that have been taken away. In order to communicate acceptance and emphasize normality, the music therapist has offered some information about the importance of staying connected to people who have died through dreams, talking, linking objects and memorializing. The group has also decided that even if the loss is of hopes and plans, it is important not to give up. They have therefore decided to keep the final line of the chorus from the original song, knowing that it represents the things that matter – staying connected to dreams and loved ones. The chorus is simple but powerful. It offers hope and acknowledgment.

> Grief can make you want to hide
> Rip your dreams apart inside
> But nothing else matters. (Metallica 1991)

They record the song in the next 20 minutes and still have sufficient time for transition and closure. The music therapist promises to drop the CDs to the office in the next week and discusses what it will be like to hear the song again and who will want to hear it. These are important themes, and the music therapist repeats this discussion with the professionals she speaks to when she drops the CDs in.

EVALUATING EFFECTIVENESS

The brief nature of this workshop programme makes it difficult for the music therapist to ascertain effectiveness. It is a whirlwind process of warming up, diving in and accessing emotions, processing and articulating some of the unexpressed ramifications of grief, and then quickly providing adequate closure so that the young person is not left feeling sad and vulnerable. This is particularly important in a substance misuse programme, because the most common use of substances is to cover up emotional pain, and these young people are particularly sensitive to uncomfortable feelings. Since the aim is not for the young person to walk out of the programme and off in search of a hit, finishing with a sense of empowerment is critical.

Follow-up interviews at a later date may be insightful, but because the music therapist is not attached to the programme this would not be a standard procedure. It is more feasible to follow up with professional support workers after some time has elapsed. Those in regular contact with the young person will be able to offer feedback on any ramifications of the workshop, either perceived or acknowledged. The music therapist could request her contact person to gather responses from these workers for her in order to give her feedback and help with gauging effectiveness.

KEY POINTS

- In running workshops, it is crucial to be conscious of time and to allow space for warm up and closure.

- Food is critical to most workshop events and young people need to have energy reserves to draw on when grappling with grief.

- Music is a powerful way of accessing feelings and this should be harnessed and utilized – certainly not underestimated.

- Young people in crisis need containment for experiences of intense emotion.

- A blend of improvisations and songwriting can provide both structure and release.

- It is possible that many young people have not discussed grief-related feelings before, so highlighting similarities is helpful.

- Directing young people towards hope for the future is an important part of dealing with grief.

- Young people who misuse substances are often very tender emotionally and also vulnerable to reusing substances as a coping strategy for emotional pain. Normalization and understanding will make a difference to this, but equally, it is important to offer closure.

Adolescents, music and grief: workshops for youth professionals

There are not enough music therapists to work with the vast number of teenagers who could benefit from more opportunities to engage therapeutically with music. One way of widening the circle of influence is to function as a consultant for youth organizations and provide train-the-trainer workshops. There are many professionals involved in the support of young people – youth workers, social workers, psychologists, paediatricians and counsellors are common in the community, and in institutions there are also teachers, nurses, allied health professionals and psychiatrists. Each of these has a specialty, but all are committed to the support of teenagers as they progress through either a crisis, an ongoing challenge or simply the turmoil which sometimes accompanies adolescence. As illustrated in the previous vignette, grief and loss are attached to most challenging situations, and the links between teenagers, music, emotions and grief are powerful. In working towards facilitating the *development* of teenagers, it can be helpful to provide information to those who support them more regularly so that they have better access to musical engagement that is not dependent on music specialists.

SETTING AND PURPOSE

When facilitating workshops for professionals who work with adolescents, it is important to draw heavily on experiential learning. The theoretical details of how music therapy works and why it is a valid and important profession are already apparent to those professionals who have registered for the workshop. They have come to hear an expert on the topic. Most creative professionals working with teenagers will have recognized what a powerful force music can be and have perhaps already attempted to harness it. An important function of the workshop is to help these youth workers anticipate the strong reactions that musical engagement can evoke and provide musical strategies for dealing with these. Music therapists are conscious of the unexpected responses to music, where other professionals may assume a more simplistic and positive response. Experiential learning will ensure that the participants know how complex a relationship with music can be, because they will experience it. By using powerful music therapy methods such as improvisation and songwriting, situations will arise that illustrate how even professionals cannot predict their responses and inherent biases towards music. Participants will be more convinced about how music can work therapeutically, and also more careful.

In facilitating workshops for fellow professionals working with young people, the following plan may be helpful. It provides a taste of the most common music therapy methods for working with teenagers, and it is an engaging day of musicianship and learning.

Table 9.2: Session plan for adolescents, music and grief workshops for professionals

Introductions

Activity: Verbal introductions round circle, beginning with facilitator
Purpose: Allowing for late arrivals, conveying facilitator and group expertise, ascertaining expectations for day
Time: Approximately 20 minutes

Warm-up

Activity: What kind of music did you like when you were 5, 15, 25?
Purpose: Remembering how powerful the relationship with music is during adolescence
Time: Approximately 1 hour

Music listening exercise

Activity: Listen to Hole, Wagner, Tony O'Connor and share descriptors of your reaction to each type of music that the facilitator writes on the board to emphasize diversity
Purpose: Understanding that each young person's relationship to particular types of music will be personal and may differ to what may be assumed from the sound of the music
Time: Approximately 30 minutes

Improvisation

Activity: Free improvisation and then playing different feelings in order to emphasize the expressive capacity of music
Follow with verbal processing of how we represent ourselves in groups – quiet/dominant; comfortable/annoyed. Who did you hear? This is a way of communicating how music reflects group dynamics
Purpose: Re-experiencing how powerful the emotional elements of music are and also how it does reflect group dynamics
Time: Approximately 1.5 hours

Songwriting

Activity: Identify a song that is known to all the group and then use a lyric substitution process to write a song about teenagers, grief and music
Purpose: Reviewing information, illustrating how easy and fun it is to do lyric substitutions
Time: Approximately 1.5 hours

Reflections and feedback

Activity: Discussion of learnings from and responses to the day
Purpose: Evaluation and facilitator feedback
Time: Approximately 30 minutes

ILLUSTRATIVE VIGNETTE

Music blares from the speakers in the front of the room. Thrash metal is fast, frenetic and furious and for those who are unfamiliar with the nuance of the genre, it is usually quite disturbing. On the positive, the songs are only around two minutes long because no musician can maintain the pace for much longer, so the pain is over quickly. As the song comes to an end, the music therapist steps up and hits the stop button and then turns to the group of 20 professionals sitting in a semi-circle, facing forwards. 'So what words would you use to describe that music?' she asks, whiteboard marker poised in hand. 'Angry,' says one of the middle-aged women immediately. 'That sounds disturbed to me.' 'Angry. Disturbed.' The music therapist writes the two words on the whiteboard. 'What else?' 'Energetic,' calls out one of the older women. 'Passionate,' shouts one of the young men. The music therapist nods and turns to write these on the board. More words are called out as she writes and the participants are insightful enough to see that there is a real diversity in people's perceptions. After a couple of minutes there are 20 words on the board and the music therapist turns back to the group. 'Do any of you actually recognize that song?' she asks, and one of the youth workers with dreadlocks holds up his hand. 'What do you think it's about?' asks the music therapist. 'It's a commentary on the last American election,' he replies, 'and the lies that the politicians were prepared to tell just to get themselves elected.' 'Yes, it's political,' responds the music therapist. 'For those of you who didn't know the song, did you get that side to it?' Most of the group shake their heads. 'You couldn't understand the words at all,' says an older man, 'I would never have guessed that.'

The music therapist moves on to a classical piece of music and works through the same routine. She then plays a New Age piece. 'So it's clear that different people have different responses to the same piece of music isn't it? Some people get frustrated by the sounds of rainforests and others are disturbed by crashing cymbals and incomprehensible lyrics. What's my point?' The group look at the music therapist for the answer. When nothing is forthcoming, one young woman speaks up. 'That we all have different taste? But we talked about that in the first exercise.' 'Yes, it's extending on that to say that not only do we all have different tastes, but that we make unconscious judgements about other people's music. For example, if a teenager is listening to a rap song and they let you listen and you partially make out the words kill, and mother-f*ker, it is easy to assume that the music is negative. But the question you need to ask the young person is "What do *you* like about this song?" You have to put your own response aside and find out what their response is. I can guarantee you that 90 per cent of the time you'll be surprised at the answer!'

There is murmuring around the group and the music therapist draws the two previous exercises together. 'It's the same as when Helen said that she was a fan of Pink Floyd as a teenager. You were all surprised. But Helen didn't listen to Pink Floyd because she was alternative, she enjoyed the guitar solos and she loved the graphics they used on their albums to their early film clips. Now which of you could have predicted that?' More murmuring. 'Are there any teenagers you work with who you worry are listening to too much negative music?' Almost half the participants raise their hands. 'Actually, I'm thinking of my son,' says one of the men. 'Me too – my daughter,' says a woman. The group laugh and so does the music therapist. 'Better still,' replies the music therapist, 'go home tonight and ask if you can listen to their music, then try and find out why they like it. It's hard to hold back your own responses, but it's really critical if you are going to work with teenagers and their music. If you ask a grieving teenager to bring in a song to play for you that says something about their grief, you are potentially opening up an important opportunity for dialogue. But not if you close it down with your prejudices. And as we know, most prejudices are built on unfamiliarity!'

EVALUATING EFFECTIVENESS

Although brief surveys are the most common approach to evaluating professional development workshops, written responses will invariably be positive after a day of active and engaged music making. Soliciting immediate verbal feedback at the end of the workshop can be a far more informative and useful way to discover what was more and less effective on the day. Asking the group to reflect on whether the information addressed their initial goals for attendance is a useful question to discuss. Not only can this inform the therapist's practice, but any discrepancies can be immediately addressed which may further enhance learning if the therapist is able to piece together any missing links.

KEY POINTS

- It is a part of our role as music therapists to ensure that the relationship between teenagers and music is better understood.

- It is unrealistic to expect that every adolescent specialist service will employ a music therapist, therefore it is valuable to offer information to colleagues who may be able to use musical engagement in their work with teenagers.

- The relationship between teenagers, music and grief is hinged on the emotional qualities of music, and any improvement in understanding about teenagers' music can then be directed into more successful grief work.

- The most important strategy to teach other professionals is having them ask teenagers to bring in music that is 'important to them', and then for the professional to listen to it (without talking) and find out why it is important. Other methods will usually not be taken up by non-music therapists, but experiencing them helps to understand the power of the medium.

- It is deeply satisfying to work with youth-oriented professionals using music. They are typically open-minded and creative adults who will take the opportunity to explore the musical medium with great enthusiasm and insight.

- Many professionals will have existing music skills and they should be encouraged to use them, taking into account the importance of not projecting one's own relationship with music onto the teenager.

- We should all make music and therefore music therapists should encourage this in any way they can.

CONCLUSION

There are many ways that music can be used to support teenagers who are grieving. The impact of grief is not usually so strong that intensive treatment is required, although grief often plays a role in other conditions requiring concentrated approaches. In the majority of cases, however, music therapy is working towards preventative or indicated goals and therefore long-term interventions are not required. Workshops, monthly support groups or short programmes can be very effective in ensuring that resilient approaches are being adopted by young people. Ensuring that support networks are in place by encouraging musical connections both within and beyond the group is an important outcome of brief music therapy interventions with grieving teenagers. Identity formation continues to be an essential force in any work with teenagers, and it is often in identifying their experience of grief as normal that young people are able to refocus on who they are in response to the loss. The fact that music is fun as well as connected to emotions means that the oscillation between grieving and distraction can be easily embraced and creatively utilized. The relationship between grief and music is a natural one, as is the relationship between teenagers and music. This can help teenagers to cross the less familiar bridge between adolescence and grief in a creative and productive way.

Chapter 10

Preparing for Performances

Some might argue that adolescence is a constant performance, given the high levels of self-awareness and the constant sense of being watched. As Lily Allen suggests in her song, 'Fear', it's more a question of how to get the performance right. The dilemma is not dissimilar in music therapy. It is less of a question about whether to perform or not, and more of a decision about who will be the audience. Music therapists sometimes expand the audience of the teenager's performance from therapy to include family, friends, professionals, interested stakeholders and sometimes even unknown audiences. This chapter examines the increasing use of performance to a wider audience as a method within contemporary practice. Successful and unsuccessful applications of this method are discussed in relation to (at least) five questions about appropriateness, and a model for evaluating the success of performances is offered.

Performance is becoming more common in contemporary music therapy practice with teenagers. In previous decades, this was not the case and depending on the orientation of the therapist, performances have often been seen as anti-therapeutic. If therapy is viewed as a private and contained process leading towards enhanced *understandings*, it is easy to appreciate why this perception is held. Personal insight is a private journey, whether it takes place in groups or individual work. The desire to share it publicly is therefore considered to be dubious. What does the adolescent or therapist seek to gain from sharing their private story? Alan Turry (1999) was one of the first contemporary music therapists to outline this contradiction. He noted that performances have historically been used by music therapists practising with an intention of facilitating *development* (what he calls recreational music therapy), but that the consideration of performance for fostering *understanding* requires a different examination. He briefly touches on the complex dynamics that emerge in response to performance but ultimately proposes that acknowledgment and processing of this material can be further 'grist for the mill' of the therapeutic process.

As suggested by Turry (1999), performance is more easily understood in the context of facilitating *development* since it can be a motivation in itself and can also be an achievement. Early pioneers of music therapy did describe the use of performances (e.g. Nordoff and Robbins 2004/1971; Schmidt-Peters 1987), although Gary Ansdell (2005a) points out that performances are very rarely documented in the contemporary literature, despite being known to be an important facet of early models. Despite not being represented in the literature, anecdotally it is common practice for music therapists with a *developmental* intention to participate in Christmas concerts and choir performances since this is a motivating forum for the *development* of musical and non-musical skills. Attending, waiting, reworking, practising and performance are all skills that are useful for young people preparing for an interactive adulthood. A successful performance may even improve self-esteem, although there has been no rigorous examination of this commonly posed assumption to date.

A natural relationship also exists between performance in music therapy and a *participatory* orientation. As noted in Chapter 8, contemporary community music therapy theory suggests that performative elements are inherent in this approach (Stige *et al.* 2010). This perspective was pre-empted in the earliest attempts at explaining community music therapy. Brynjulf Stige describes his work with a man named Knut who has Down's syndrome (Stige 2002a, pp.113–133), explaining how Knut's desires influenced the development of his ideas of community music therapy as cultural engagement, where performance functions as a mechanism for *participation* in the community. All of the case examples offered in *Community Music Therapy* (Pavlicevic and Ansdell 2004) incorporated performances as one part of their descriptions, with a range of audiences and venues. However, Even Ruud's (2004) suggestion that community music therapy could be defined by 'just adding performance' (and a systemic orientation) was not accepted by the main proponents (Ansdell 2005b; Stige 2004). Performative practice is seen to incorporate the intimate revealing of self within the safe bounds of the therapeutic relationship, as well as more public performances that may have a more systemic focus – but it does not demand an audience outside of therapy. Stige (personal communication 2009) emphasizes that the young people should be the instigators of a performance, and then the music therapist with *participatory* intentions strive to assist them to achieve this goal. The idea of sharing music outside of therapy is more likely to occur to young people when an increased consciousness regarding their context is emphasized by the music therapist. Despite the fact that performance is not an essential component of community music therapy, the relationship between a *participatory* orientation and a performance outcome is unproblematic, since a relationship with the world outside therapy is important.

A different argument against performance can be made where fostering *acceptance* is the intention of the music therapist. Working towards a performance directly conflicts with being in the moment with a client. It orients to a future outcome that detracts from the present, often in a significant way. In addition, it suggests that a 'good' performance is required, instead of acceptance of any musical gesture. The journey is no longer the focus, instead the destination is prioritized. It is difficult to understand the relevance of performance when the therapist's intention is to offer unconditional positive regard to the teenager as he or she is right now, rather than saving it as a reward for a successful performance. When adopting a blended, eclectic approach to practice, these distinctions become less clear, however, and the reality is more complicated.

WHAT IS A PERFORMANCE IN MUSIC THERAPY?

Teenagers are always performing. A significant feature of this stage of development is an overly sensitive awareness of the opinions of others (Erikson 1963). Most teenagers feel that they are being watched – as they walk across a street, order a pizza, or bump into a door. They are performing their identity with every step. A similar argument can be made for music therapy, since every session is a performance. The teenager plays an instrument or uses his or her voice and the music therapist listens. This is even stronger in group work, since peers also constitute the audience, as well as taking up roles as performers themselves. Within this chapter, the definition of performance will be stricter than 'performative', and suggests an audience beyond the existing therapy boundaries.

For the purpose of this chapter, performance refers to musical events to be heard by people outside the immediate therapeutic encounter. The direction of performances is outwards and around (Stige *et al.* 2010) in order to support the aim of increased connectedness with others. Figure 10.1 outlines the two different types of performances that will be described in this chapter

– using live and recorded musical mediums. These can then be further delineated in terms of the audience, which in the case of a live performance is often restricted but may sometimes extend to a public audience. The sharing of recordings can usually be more controlled by the young person, but Figure 10.1 also highlights that this is not always the case and this potential for sharing without consent should be a recognized danger of recording therapeutic song material, and has not been discussed in the literature.

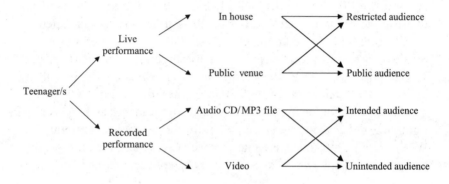

Figure 10.1: Various performances with adolescents in music therapy

KEY FEATURES OF COMMUNITY MUSIC THERAPY

In considering whether this kind of audience-oriented performance is suitable for teenagers in music therapy, five questions should be considered that parallel the key features attributed to community music therapy and used as the basis of Chapter 8 (Stige *et al.* 2010).

- Whose idea was this, anyway?

- What is the purpose of this?

- What type of performance is most suitable?

- What resources are available to make this happen?

- What are the pros and cons of this particular performance?

The answers to each of these questions will be different in each unique situation and should be contemplated afresh each time the possibility for performance arises. There are many pitfalls in the journey towards performance and it is not a process to be undertaken lightly. Nor should it be assumed to be a valuable contribution to the therapeutic process. It is often distracting and time consuming, and comes with inherent risks, such as performance anxiety (O'Grady 2008). It is best approached with the full support of the teenagers involved, the organizational structures surrounding it and with access to a wealth of resources. Performances with adolescents in music therapy are not for the faint-hearted.

Whose idea was this, anyway?

The mastermind behind a performance in music therapy assumes a great deal of responsibility. They must carry the energy for the performance, provide the focus for the process and bear the weight of responsibility for the performance, no matter what outcome. When the therapist maintains a *participatory* stance, it is assumed that the instigator will be the teenagers themselves, yet this is actually a fairly idealistic sentiment. The music therapist may have nominated performance as a potential outcome of the project, or she may have suggested it in response to material that emerged in the group process. The young people may have taken up the idea, but not actually spoken it out loud in the beginning. In reality, it can be difficult to disentangle the root of an emerging interest in performance. What is important about the *participatory* approach is that the young people own the process and take responsibility for it. The role of the music therapist is to encourage, not manage or conduct.

ILLUSTRATIVE VIGNETTES
Bereavement support group
'Alright, what are we going to do this evening?' the music therapist asks. The bereavement support group has been officially running for 30 minutes now, and so far it has been pure gossip and catching up. 'Shall we get out the picture cards and see where everyone is at?' she suggests. 'Nah,' responds Sarah, 'I can't be bothered.' 'Yeah, let's do something different,' says Tommy. 'Like what?' asks the music therapist, always open to a good idea. 'I dunno,' comes the reply, 'What haven't we done before?' 'Hmmm, well, I've spent the afternoon planning for the staff Christmas carols,' says the music therapist, 'Maybe we could do something for that?' 'Yeah, let's be the choir!' yells Melina eagerly. 'No way!' says Tommy, the only boy in the

group. 'Oh, go on, it would be fun,' replies Jane immediately, 'You could play drums!' Tommy considers this suggestion and the music therapist takes the cue to jump in with enthusiasm. 'That would be awesome,' she says, 'But it's a big commitment and it'll take a lot of time as we get closer to the event. Are you sure you're up for it?' 'Yeah!' respond the group, nodding enthusiastically.

In this situation, the music therapist has actually been the one to suggest the performance. She was genuine in only having thought of the idea in the moment and the enthusiastic response was an unanticipated surprise. The music therapist moves carefully towards giving ownership of the performance to the young people by asking them about taking responsibility. She will return to this theme again and again as they work towards the event and attempt to identify all hurdles in advance so they can be contemplated and conquered effectively.

Individual work with Garry

In the following vignette, the music therapist elects to utilize a performance as part of her intention to facilitate *development*, and the balance of power is different. The potential performance is offered to the young person as bait and the music therapist assumes responsibility for ensuring it is successful if all the required hoops are jumped through. In this case, the music therapist needs to be sure that it is both possible and feasible for the performance to take place before making the suggestion, since it is not an explorative process.

'You really love singing into the microphone, don't you?' the music therapist comments at the end of a particularly passionate rendition of 'In the Jungle'. Garry nods solemnly. 'Yeah. There's a microphone attachment on my SingStar game at home, you know.' The music therapist nods in an equally serious manner. 'Hmmmm. Maybe we should think about making a CD of your songs, since you enjoy performing so much? That could be pretty amazing.' 'What do you mean?' asks Garry. 'Well, you've been doing really well over the last few weeks. You're less aggressive towards people and have been getting into less trouble in the programme. What about if we make a CD to reward you for your self control? Each week we can record a song if you've been able to keep up this level of non-aggressive behaviour.' Garry looks at the music therapist incredulously. 'Really? We can do that?' 'Yep. We can make the CD if you can control how rough you are to other people. What do you think?' 'I'm in!' he says with passion.

'Alright,' the music therapist responds with equal enthusiasm, 'let's start right now. What song would you like to record today?' The music therapist jumps in immediately so that Garry has a chance to see how good it feels, and she has a chance to see if it works.

This classic application of a reward scenario is simple and controlled. The music therapist offers the performance for good behaviour and the adolescent accepts. They have negotiated a deal and they begin immediately. The music therapist has offered the control of the performances to the young man by connecting it to his good behaviour. The young man has not contemplated this connection very seriously as yet, but will no doubt do so as the weeks arrive and pass and he is able to record, or not. The responsibility for achieving the reward is Garry's. The music therapist is responsible for making the performance happen.

Special school concert

Another common context for performance is when it exists as a regular part of an existing music therapy programme. The idea for performance in this case can be unrelated to the therapist's orientation, since it is decided at an administrative level. It is not uncommon for music therapists to facilitate small performances as part of regular events since many people assume this is what music therapy is – making people happy. Although this is a simplistic assumption, once performance becomes tradition in an organization, it is not easy to make a case for the unique and individual teenager or group who would be better off *not* taking part in the performance. Indeed, other professional staff often get as much out of a performance as the young people do. It is as fun and rewarding for them as it is for the young people they care for.

Term 4 signifies the beginning of preparations for the end of year concert at the special school. Group music therapy sessions are often dedicated to preparing for the event and practising particular musical parts within a song framework. The music therapist is starting this journey in her work with a group of 14- and 15-year-olds who have profound and multiple disabilities. They have chosen to perform Bob Marley's 'Buffalo Soldier' using various communication strategies to vote between different songs that were played to them. Damien can hold a beater and strike a drum, so he will spend this term practising doing this on cue in the song. Nadia will attempt to play the repeating bass line on the tones of the metallaphone and that will also take a great deal of rehearsal. Mike and

Pip will sing the words and other group members will be set up with different instruments that contribute to the overall soundscape of the piece. Actually making this all happen at once on stage is a challenge, but the teacher and music therapist feel that it is feasible. The audience is made up primarily of family members and will be primed to respond to effort rather than achievement, in any case.

KEY POINTS

- The idea of performance often elicits an enthusiastic response that is quite different from the usual response to therapy.

- It should be acknowledged that this enthusiasm is as rewarding for the music therapist as it is for the young person.

- The more involved teenagers are in making this decision, the more they will take responsibility for the performance.

- Teenagers do not realize what they are committing to; only the music therapist knows how much is involved in working towards a performance.

- 'Whose idea was this, anyway?' is a simple question but it has an extraordinary influence over how the process will proceed in terms of responsibility and level of engagement.

What is the purpose of this performance?

The inclusion of a performance in the music therapy process can lead to many benefits for any combination of audience members and performers. Lucy O'Grady (2010) asserts that the music therapist needs to be clear about who is the intended beneficiary of a performance, since it should influence how the performance preparation proceeds. The many levels of potential benefit include the individual or group of performers, the known audience, or a broad and public audience that is largely unknown. Every aspect of devising the performance will be influenced by the intended audience – including setting, content, length, quality and time commitment. The way that the performance is negotiated with the teenager/s should also take the audience into account.

For the choir of bereaved teenagers, the audience is seen as the central beneficiary from the performance. Nurses, volunteers and other staff comprise the audience for the annual Christmas carols. It is seen as a time of celebration for all those who dedicate their time to the palliative care service during the year. Singing, eating and drinking are integral to the event, which is held in the fresh December air on a weekday evening in the Australian summer. Some staff bring their children to the event and family are welcomed. The involvement of the bereaved young people will add poignancy to the event, and these teenagers want to give something back to the service that cared for their deceased parent. Unbeknown to the young people, the bereavement support group does sometimes attract the attention of management, who question why these teenagers require ongoing support over such a long period of time. The truth is that they enjoy the group, the friendships and the opportunity to work with grief-related issues, but it is equally true that they are no longer 'at-risk' and therefore the service could be considered unnecessary. An additional systemic benefit of their involvement in the performance will therefore be to highlight the value of their connectedness to the organization, reminding administrators of the philosophy of palliative care and how well the service cares for the needs of the whole family. Any sense of satisfaction or pride that is experienced by the young people is an additional benefit, but it is not the primary purpose of their involvement.

ILLUSTRATIVE VIGNETTES
Bereavement support group
The music therapist steps up to the microphone once the Chief Executive Officer has made her introductory speech. 'We have a special surprise for you this evening,' she begins. 'The carols this year will be led by the young people who have been involved in the adolescent bereavement support group over the past couple of years. These committed and creative young people have selected the carols, helped to make the programmes and have been practising for this event over the past couple of months. Please welcome Jane, Sarah, Melina, Freya and Astrid, and the magnificent Tommy on drums!' The crowd applauds and hoots as the young people enter the stage wearing Santa hats and casual clothes. They shuffle to the side of the space and huddle together. Jane and Melina beam brightly and stand tall, while Freya, Sarah and Astrid hunch behind them looking a little embarrassed. Tommy is hidden behind the drum kit, and the music therapist decides to move her keyboard to centre stage to take some pressure off the group, who are more nervous than they had expected. After the first

couple of carols, she invites Melina to the main microphone. The plan is for each teenager to invite his or her favourite nurse up on stage to join in a song, and the music therapist thinks Melina will be confident enough to start this process. Adding further weight to this decision is the fact that the nurse who worked closely with Melina's family is a rowdy Scottish extrovert with a hearty voice. It should be a laugh to watch them sing 'Rudolph the Red Nosed Reindeer', and the teenagers have a number of props planned to keep things rolling.

A great deal of thought has gone into making this event rewarding for the audience. The young people have considered individual members who will be present and how they will engage their interest and attention. Although they are naturally a little embarrassed to be on the stage (wearing silly hats) their commitment to the audience is clear, and this is the shared focus of the teenagers and the music therapist.

Individual work with Garry

The purpose of performance for Garry is distinctly different. The performance will be used to address his individual goals and objectives. The audience for his CD will be more important in the anticipation than they will be in actually listening to the audio recording. The idea of people listening to him will be used as a motivator and the actual recording will then be the reward. The relevant goals and objectives for Garry are therefore as follows:

- For Garry to reduce his aggressive behaviours towards peers in the programme

    ○ to participate in positive unstructured interactions with peers

    ○ to abstain from striking people when frustrated

    ○ to use mature strategies for gaining attention.

- For Garry to create a CD of himself singing and playing

    ○ to achieve a reduction in aggressive behaviours (see previous goal)

    ○ to engage enthusiastically in practising selected songs for recording

    ○ to remain focused during the recording aspects of sessions.

'So I hear that you've had a peaceful week, Garry,' the music therapist comments once Garry finishes playing on the drum kit. 'Dunno,' he replies. 'Oh. It wasn't intentional then?' the music therapist queries. 'Well, I been trying to count to ten before I hit anyone,' Garry responds, 'and Marcus isn't here any more, and he used to drive me crazy, so that helps.' 'Hmmm,' says the music therapist. 'Well, we have made this plan to create a CD to reward you when you can control your aggression. It seems to me that you have been doing that, but you're not really giving yourself much credit for it.' 'Yeah! I have been good enough haven't I? I almost forgot. We haven't done a recording in weeks. Let's do it.' Garry is on a high now, and is moving around the room looking for the recording equipment. 'Okay Garry, I do think it's great that you've been controlling your behaviour, and counting to ten seems to be working for you. If you want to get the microphone out it's in that cupboard there. I'll set up the mixing desk.' Ten minutes later the room is transformed into a simple studio. 'Why don't we record that love song you wrote last week?' proposes the music therapist. 'Ahhhh, that's too embarrassing,' responds Garry. 'Okay, you choose,' says the music therapist. 'Well, I 'spose it would be good to record that one, actually,' says Garry, changing his mind. 'I don't mind, is there a different song you would prefer?' clarifies the music therapist. 'Nah, let's do that one. Do you remember the words?' The music therapist pulls out the lyrics from a folder where she keeps Garry's material. 'I typed them up for you – is that font large enough for you to read?' 'Yeah. Let's do it. Will I press record?' Garry is racing ahead and the music therapist moves to alter the pace so that his objectives are addressed in the process. 'Hang on, Garry. We need to rehearse it a few times and make sure you remember it, as well as decide on what instruments we will use. We've still got 25 minutes, so we don't have to rush.' 'Okay, okay. Can I practise with the microphone, though?' he responds.

The purpose of the performance influences each step of the recording process. The focus is not on the performance itself, it is on the achievements that are made to get to the performance. Garry is required to pace himself in the sessions, control himself outside of the sessions, and work hard to achieve the reward that is dangled in front of him. The music therapist is responsible for these steps and also works hard to ensure that they are achieved according to the plan.

Special school concert

When there is an expectation of performance in an institution, the intended beneficiaries obviously include those who have created this expectation. A concert provides an important platform for administrators and professionals when advocating for their services. They can describe the event to potential service users, emphasizing its role in bringing families together in celebration of the capacity of the young people in the facility. Administrators can use the concert to differentiate their service from their competitors, highlighting how creativity plays an important role in their service. These managers also benefit from attending the performance and having the opportunity to feel pride in what they have been able to achieve with their clientele. Other audience members also benefit similarly, with families enjoying the idea of their child participating in a normal school event such as a school concert. At the event they will have the opportunity to socialize with other families in similar situations to their own and also to feel connected to the school. The benefits to the teenagers are less important. They may be conscious of the excitement and energy that builds as the event comes closer, but they will also sense the pressure of having to perform. Rehearsals may have been pleasurable at times, although the more flexible and dynamic group sessions that they have replaced could also have fulfilled this function. It is important to keep the more systemic beneficiaries in mind during the preparation for a performance event such as this, since focusing on individual benefits would likely challenge the music therapist who may feel doubtful that the experience was worthwhile for the teenagers involved.

As the final act draws to a close on the annual concert a slide show begins and the music therapist changes the voice on the keyboard to 'Hammond Organ'. She plays in a syncopated 12/8 waltz style, moving through a circular chord progression that she will be able to maintain for what is approximately ten minutes of photos. They have been using slides to end the concert for the past two years and it invariably triggers laughter and tears in the crowd. The photos capture achievements over the year gone by and they provide a safe ending to the concert. It also gives teachers a chance to organize all the students in a line so that they can re-enter the stage for a final bow. When the moment for this final entry arrives, the music therapist puts the 1997 hit 'Mmmm Bop' by Hanson into the sound system and joins the students and teachers on the stage. She raises her hands and gets the audience to clap in time to the steady beat of the song. The students are all familiar with the song, since it has been playing regularly in classrooms in preparation for this event. As the chorus begins, the whole school team sings along and family members join in with gusto. It is a successful conclusion and staff members begin to feel a wave of relief.

The audience is the primary focus of each stage of the performance. Staff members are aware that parents will want to see their children perform, and also see their photos in the slide show. Effort is directed towards equal representation of all students, not for the students themselves, but for the audience who will experience this equality. The quality of the performance is also significant to the audience, and the less sympathetic they need to be in their appreciation of the event, the more successful it has been.

KEY POINTS

- Knowing who will benefit from a performance is very helpful during the most stressful moments of preparation.

- The purpose of the performance dictates the level to which the young people are involved in decision making.

- It also influences what level of quality is required of the performance.

- The role of the audience may be actual or imaginary and the role of the performers may be critical or secondary. It is important to be clear about what combination is relevant in each performance.

- The benefit may occur before the performance, during the performance, or long after the performance has finished.

What type of performance is most suitable?

Once the idea has been generated and the intended beneficiaries clearly identified, there are a number of options that may be suitable for a performance. Not all performances need to be live events and although this seems like the most obvious option, it is also the most complex and time consuming. Recordings require another type of performance that can be suitable to address different outcomes from the music therapy process, and sometimes a combination of recording and performance may even be warranted. To a certain degree, the decision may already be apparent from the answers to the previous two questions. Performance anxiety may also be a crucial determinant in this decision, since the degree of pressure does vary between live and recorded performances. The goodness of fit between ownership, purpose and mode of performance is crucial to a successful performance. If a mode of performance is selected that does not suit the intention of the therapist and the purpose of the performance, the results can be dramatic.

ILLUSTRATIVE VIGNETTES
Bereavement support group
This is not the first time the music therapist has suggested a performance to a bereavement support group. Two years previously she had asked a different group if they would be interested in performing for a professional symposium she was hosting at the facility. The young women's response had been similarly enthusiastic, but the degree of ownership was vastly different. On that occasion, the music therapist had continued to offer *acceptance* while preparing for and hosting the performance. She had theorized that it would be good for the young women's self-esteem to participate successfully in a public performance of an original song they had written about grief. In the weeks leading up to the performance she had arranged some extra rehearsals, but they were not well attended and she chose not to follow up group members because she didn't want to pressure them to perform. On the day of the symposium, only three of the eight young women arrived.

'I'm nervous,' whispers Carolyn to the music therapist as they stand at the back of the room waiting for their entrance in five minutes time. 'Oh, that's natural,' the music therapist replies reassuringly, 'I'm a bit nervous myself!' 'I don't think I want to do it,' replies Carolyn. 'Oh.' The music therapist is stuck. On the one hand, her instinct is not to place pressure on this bereaved young woman, but on the other, they have an audience waiting. 'How are you guys feeling?' she asks, turning to the two sisters behind them. 'I'm terrified,' Meagan responds. 'I'm not, I'm excited,' says her sister. The music therapist breathes an inaudible sigh of relief. 'Alright, Katie, how can we get these two excited too? What are you thinking about?' 'Oh, you know, whatever. I just like being on stage,' she replies, casually fluffing her hair. 'Yes, and you look good, too,' responds the music therapist, 'These outfits look so Britney Spears!' It's a desperate situation and the music therapist feels very uncomfortable at placing pressure on these young women. Just then they are called to the stage and move forwards en masse to sing their song. It is a tentative beginning, but the young women are singing strongly by the first chorus and they do a reasonably good performance. Afterwards, they are glowing with pride and bouncing up and down with excitement. 'That was soooo fun!' exclaims Meagan, 'We sounded great.' 'I'm glad you enjoyed it,' says the music therapist, 'I started to feel really pushy when you were nervous beforehand.' 'Nah,' says Carolyn, 'I'm always like that before a performance; you just have to get me out there.'

For these young women, a safer mode of performance may have been better suited to the music therapist's intentions. Neither the music therapist nor the young women were prepared for the pre-performance anxiety, and this was challenging to manage without an abrupt shift on the part of the therapist. Although it was a positive outcome, the missing participants also suggest that there is more to the story. These young women had already recorded their song to CD, and it may have been more suitable to remain at the more private level of performance if the therapist planned on maintaining her *accepting* stance. An alternative would have been to actively engage them in contemplating how their performance may benefit the audience by having them consider what impact it will have, and therefore foster a stronger sense of audience to draw upon in the inevitable moment of anxiety.

Individual work with Garry

Garry is poised and ready to record. He has practised the song nearly five times and on the last rehearsal it was nearly perfect. 'Ahhh, come on, let's record it now,' he pleads with the music therapist. 'Do you really think it's ready?' she asks, trying to draw out his focus on the recording as per his goals and objectives. 'It definitely is!' he replies, and the music therapist concedes. 'I think you're probably right,' she says, 'Do you want to stand up while you're singing it for the recording? You get more air in your lungs that way and the sound is usually better.' Garry pushes the chair back and waits. The music therapist moves to the mixing desk and gets things going before moving back into place with the guitar on her lap. They record the song three times before Garry makes it through the whole song without an obvious error. This is fairly normal for recording, and the music therapist commends Garry. 'Well done. And we've still got time to listen back to it. Do you want to come and sit over here?'

As the music starts playing, Garry listens intently. Once his voice joins the guitar sound he moves out of his chair and starts pacing around. 'I think you sound good Garry. What do you think?' the music therapist enquires. 'I messed that bit up,' he replies. 'That was pretty small though, it's hard to get it exactly right. In the big studios they might take a whole day to do one song; some people even take weeks.' Garry is not consoled, however, and after another minute he starts hitting the drums and is no longer listening to the CD. The music therapist tries to process it further but he is not interested and the session time is nearly over. The next week she presents the CD to Garry and he shows little interest and then leaves it behind at the end of the session.

If the music therapist was working towards fostering *understanding* of the personal issues underlying this young man's behavioural problems, this scenario would present an opportunity for insight and consideration. But in that mode, the recording would not have had an intended audience other than the music therapist and the young man, and therefore there would not have been a drive for quality. Instead, the CD has been created with a clear orientation towards *developing* skills, using a traditional reward structure. It is the awareness of audience that is challenging for Garry, who envisages himself as a rock star as he sings into the microphone, and then hears himself as a 14-year-old singing along with an acoustic guitar when he hears the recording. Not only is the link between his behaviour and the reward seemingly tenuous, but the reward is no longer rewarding. The match between purpose and outcome via the performance is not close enough. This suggests that time could have been spent working towards his goals in more effective ways.

Special school concert

Petter is a 16-year-old with multiple and profound disabilities, and for him the term spent in preparation for the end of year concert has not been very successful. He has been far less engaged in the group music therapy sessions, and although he has had the opportunity to communicate his instrument choice each week, the responsive and interactive nature of sessions has been missing and he has sometimes fallen asleep or simply not participated. On the day of the concert he returns to school after being sick for a week and is still a little frail. 'Where do you want me to put Petter?' an assistant calls out to the music therapist as she arrives at the performance venue. 'His group is over there,' the music therapist replies, stopping briefly to bend down to eye level and acknowledge Petter. He does not respond and she bends more deeply and begins to sing a familiar 'Hello Song' that they usually share at the beginning of sessions. Petter holds his head up and looks towards the music therapist. She gets the sense that if she persisted for a couple more minutes he might use his voice to interact with her, but there is no time. 'I'll catch you after the performance, Petter,' she says gently before moving away to keep organizing the logistics of the performance.

Some of the groups have to wait in the slightly draughty and dull 'green room' for 45 minutes before going on stage, and Petter is in one of the last groups to perform. As he is wheeled up the ramp the lights shine on him and he begins to sweat profusely in response to the sudden temperature change. As the song starts, the lights change colour a few times. The teachers are conscious of not triggering seizures with the lighting and have rehearsed these lights over the past week with the different groups, but Petter has been away. He looks surprised and then starts to become agitated. He rocks backwards and forwards in his chair and pushes the wind chimes aside as he bangs into them. The classroom assistant, who knows him well, quickly moves the chimes out of the way and stands next to him talking quietly and patting his arm as the rest of the group perform. He calms down and the lighting does too. As the familiar song comes to a conclusion he uses his voice a little, and the assistant standing behind him points to him and cheers so that his parents know he has made a contribution. By the time all the students enter the stage for the final song he is asleep in his chair and does not wake during the song.

The reality of a large-scale performance is that it is hard work for all those involved. There is enormous planning and preparation involved, with teenagers either contributing to that or experiencing the stress of it second-hand. In the case of an annual event, there is an assumption that being involved in this kind of event as 'normally' as possible is an important part of the experience. In reality, many teenagers would find this kind of repetitive practice dull, and there will necessarily be time spent sitting around with very little relevance to the individual. Coincidentally, this is also a good description of the daily life of a teenager with profound and multiple disabilities, and it is a complete contrast to what the music therapist would usually be striving towards in sessions with this group of teenagers. The performance itself is usually the justification for this expenditure, but as can be seen for Petter, this is not always the case. In fact, many young people do not enjoy the pressure of performances. He has not been able to anticipate it in the same way the bereaved teenage girls did because of his limited cognitive capacity. On the day, the unexpected performance issues are managed well and Petter's sickness was a contributing factor to his reaction, which his parents will understand. Because of the more systemic focus of the event, with the 'greater good' being nominated as a priority for the performance, this unfortunate personal experience does not detract from the success of the event. However, it is worth noting and acknowledging for the 'Petters' of a regular performance.

KEY POINTS

- An awareness of both purpose and intended audience needs to be cleverly matched with the right mode of performance for the individual or group.

- Performance anxiety is a normal reaction of all people to this level of pressure – it should *always* be expected.[1]

- Practice is the best strategy for overcoming performance anxiety, since the more confident the performer is, the better the outcome.

- Knowing the audience and the reason for communicating with them is empowering.

- The anticipation of a performance, either live or recorded, is not necessarily a good indication of the actual emotional experience of being heard live.

- The music therapist should be ready for anything at a performance and be prepared to do what is necessary to achieve the intended outcome. The teenager should never be sacrificed to the cause.

What resources are available for this performance?

Valuing and drawing on the abilities of teenagers is central to the decision to use performances within music therapy. Performance necessarily focuses on the capacities of the young people, with the intention of sharing those

---

1   An exception is young people on the autistic spectrum, who often make excellent performers because they are not as concerned with the response of the audience.

with an audience. It is not a private valuing that is acknowledged through offering *acceptance*. It is, to varying degrees, a public performance that is related to what resources are available from within the young person. Resources can be understood as existing at multiple levels, from the most obvious level of musical abilities, to the most subtle level of altruism. Music therapists are less inclined to emphasize musical abilities, since our focus is usually on the psychosocial–emotional abilities of the individual or group. In a *participatory* model, however, musical resources can be an entirely valid reason to choose to work towards a performance. It opens up the question of how this talent might be used to reach beyond the moment and into the systems surrounding the teenager/s. Other strengths can also be highlighted through performances, either through the revealing nature of lyrics or by physically conquering the mechanics of performance.

Another level of resources is also critical to performances and these involve material goods. Without access to appropriate equipment, venues, time and other organizational capacities, performances can become an impossible feat. Even the simplest strategy for the creation of a CD requires some kind of recording device that is then downloaded into audio software and converted into CD burning format. The quality of this type of recording is nowhere near the level of multi-track recording, which ideally takes place in some kind of studio environment. Once recordings are being created at this level of quality, a new question emerges about who should perform the material. This kind of investment in quality may benefit from the services of a professional performer in order to render an excellent quality sound, as Emma O'Brien (2004) chose to do when presenting songs written by oncology patients. With the creation of CDs come covers and track information, as well as decisions about how the material is shared, or even distributed. Although making a CD can be quite simple, it can quickly become complex.

Live performances require even greater levels of preparation and often more physical resources. Venues need to be sourced and audiences need to be made aware of the performance. Within the venue some kind of amplification is usually required, at the simplest level requiring microphones plugged into a mixing desk and output through portable speakers. Once instruments such as drum kits are included, it is important that individual instruments are amplified and that someone is designated to mix the levels of sound. Once this degree of performance has been taken into account, lighting and other mechanical aspects of the performance need to be considered, with someone functioning in the role of director. From there it is only a small step away to also needing a stage manager and at the very least a detailed plan of events. Tickets or some kind of welcoming party are required for the audience, and someone to introduce and thank guests is usually helpful. None of this is necessarily related to the kinds of resources discussed initially, at the level of the individual or group of teenagers. A focus on strengths is one thing. The ability to create a successful performance is quite another.

ILLUSTRATIVE VIGNETTES

Bereavement support group

The day of the Christmas carols begins with grey clouds and an ominous light. The carols are always held outside because it is usually a hot and balmy Australian December night, but this can never be guaranteed. The music therapist meets the equipment hire people at the facility early in the afternoon. 'What will we do if it rains?' she asks them as she offers directions regarding placement of speakers and where to set up the mixing desk. 'Oh well, you'd have to pack it up quick smart,' comes the reply. 'Do you think it will?' the music therapist asks, seeking reassurance. 'Hard to say,' the man states, 'but you'll have to pay for any equipment that gets wrecked, that's for sure.' 'So, should we be setting this up out here?' asks the music therapist nervously. 'Up to you, mate. It's your gig.'

As it turns out, the rain never eventuates since a cool breeze blows the clouds through. The change in temperature does catch people by surprise, though, and those dressed for the humidity find themselves surprisingly cool in the evening air. The music therapist does not take responsibility for this, however, and is busy doing a sound check as the teenagers arrive and rush out the back excitedly. 'Make sure you put your mouth really close to the microphone,' she advises the teenagers. 'They're uni-directional, so they won't pick you up if you're too far away.' The music therapist reflects on how such a simple instruction is usually quite difficult for performers to remember, and cranks the volume up for the vocal microphones. As she hears feedback she turns it down a little and goes to reorganize the gear. 'Jane, can you adjust that first dial on the right hand side when I tell you?' she asks one of the young women. 'Which one?' calls back Jane, as she reaches the mixing desk. 'On the right.' 'At the top?' 'No, the bottom.' Somehow the sound levels are set and the group gathers in the front room to prepare for the performance.

'Thanks so much for being involved in this, you guys,' starts the music therapist. 'I'm sure that the nurses and staff will be thrilled to see you and hear you.' 'Will Kai-Wan be here?' asks Tommy. 'I haven't seen her today, Tommy, but she said she was coming. I hope so,' replies the music therapist. 'If she's not, is there another nurse who was helpful to you?' 'Nah, but the psychologist lady was pretty nice,' Tommy offers. 'Lucy? She's definitely going to be here. So if Kai-Wan isn't in the audience, we'll get Lucy to sing with you. Now shall we talk about what we are trying to achieve before we go out there?' The group discuss their plan for the event and the strategies they have in place to achieve it. 'Right, hats. We need hats,' says the music therapist, looking about. 'I've got them!' calls Freya, 'I even brought one for you, coz I knew you'd forget to bring one.' The music therapist smiles gratefully at the young woman. 'You rock,' she says, 'Now, let's go and sing some carols with these people!'

This performance is a small-scale event in the back yard of the facility and yet it still involves considerable material and individual resources. During the preparation stages, amplification needed to be sourced and set up. Ongoing mixing and monitoring will be required during the performance and seats for the audience need to be set up. Carol books have been compiled with the songs in them and candles have been purchased, as well as safety plates for the candles so that occupational health and safety measures are met. Costumes and entrances have been planned, as well as different musical strategies for the concert. The teenagers have rehearsed the songs on three occasions including working with Tommy on the drums, and the music therapist has spent some time ensuring that she can play the songs without needing to look too often at the music. She will be busy cueing singers, leading singing, and monitoring the performance for the duration of the concert. All in a day's work, really.

The resources that have led to the participatory orientation of this performance come from within the young people and will be used to advocate for the service itself. Their enthusiasm, altruism and musical abilities are central to the decision to be involved in the performance. As a group, they are committed to supporting one another, as well as to offering something back to the organization that cared for their dying parent. Seeing the nurses and staff again will no doubt have emotional moments, but these young people have been working together for more than a year and have developed a strong understanding of their grief and the strengths they have been forced to acquire in coping with it. They want to give something back to the systems that have supported them, and this is a creative and fun-filled way of doing so.

Individual work with Garry

When Garry goes to get the microphone from the cupboard of the music room, he selects the vocal mike that he has used on previous occasions from the array of microphones available. He goes to another cupboard to select a microphone stand and to choose a lead that will connect the microphone to the mixing desk. He attaches the mike lead to the mike, cradles it in the stand and then goes over to the desk and attaches the other end of the lead to the back of the desk. He then moves the slider up to increase the volume and checks that the master volume control is at a reasonable level. Garry has been through this process many times and shown interest in the mechanisms of recording, so he has acquired the skills relevant to his interest. The music therapist takes responsibility for recording the amplified sound. The gear is not linked to a computer because it has been set up with the idea of live performances in mind, rather than recordings. Instead of recording directly into computer software, the music therapist creatively positions the MP3 recording device between the speakers so as not to produce feedback. It is a tricky game of placement in this improvised recording set-up, particularly since her acoustic guitar is not amplified, but is crucial to the sound. She and Garry have experimented with a number of strategies and have agreed the best placement under the circumstances, which they both recognize is not perfect.

Garry is full of bravado regarding his role as singer, and enjoys a fantasy identity that he employs while singing in sessions. The music therapist has attempted to discuss this bravado in working towards greater *understanding* in previous sessions, but Garry is not interested in the discussion and tends to move away and play instruments when these kinds of verbal dialogues are initiated. Instead of focusing on this as denial or resistance, the music therapist utilizes his performing confidence as a resource for the use of performance in the therapy process. Although Garry does not sing in a particularly melodic way, his passionate style of singing is both engaging and convincing and this is also fundamental to his presentation. Today they will record an original song he has written about a girlfriend who seems to be about to dump him, and he laments this in the song lyrics. Whether or not the song is fact or fantasy is not entirely clear, but Garry's passionate portrayal of the topic is real.

While this programme is relatively well resourced and the music therapist has taken the additional step of allowing for electric as well as acoustic instruments, it is not set up for recording. Musical recording is a complex and expensive business and the degree to which it is embraced is probably related to the interest of the music therapist and the level of technical support and professional development time available. Not only is every part of this process expensive, it is constantly changing and so requires updating and re-training. This can be stimulating for a music therapist who uses a lot of performance in practice, but may not be as interesting for those who do not consider it a priority. If the employer is resource-poor, a simple recording device such as an MP3 recorder with a mini condenser microphone can suffice when combined with basic software. Recording can be a reality for less than £500, and many people will not be able to tell the difference between this and multi-track professional recording from a sound studio. But some definitely will.

Special school concert

With each passing year, the expectations of the annual concert increase. Technology is always improving, and what used to be a fairly simple event has become a large-scale, multi-media extravaganza. A team of staff members is formed in the middle of the year with the dictate of organizing the event, and a number of enthusiastic teachers, administrators, technical support and allied health professionals work together to design and implement the production. This process is not dissimilar to the commitment made by many good schools to an annual performance, and it is important to this special school that their students have equivalent opportunities.

The team of ten professionals navigate their way through planning, drawing on the expertise of those who have been involved previously as well as the naïve enthusiasm and energy of those who have not. They report regularly to staff meetings and begin to make requests of all class groups in terms of music, themes, photographs and time. The final school term is dedicated to the event and it is impossible to calculate the time poured into the performance. The material resources are more identifiable and are mostly owned by the school, since this is a regular event. Testing of equipment is undertaken and new equipment purchased where necessary.

The theme of the Australian Bush has been selected for this year in response to the bushfires that have ravaged the state. The impact of the country fires has been felt even within the metropolitan city, with many students beings hospitalized due to poor lung capacity and high levels of smoke. This theme allows for 'Australiana' at many levels and some teenagers have particular skills to display. One of the non-verbal young men can sing the song of his favourite football team and this will be incorporated into the performance. Another student has a pet cockatoo and the family has agreed that she can be bought to the school for the event. Some of the students in the senior class have a particular love of Rolf Harris, a classic Australian country singer, and can do a hearty rendition of 'Tie me Kangaroo Down, Sport!' Each of these resources will be drawn upon in relation to the theme, as well as the musical or other dramatic skills which are known to the music therapist and teachers. The art teacher will engage all the class groups in making backdrops out of gum leaves and yellow bush blossom and the school hall will be adorned with their work. In this way, the production is a team effort, with the young people working alongside professionals to create an event to be proud of.

Without the commitment of the entire school community, from the highest levels of administration to the youngest child in the school, this kind of event would not be possible. Parents will be engaged in making costumes and preparing food for the celebration after the event. It is truly a community affair. The resources are therefore vast at all levels, and the long tradition of the event means that expectations are appropriate for the capacities of the performers. The audience is well known and the importance of the event is agreed. Although some individuals may find the event challenging or over stimulating (such as Petter), others may find it boring and teenage siblings have been known to look unimpressed. Nonetheless, the alignment of intentions, purpose, forum and resources is strong and even an electrical short circuit could probably not detract from the overall success of the event.

What are the pros and cons of the performance?

Active reflection is evident at each step of the process outlined above. It is required for advanced planning and for ensuring that there is coherence between the music therapist's intentions, the outcomes and the nature of the performance. Table 10.1 provides a useful summary of the active reflections made in relation to the three vignettes. Structuring these reflections as pros and cons serves the purpose of highlighting that using performance in music therapy is not necessarily good or bad. It could be either. This list is not comprehensive, but it does illustrate the considerations to some degree.

Table 10.1: Areas for consideration in deciding to use performance in music therapy

Pros	Cons
An opportunity to give back to a community	The need to acquire significant material resources
A chance to showcase capacity	Potentially poor quality product
A forum for communicating important messages	The risk of embarrassing disclosures of private material
An incentive to achieve non-musical goals	A distraction from being in the moment
A reward for positive achievements	Being confronted by the difference between actual musical abilities and fantasized abilities
An exhilarating experience	An over stimulating experience
A strategy for advocacy	Wasting time that could have been spent more therapeutically

Evaluating effectiveness

It is not a simple task to determine whether community understandings have been changed by a performance, or to measure whether the altruistic desire to give something to an audience has been worthwhile. When the audience is the intended beneficiary of a performance, it is unlikely that evaluation will be undertaken since this may detract from their experience. One potential strategy is to evaluate how effective the performance was in and of itself. There are a number of indicators that address the quality of a performance in music therapy and therefore suggest that intended outcomes have been achieved. These indicators are observable by necessity, since internal processes are impossible to gauge in this way. They are based on how both the leader and the teenager/s perform at the event, the success of the musical material, and the roles adopted by the music therapist and the audience. Each of these elements can be considered in a number of ways and a complete evaluation takes each into consideration in a balanced way. These criteria are listed in Table 10.2.

Table 10.2: Criteria for evaluating performances

Leader's performance

Familiarity with musical material

Accuracy of performance

Appropriate level of complexity of musical material played

Suitable incorporation of props/costumes/lighting/other art forms

Teenagers' performance

Appropriateness of roles for different participants

Apparent level of satisfaction with performance

Level of rapport between group members

Number of rehearsals attended

Musical material

Relevance of material to group membership

Appropriate level of complexity for abilities

Appropriateness of performance venue

Leadership role

Level of support provided to group

Ability to take varying levels of responsibility for performance depending on presenting needs

Level of expression modelled in the performance

Audience role

Appropriateness of audience for performance

Consideration of audience as beneficiaries evident in performance strategies

Number of audience members recruited for performance is appropriate

CONCLUSION

There are many perils when incorporating performances into the music therapy process. Not only does it distract from the moment of being in therapy, but it places inestimable amounts of pressure on both the teenager and the music therapist to perform. It is not surprising that this idea was the target of suspicion in conventional models of music therapy. In order to justify the potential benefit of incorporating performances into music therapy, it is important to reflect actively upon a range of questions, such as those suggested above, and to anticipate challenges that may arise. Performances create dynamics that music therapists often strive to avoid

– pressure, anxiety, expectations. A simplistic expectation that performance will lead to an increase in self-esteem does not, in itself, justify a decision to use performances rather than other music therapy methods that focus on more immediate experiences. Teenagers may respond with enthusiasm to the idea of performance, but usually this is not based on any understanding of what working towards a performance involves. It is the responsibility of the music therapist to foresee how performance will impact upon the therapeutic process. This chapter provides a balanced discussion of what is required and what can happen when performances are included in music therapy. When a *participatory* stance is assumed, the possibility for performances increases and it is likely that they will become more common as a part of music therapy practice. Sometimes it is good. Sometimes the outcomes are not so good. Nothing should be assumed.

Conclusion

It does take courage to work with adolescents. I have worked with teenagers in a wide array of settings now, and it is never easy work. I can honestly describe it as powerful or stimulating or rewarding or exciting; there are many positive descriptors, but not 'easy'. Just this week, as I draw together my final thoughts, I once again find myself in the situation described in the introduction (p.17). I have been wondering if what I am doing is of any value. If I am really honest, my adolescent self is simultaneously thinking: 'Maybe they don't like me.'

I have been working at this particular organization running a weekly group programme for 16 weeks, and this is the second crisis of confidence I have had. The mostly homeless youth are sporadic attendees at best, and when a couple of weeks pass with only one or two young people staying behind for the music programme, I start to question myself. I notice that I feel tense on the day of the programme and the feeling only passes when I arrive and start 'doing it'. In between times I thrash about for new ideas and notice an urge to control the process, an instinct which I interpret as intersubjective counter-transference since it is an unwarranted reaction (Bruscia 1998b, p.86). Alice Morgenstern (1982) describes the way that music therapists often respond to group conflict in more lay terms, saying that 'Music therapists often respond frantically and switch from one activity to another without much success, as if by finding the "right" activity everything could be fine' (p.19). This quote often comes back to me at these times in a group process and I try to learn from her wise words, but the emerging dynamics of group work with adolescents are powerful and it is difficult to resist being pulled into them.

There are many guides for understanding the fairly consistent stages of group development that are relevant to music therapy with adolescents.

Irvin Yalom (1995) is regarded as the best-known theorist on group process across many disciplines, including music therapy. He advises that 'If you are to perform your task of assisting the group to form therapeutic norms and to prevent the establishment of norms that hinder therapy, then you must have a clear conception of the natural, optimal development of a therapy group' (p.294). Both Yalom and Morgenstern are effectively arguing that the music therapist needs to hold his or her ground rather than retreat from the intensity of group dynamics during difficult times. This is similar to Andy Malekoff's (1997) advice that adolescents need someone who can survive the intensity as they grow increasingly honest and vulnerable within the therapeutic process. This kind of advice is most relevant for music therapists who are focused on fostering *understandings* or offering *acceptance*.

A slightly different perspective on group dynamics may be more useful for music therapists who operate primarily with the intention of facilitating *development* or encouraging *participation*. Although dated, Bruce Tuckman's (1965) insightful review of the literature proposed four stages of Forming, Storming, Norming and Performing as representative of the reasonably predictable path that many groups travel. This model continues to be adapted and applied to contemporary team development, with an emphasis on managing the 'storming' stages, more than accepting them. If a group has chosen to work towards a performance, for example, or if a particular skill is being targeted, too much focus on allowing group dynamics will distract from the therapeutic task at hand. In my experience as a music therapist who blends different intentions and uses approaches in an eclectic way, I find considering these two approaches particularly relevant during difficult stages of group development. Sometimes this involves offering something new to focus on that will keep the group on track; at other times it involves working steadily to ensure that all members are surviving the chaos alongside me.

I have previously categorized a number of indigenous models of music therapy group development (Achenbach 1997; Bruscia 1987; James and Freed 1989; Morgenstern 1982; Plach 1996) within a Symphonic framework (Skewes 2001) and this may be a helpful way for music therapists working with adolescents to contemplate group development. The Symphonic analogy was selected because both physicists and musicians alike consider symphonic form to bear a relationship to natural organic growth. The proportions of the form are described as being in 'golden ratio', having optimal balance between different sections (Howat 1983, p.9). Tony Wigram (2004) initially identified this idea, relating the organic structure of many improvisations to Sonata Form, which is very similar to Symphonic Form.

This model is presented in Table c.1, where musical features, therapeutic indicators and the therapist's role are all delineated. A comparison between this theoretical model and the musical data resulting from my doctoral investigation showed a high level of affinity between the predictions made by the model and the improvisations that were analysed from each of the ten sessions. Although this model focuses on improvisation with a blend of therapeutic intentions including fostering understanding and offering acceptance, it has potential application to all forms of music making in music therapy groups. I have found it useful in contemplating my musical and therapeutic role at different stages of group development.

The Symphonic model of group development shows that after an initial Introduction stage, the Exposition marks the real beginning of the group where the major themes are introduced – the personalities, the issues, the methods. The Development section is the stage I am referring to above, where things that seemed to be going well suddenly are not. Attendance dwindles. Infighting occurs. The real picture becomes more obvious after the niceties of the Exposition. If the music therapist survives this stage without retreating, the Recapitulation is where the potential for significant growth occurs. Having been accepted and/or understood just as they are, the group members are able to begin processing the most relevant issues and grappling with the possibility of change. The Coda then functions as closure, allowing for a return to the polite behaviours of the Exposition, but informed by the growth that has occurred. It is an opportunity for reflection that should always be celebrated. Australian teenagers usually like to do this with fizzy drinks and crisps.

Despite the fact that group development is a theoretical construct rather than a reality, it is my experience that the dynamics do proceed in the expected direction more often than not. At the same time as I am working with the highly industrialized young people in the city, I am concurrently working with another group of teenagers who have survived some of the worst bush fires in Australia. I drive for two hours to run back-to-back groups at a small country high school that was severely affected by this natural disaster at the beginning of 2009. In some ways, my work with these groups is very different to my work in the city, and there is a strong sense of community apparent in the way the young people interact in comparison to the fierce independence of their city peers. There are no secrets in these country towns and the teenagers have a much more developed consciousness of how their behaviour impacts on

Table c.1: A Symphonic model of music therapy group development

Symphonic structure	Musical milestones	Therapeutic indicators	Therapist's musical role
Introduction	• The group plays together in highly structured improvisations	• Development of rules • Clarify purpose of group and members' expectations	• Create musical environment for participants to step into and shape the musical experience to encourage participation • Offer unconditional positive responses to musical material generated regardless of aesthetic pleasingness or expressive qualities
Exposition	• The group begins to play spontaneously • The group frequently plays together in time • Beginning to explore a variety of musical styles: dynamics, rhythms, attack and orchestration	• The group identifies similarities between members • Individual participants begin to feel trust and support • Beginnings of interactions and relationships including establishment of hierarchy with counterparts, alliances and expected patterns of behaviour	• Provision of exercises to encourage different musical experiences such as inclusion of themes, games and imagery • Model variations on playing styles and behaviour
Development	• Resistance or refusal to play together • Expressed dislike of others' musical material • Musical risk taking • Increased differentiation in tempi and different beats • Harmonic dissonance • Musical competing expressed through dynamics and orchestration	• Recognition of differences between participants • Working through communication problems, uncovering maladaptive strategies and extreme behavioural reactions • Disintegration and conflict • Confrontation of issues leading to the discovery of resolutions	• Support individual members' musical material by facilitating dyadic musical interactions within the group sound • Decrease centrality of role through selection of quieter instruments, supporting rhythmic grounds and patterns of other players • Leadership may be challenged musically and important to separate from leadership role and handover responsibility

continued

Table c.1: A Symphonic model of music therapy group development *cont.*

Symphonic structure	Musical milestones	Therapeutic indicators	Therapist's musical role
Recapitulation	• Flexibility in playing • Increased ability to listen to the music of others and play in a communicative way • Freedom of movement between different styles of playing • Individual musical material is related to the central form and is also differentiated from it • Musical material is sometimes aesthetically pleasing in a traditional, improvised sense	• Acceptance of difference within group membership with intermittent return to conflict • Personal involvement with dynamics, interactional self-disclosure and insights • Open expression of feelings and sharing of intense and stressful emotions • Experimentation with new patterns of behaviour	• Group is self-led • Individual role within group sound that complements and supports others' musical material • Incorporation of verbal insights • Assist in bringing blocked issues to the surface
Coda	• Group improvisation without leader or presented to others	• Achievement of independence • Variety of coping strategies and behaviours relating to loss and separation • Reflection and planning for ongoing work	• Acceptance of variety of coping strategies expressed musically

others. The preferred musical genres are also distinct. The disenfranchized metropolitan teenagers are committed to hip-hop and alternative rock. The traumatized bush teenagers are rock and pop focused, with more individual variations. Yet despite these differences, the intensity of the group dynamics is remarkably similar and during the developmental stage of each group, the same questions arise. On this occasion, however, I am co-facilitating the groups with a colleague, Kate Teggelove, and have the opportunity to observe my responses to each week through our dialogue. The peer supervision we offer one another allows my 'adolescent voice' to have its say. Last week we began to worry about our effectiveness, and as we finished making plans for what we would consider for the next week I made a casual comment.

> 'You know, it seems to me that every time I reach this point with a group of adolescents, it means they are just about to turn a corner. I get this feeling of tension and put a lot of effort into making back-up plans, just in case, and then the situation resolves itself and my plans are redundant.'

Sure enough, when we facilitated the groups the next week, we had turned a corner. Lyrics that had previously been written about fantasies and jokes were replaced by poignant commentaries on the individual situations being faced by each of these brave young people. They began to try to blend together the trauma of the fires and the ongoing challenges of peer relationships with the emergence of love and frustration. We had survived the Developmental stage and they had decided to trust us.

The strength of the therapist's counter-transference reactions in music therapy with adolescents is a good indicator of the need for professional or peer supervision. Although working with teenagers in special education evokes fewer complex reactions, group work with adolescents is often and inevitably evocative of one's own history. For this reason, it is important to seek the opportunity to discuss responses to group processes and individual encounters (Forinash 2001). Speaking with colleagues is an invaluable part of my own professional experience, but I also maintain an active awareness of my inner workings through a combination of personal therapy and professional supervision. As may be obvious from the existence of this book, I find it quite easy to articulate my experience of working with teenagers, but I still find it helpful to take care of myself so that the feelings of adolescent insecurity are kept in their place.

It is inevitable that one's own experiences of adolescence are retrieved while working with adolescents. The same is true for every field of music therapy work. Working with people who have cancer will undoubtedly touch upon personal experiences of cancer or other life-threatening illness. It happens when the people we work with have dementia, autism, multiple sclerosis, attention deficit hyperactivity disorder. But adolescence is unique because none of us have been able to avoid being there, and each of us carries our own experiences as representative of that time. For this reason, it is important to be prepared to revisit this stage of life. This is why I believe the Map can be a valuable frame of reference.

I have suggested in Part One that it is helpful for music therapists to locate themselves on the Map in terms of their preferred theoretical orientation, their personal stance, their intention for therapy and the kinds of outcomes they are working towards (see Figure 2.2; Figure iv.1). Having shared examples of some of the extraordinary young people with whom I have had the privilege to work, it is now possible to change the orientation of the Map. The next variation of the Map is an attempt to represent what music therapists really do, which is to focus on the presenting needs of the young people in the moment, rather than on some distant theoretical inclination. In Figure c.1, I have removed the theoretical framework and replaced it with references to the teenagers themselves. I hope that you can picture the young people I am referring to by these brief snippets. For me, when I think about the completely lost teenagers I have worked with I hear emo and metal music. For those that are trying valiantly I hear rap and rock. Those teenagers needing more concrete types of help might be represented by more conservative genres, such as classic hits and even classical music. And for the final group of young people who are up for a challenge, I can hear Top 40 songs, although these teenagers would probably be willing to listen to just about anything. This variation on the Map is no longer a therapist-centric representation of how music therapy can be with adolescents; it is closer to a real life picture of the young people that we meet and what they want from us.

WHERE TO FROM HERE: TALKING RESEARCH

This book has outlined a very practical approach to working with teenagers in groups and individually, using songs, improvisations and performances in a blended and eclectic way. Much of what has been

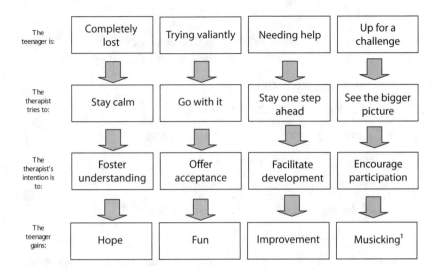

1. Small 1998

Figure c.1: How music therapy can help teenagers

written is underpinned by research, and the literature on music therapy and adolescents was canvassed and presented in Chapter 1. What became evident from that review of the literature is that there is very little research that specifically addresses the value of music therapy for adolescent clients. The research that has been conducted is typically organized around the conditions challenging the teenagers rather than any particularly adolescent needs. For this reason, when more than one participant was involved, the research often combined age groups, incorporating either children and teenagers, or young adults and teenagers. Even the individual case studies seemed to regard adolescence as a coincidence in the main, rather than as a central figure in the equation. This is a valid position to take if Robert Epstein (2007) is right in suggesting that the label of adolescence is both unnecessary and unhelpful. But is it?

One of my own investigations with Felicity Baker (Baker and McFerran 2006) focused solely on hospitalized adolescents and revealed that identity formation issues were critical in their use of music therapy. Our analysis revealed that lyrics describing 'identify formation' were the most common focus of material within the songs (28.2%). Lyrics were classified to this grouping when they were in line with the two personally oriented categories identified in the literature review in Chapter 1 – describing either the intra-personal or inter-personal discoveries about self. The sub-categories within identity formation included the following:

- comparing self with others
- considering how viewed by others
- expressing emotions or views about peers
- autonomy, independence from family
- exploring new behaviours, positive self-talk
- exploring limitations of world and of self
- self reflection – who am I?

A number of other themes emerged from the songs that are closely related to identity formation, such as emotional awareness (17.2%), relationship dynamics (17.4%), aspirations for the future (16.6%), as well as reference to the disorder and its impact on their lives (15.2%). A retrospective content analysis such as this provides an opportunity to contemplate how adolescent clients perceive the purpose of therapy and what they utilize it for. In this case, the young women spent a lot of time considering themselves in relation to others.

Another important theme that has emerged from my research into music therapy with adolescents is the importance of balancing fun and enjoyment with opportunities for choice and control. In a phenomenological analysis of the perspectives shared by six bereaved teenagers who had participated in ten weeks of music therapy, this finding was the most conspicuous (Skewes 2001). A follow-up study of bereaved teenagers where we conducted focus groups to collect the teenagers' opinions on the music therapy groups highlighted this perspective once again. The theory that emerged from the second study suggested that 'bereaved teenagers feel better if they have opportunities for fun and creative expression of their grief alongside their peers' (McFerran 2010, p.23). Once again, the combination of emotional expression and chaotic creativity was endorsed unanimously by the young people who found it valuable. This emphasis was confirmed in a study by Susan Gardstrom (2004) who investigated her work with six teenagers struggling with severe emotional and behavioural disorders within a residential treatment setting. Yet again, the young people involved in improvisational music therapy noted that music evoked and allowed for the expression of emotions, while also being energizing and motivating, a much valued novelty that was described as 'having fun'. Trygve Aasgaard's (2000) research has also emphasized the importance of promoting fun and laughter in his work in paediatric hospitals. Aasgaard's participants were not exclusively adolescents, however, nor is the concept of having fun limited only to the younger participants he describes. As an example, he quotes a 13-year-old girl who, upon discovering he was yet another 'therapist', expressed her disappointment and assumed that he too would focus on her numerous problems. She whispers, 'I had hoped we would just make music together' (Aasgaard 2004, p.157), and Aasgard responds with humour and a pleasure-oriented music therapy experience. Taken together, these rigorous qualitative investigations suggest that there is something unique about the way that teenagers perceive the potential of music therapy to oscillate with them from one emotional extreme to another.

A further outcome that is emerging across a number of meticulous qualitative studies is related to self-knowledge. Gro Trondalen's (2003) improvisational music therapy work with a young woman suffering from anorexia revealed a new awareness of personal connectedness in time and space as a result of therapy. Trondalen's focus was on emphasizing personal resources and fostering expression, which promoted an increased ability for the young woman to regulate herself in relation to another person – and sometimes in relation to food. A similar result was identified in another investigation of young people with disordered eating, this time participating in vibro-acoustic music therapy (Ruutel et al. 2004). Grounded theory analysis of the young people's perceptions revealed that one of the important roles of music therapy was providing opportunity for self-discovery. The participants felt that the music therapy sessions enhanced coping, self-knowledge and self-awareness as a result of the combination of relaxation and reflection. Although the journey of self-discovery is not limited to adolescence, these years mark the beginning of cognitive capacity for the self-reflective aspects of this journey. These two key themes emerging from qualitative investigations of music therapy with teenagers suggest that they use music therapy in the ways that they use music: to have fun, to express something of who they are, and to explore who they might become. These themes should be used systematically in further investigations of music therapy with adolescents.

The music therapy research literature on adolescents is marked by a consistency between selected research design and the theoretical orientation of the music therapy programme being investigated. In all cases, the approach used was well placed to ascertain whether the intended outcomes were being achieved. In the literature on teenagers with disabilities there was a steady emphasis on applied behavioural analysis, with control conditions being utilized in most studies. These studies measured whether music therapy helped to develop postural control and engagement levels, and whether it impacted on other behaviours such as reducing self-stimulating behaviour. The research into at-risk adolescents incorporated the greatest proportion of qualitative investigations that asked clients about their perceptions. Appropriately, what quantitative studies were undertaken with these young people focused on measures of coping and self-confidence, as well as anxiety. In the studies of those classified as having behavioural problems, the researchers often measured the frequency of the problem behaviours in the classroom. In residential treatment programmes there was greater emphasis on measuring the participants' perspectives, either through self-concept or therapeutic effectiveness measures. In the field of mental illness there was a tendency to focus on comparisons of different methods rather than targeting outcomes. Similarly in hospital settings there was some measurement of the emotional elements of treatment, namely anxiety, but few attempts at outcome measures.

The idea of selecting appropriate designs for research can also be attached to the Map, and Figure c.2 suggests what positions may be broadly appropriate for researchers identifying with one dominant stance. The alignment between therapeutic intentions and research approaches proposed in Figure c.2 is partly conjecture on my part, built on a combination of patterns from the literature and my own experiences of research with each of the methodologies being suggested. It is not intended to be a strict set of rules and there could be good reasons to justify a re-ordering of the categories for any particular project. My use of terminology is strongly influenced by the qualitative research frameworks outlined by Egon Guba and Yvonna Lincoln (2005), as well as the explanations of the various methodologies offered by music therapy experts in *Music Therapy Research* (Forinash and Grocke 2005; Hanser 2005; Smeijsters and Aasgard 2005; Stige 2005).

It is my view that a pragmatic approach should be adopted for research in a similar fashion to my preference for blended, eclectic approaches to practice. Rather than locating oneself as attached to a particular paradigmatic stance (and associated ontological and epistemological positions), a commitment to adopting the most suitable approach to the research question offers a more flexible position. John Creswell (2003)

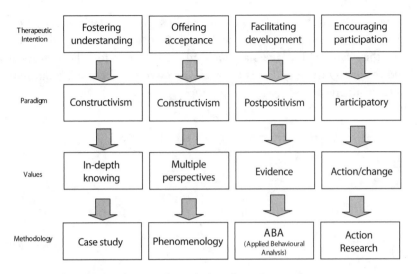

Figure c.2: Aligning research approaches with clinical stance

describes this pluralistic orientation as 'opening the door to multiple methods, different worldviews, and different assumptions' (p.12) that best address the problem at hand and take into account the intended audience. While he advocates for mixed methods designs, this can equally mean aligning with a particular stance in one project (for example, using Action Research when investigating a community music therapy project), and then adopting another focus when asking a different question in another setting (for example, using applied behavioural analysis for a study of improved communication skills in special education).

FINAL THOUGHTS

Pragmatic and flexible. Pluralistic and eclectic. Creative and thoughtful. Fun-filled and seriously attentive. A great many of the ideas proposed in this book on how to do music therapy with adolescents represent my perspectives on music therapy in general, as much as they are to do with teenagers in particular. Although some of the ideas may be overly simplistic, my fundamental intention has been to provide a Map, or a guide, that encourages music therapists to approach adolescents in their own way. I am not suggesting that there is one single best way, but approaching a teenager with the confidence of knowing where you are located is an important beginning. I started this chapter by saying that it takes courage to work with adolescents, and I will end by saying that our main purpose in working with adolescents is to help them have the courage to be the best they can be. Teenagers are looking for someone to believe in them, and sharing music together is a powerful way of communicating our faith in their inherent capacity to grow. I hope you have some fun.

List of literature reviewed
for Chapter 1

Aasgaard, T. (2003) 'Musical Acts of Love in the care of severely ill and dying children and their families.' Available at www.musictherapyworld.de/modules/archives/papers/show_abstract.php?id=51, accessed on 25 October 2009.

Abad, V. and Williams, K. (2006) 'Early intervention music therapy for adolescent mothers and their children.' *British Journal of Music Therapy 20*, 1, 31–38.

Agrotou, A. (1994) 'Isolation and the multi-handicapped patient: An analysis of the music therapist–patient affects and processes.' *The Arts in Psychotherapy 21*, 5, 359–365.

Aldridge, D. (1993) 'Music therapy research 1: A review of the medical research literature within a general context of music therapy research.' *The Arts in Psychotherapy 20*, 11–35.

Baker, F. and Jones, C. (2005) 'Holding a steady beat: The effects of a music therapy program on stabilising behaviours of newly arrived refugee students.' *British Journal of Music Therapy 19*, 2, 67–74.

Baker, F., Kennelly, J. and Tamplin, J. (2005) 'Themes in songs written by patients with traumatic brain injury: Differences across the lifespan.' *Australian Journal of Music Therapy 16*, 25–42.

Bednarz, L.F. and Nikkel, B. (1992) 'The role of music therapy in the treatment of young adults diagnosed with mental illness and substance abuse.' *Music Therapy Perspectives 10*, 21–26.

Boswell, B. and Vidret, M. (1993) 'Rhythmic movement and music for adolescents with severe and profound disabilities.' *Music Therapy Perspectives 11*, 37–41.

Breaswell, C., Brooks, D.M., Decuir, A.A., Humphrey, T., Jacobs, K.W. and Sutton, K. (1986) 'Development and implementation of music/activity therapy intake assessment for psychiatric patients. Part II: Standardization procedures on data from psychiatric patients.' *Journal of Music Therapy 23*, 3, 126–141.

Brooks, D.M. (1989) 'Music therapy enhances treatment with adolescents.' *Music Therapy Perspectives 6*, 37–39.

Buchanan, J. (2000) 'The effects of music therapy interventions in short-term therapy with teens at risk: An opportunity for self-expresssion in a group setting.' *Canadian Journal of Music Therapy 7*, 1, 39–50.

Cassity, M.D. (1981) 'The influence of a socially valued skill on peer acceptance in a music therapy group.' *Journal of Music Therapy 18*, 3, 148–154.

Cassity, M.D. and Cassity, J.E. (1994) 'Psychiatric music therapy assessment and treatment in clinical training facilities with adults, adolescents, and children.' *Journal of Music Therapy 31*, 1, 2–30.

Cassity, M.D. and Cassity, J.E. (1996) *Multimodal Psychiatric Music Therapy for Adults, Adolescents and Children: A Clinical Manual.* Third edition. London: Jessica Kingsley Publishers.

Castellano, J.A. and Wilson, B.L. (1970) 'The generalization of institute therapy to classroom behavior of an electively mute adolescent.' *Journal of Music Therapy 7*, 139–143.

Chester, K.K., Holmberg, T.K., Lawrence, M.P. and Thurmond, L.L. (1999) 'A program-based consultative music therapy model for public schools.' *Music Therapy Perspectives 17*, 2, 82–91.

Choi, C.M.H. (2007) *Music Therapy Program on the Psychological Conditions of Refugee Adolescents from North Korea.* New York, NY: Columbia University.

Clark, S.L. (1995) *Current Practices in Music Therapy for Grieving Children, Adolescents, and Their Families.* Kansas City, MO: Kansas City University.

Clarkson, A.L. and Robey, K.L. (2000) 'The use of identity structure modeling to examine the central role of musical experience within the self-concept of a young woman with physical disabilities.' *Music Therapy Perspectives 18*, 2, 115–120.

Clendenon-Wallen, J. (1991) 'The use of music therapy to influence the self-confidence and self-esteem of adolescents who are sexually abused.' *Music Therapy Perspectives 9*, 73–81.

Cohen, N.S. (1988) 'The use of superimposed rhythm to decrease the rate of speech in a brain-damaged adolescent.' *Journal of Music Therapy 25*, 2, 85–93.

Coulter, S.J. (2000) 'Effect of song writing versus recreational music on Posttraumatic Stress Disorder (PTSD) symptoms and abuse attribution in abused children.' *Journal of Poetry Therapy 13*, 4, 189–208.

Dalton, T.A. (2006) 'The grief song-writing process with bereaved adolescents: An integrated grief model and music therapy protocol.' *Music Therapy Perspectives 24*, 94–107.

Dalton, T.A. and Krout, R.E. (2005) 'Development of the grief process scale through music therapy songwriting with bereaved adolescents.' *The Arts in Psychotherapy 32*, 131–143.

Darrow, A. and Cohen, N. (1991) 'The Effect of Programmed Pitch Practice and Private Instruction on the Vocal Reproduction Accuracy of Hearing Impaired Children: Two Case Studies.' In K. Bruscia (ed.) *Case Studies in Music Therapy*: Gilsum, NH: Barcelona Publishers.

Darrow, A., Johnson, C.M. and Ollenberger, T. (1994) 'The effect of participation in an intergenerational choir on teens' and older persons' cross-age attitudes.' *Journal of Music Therapy 31*, 2, 119–134.

Daveson, B.A. (2008) 'A description of a music therapy meta-model in neuro-disability and neuro-rehabilitation for use with children, adolescents and adults.' *Australian Journal of Music Therapy 19*, 70–85.

Daveson, B. and Kennelly, J. (2000) 'Music therapy in palliative care for hospitalized children and adolescents.' *Journal of Palliative Care 16*, 1, 35–38.

Daveson, B. and Skewes, K. (2002) 'A philosophical inquiry into the role of rhythm in music therapy.' *The Arts in Psychotherapy 29*, 265–270.

Davies, A. and Mitchell, A.R.K. (1991) 'Music therapy and Elective Mutism: A case discussion.' *British Journal of Music Therapy 5*, 2, 10–14.

Davis, G. (2005) 'Living Community: Music Therapy with Children and Adults in a Hospice Setting.' In M. Pavlicevic (ed.) *Music Therapy in Children's Hospices.* London: Jessica Kingsley Publishers.

de Aisenwaser, V. (1975) 'Music therapy with a mentally deficient girl.' *British Journal of Music Therapy 6*, 2, 2–8.

di Franco, G. (1999) 'Music and Autism: Vocal Improvisation as Containment of Stereotypes.' In T. Wigram and J. De Backer (eds) *Clinical Applications of Music Therapy in Developmental Disability, Paediatrics and Neurology.* London: Jessica Kingsley Publishers.

Dixon, M. (2002) 'UK: Music and Human Rights.' In J. Sutton (ed.) *Music, Music Therapy and Trauma: International Perspectives.* London: Jessica Kingsley Publishers.

Dorow, L.G. and Horton, J.J. (1982) 'Effect of the proximity of auditory stimuli and sung versus spoken stimuli on activity levels of severely/profoundly mentally retarded females.' *Journal of Music Therapy 19*, 2, 114–124.

Dvorkin, J.M. (1991) 'Individual Music Therapy for an Adolescent with Borderline Personality Disorder: An Object Relations Approach.' In K. Bruscia (ed.) *Case Studies in Music Therapy.* Gilsum, NH: Barcelona Publishers.

Edenfield, T. and Hughes, J. (1991) 'The relationship of a choral music curriculum to the development of singing ability in secondary students with Down Syndrome.' *Music Therapy Perspectives 9*, 52–55.

Edwards, J. (1995) '"You are singing beautifully": Music therapy and the debridement bath.' *The Arts in Psychotherapy 22*, 1, 53–55.

Eidson, C.E. (1989) 'The effect of behavioral music therapy on the generalization of interpersonal skills from sessions to the classroom by emotionally handicapped middle school students.' *Journal of Music Therapy 26*, 4l, 206–221.

Elefant, C. and Wigram, T. (2005) 'Learning ability in children with Rett syndrome.' *Brain and Development 27*, 1, 97–101.

Ford, T.A. (1988) 'The effect of musical experiences and age on the ability of deaf children to discriminate pitch.' *Journal of Music Therapy 25*, 1, 2–16.

Frank-Schwebel, A. (2002) 'Israel: Developmental Trauma and its Relation to Sound and Music.' In J. Sutton (ed.) *Music, Music Therapy and Trauma: International Perspectives*. London: Jessica Kingsley Publishers.

Gardstrom, S.C. (2004) 'An Investigation of Meaning in Clinical Music Improvisation with Troubled Adolescents.' In B. Abrams (ed) *Qualitative Inquiries in Music Therapy: A Monograph Series 1*, 77–160.

Ghetti, C.M. (2002) 'Comparison of the effectiveness of three music therapy conditions to modulate behavior states in students with profound disabilities: A pilot study.' *Music Therapy Perspectives 20*, 1, 20–30.

Gilbertson, S. (1999) 'Music Therapy in Neurosurgical Rehabilitation.' In T. Wigram and J. De Backer (eds) *Clinical Applications of Music Therapy in Developmental Disability, Paediatrics and Neurology*. London: Jessica Kingsley Publishers.

Gold, C., Voracek, M. and Wigram, T. (2004) 'Effects of music therapy for children and adolescents with psychopathology: A meta-analysis.' *Journal of Child Psychology and Psychiatry 45*, 6, 1054–1063.

Gold, C. Wigram, T. and Voracek, M. (2007) 'Predictors of change in music therapy with children and adolescents: The role of therapeutic techniques.' *Psychology and Psychotherapy: Theory, Research and Practice 80*, 577–589.

Grant, R.G. (1986) 'Effects of sensory mode input on the performance of rhythmic perception tasks by mentally retarded subjects.' *Journal of Music Therapy 23*, 1, 2–9.

Greenwald, M.A. (1978) 'The effectiveness of distorted music versus interrupted music to decrease self-stimulatory behaviors in profoundly retarded adolescents.' *Journal of Music Therapy 15*, 2, 58–66.

Grossman, S. (1978) 'An investigation of Crocker's Music Projective Techniques for emotionally disturbed children.' *Journal of Music Therapy 15*, 4, 176–184.

Han, P. (1998) 'The use of music in managing pain for hospitalized children.' *Australian Journal of Music Therapy 9*, 45–56.

Henderson, H. (1991) 'Improvised Song Stories in the Treatment of a 13-year-old Sexually Abused Girl from the Xhosa Tribe in South Africa.' In K. Bruscia (ed.) *Case Studies in Music Therapy*. Gilsum, NH: Barcelona Publishers.

Henderson, S.M. (1983) 'Effects of a music therapy program upon awareness of mood in music, group cohesion, and self-esteem among hospitalized adolescent patients.' *Journal of Music Therapy 20*, 1, 14–20.

Hendricks, C.B. and Bradley, L.J. (2005) 'Interpersonal theory and music techniques: A case study for a family with a depressed adolescent.' *The Family Journal 13*, 400–405.

Hilliard, R.E. (2001) 'The use of cognitive behavioural music therapy in the treatment of women with eating disorders.' *Music Therapy Perspectives 19*, 2, 109–113.

Hilliard, R.E. (2003) 'Music therapy in pediatric palliative care: Complementing the interdisciplinary approach.' *Journal of Palliative Care 19*, 2, 127–132.

Hobson, M.R. (2006a) 'The collaboration of music therapy and speech-language pathology in the treatment of Neurogenic Communication Disorders: Part 1 – Diagnosis, therapist roles, and rationale for music.' *Music Therapy Perspectives 24*, 2, 58–65.

Hobson, M.R. (2006b) 'The collaboration of music therapy and speech-language pathology in the treatment of Neurogenic Communication Disorders: Part II – Collaborative strategies and scope of practice.' *Music Therapy Perspectives 24*, 2, 66–79.

Holloway, M.S. (1980) 'A comparison of passive and active music reinforcement to increase preacademic and motor skills in severely retarded children and adolescents.' *Journal of Music Therapy 17*, 2, 58–69.

Hooper, J., McManus, A. and McIntyre, A. (2004) 'Exploring the link between music therapy and sensory integration: an individual case study.' *British Journal of Music Therapy 18*, 1, 15–23.

Howard, A.A. (1997) 'The effects of music and poetry therapy on the treatment of women and adolescents with chemical addictions.' *Journal of Poetry Therapy 11*, 2, 81–102.

Humphrey, T. (1980) 'The effect of music ear training upon the auditory discrimination abilities of trainable mentally retarded adolescents.' *Journal of Music Therapy 17*, 2, 70–74.

Hunt, M. (2005) 'Action research and music therapy: Group music therapy with young refugees in a school community.' *Voices: A World Forum for Music Therapy*. Available at www.voices.no/mainissues/mi40005000184.html, accessed on 25 October 2009.

Ibberson, C. (1996) 'A natural end: One story about Catherine.' *British Journal of Music Therapy 10*, 1, 24–31.

Ibberson, C. (2005) 'The Beginnings of Music Therapy in our Hospice.' In M. Pavlicevic (ed.) *Music Therapy in Children's Hospices*. London: Jessica Kingsley Publishers.

James, M. (1986) 'Neurophysiological treatment of cerebral palsy: A case study.' *Music Therapy Perspectives 3*, 5–12.

James, M.R. (1988) 'Self-monitoring inclinations and adolescent clients with chemical dependency.' *Journal of Music Therapy 25*, 2, 94–102.

Jellison, J. (2000) 'A Content Analysis of Music Research with Disabled Children and Youth (1975–1999): Applications in Special Education.' In American Music Therapy Association (ed.) *Effectiveness of Music Therapy Procedures: Documentation of Research and Clinical Practice*. Third edition. Silver Spring, MD: American Music Therapy Association.

Johnson, E.R. (1981) 'The role of objective and concrete feedback in self-concept treatment of juvenile delinquents in music therapy.' *Journal of Music Therapy 18*, 3, 137–147.

Justice, R.W. (1994) 'Music therapy interventions for people with eating disorders in an inpatient setting.' *Music Therapy Perspectives 12*, 104–110.

Kennelly, J. (1999) '"Don't give up": Providing Music Therapy to an Adolescent Boy in the Bone Marrow Transplant Unit.' In R.R. Pratt and D.E. Grocke (eds) *MusicMedicine*, Volume 3. Melbourne, Australia: Faculty of Music, University of Melbourne.

Kennelly, J. (2001) 'Music therapy in the bone marrow transplant unit: Providing emotional support during adolescence.' *Music Therapy Perspectives 19*, 104–108.

Kim, S., Kverno, K., Lee, E.M., Park, J.H., Lee, H.H. and Kim, H.L. (2006) 'Development of a music group psychotherapy intervention for the primary prevention of adjustment difficulties in Korean adolescent girls.' *Journal of Child and Adolescent Psychiatric Nursing 19*, 3, 103–111.

King, B. (2007) *Making a Connection: The Potential Impact of Musical Contribution on the Therapeutic Alliance with Adolescents*. Chicago, IL: The Chicago School of Professional Psychology.

Kivland, M.J. (1986) 'The use of music to increase self-esteem in a conduct disordered adolescent.' *Journal of Music Therapy 23*, 1, 25–29.

Knight, M.R. (1974) 'Music therapy with a blind boy.' *British Journal of Music Therapy 5*, 3, 19–21.

Krout, R. (1988) 'Using computer and electronic music resources in clinical music therapy with behaviorally disordered students, 12 to 18 years old.' *Music Therapy Perspectives 5*, 114–118.

Laiho, S. (2004) 'The psychological functions of music in adolescence.' *Nordic Journal of Music Therapy 13*, 1, 47–63.

Lang, L. and McInerney, U. (2002) 'Bosnia-Herzegovina: A Music Therapy Service in a Post-War Environment.' In J. Sutton (ed.) *Music, Music Therapy and Trauma: International Perspectives.* London: Jessica Kingsley Publishers.

Larson, B.A. (1981) 'Auditory and visual rhythmic pattern recognition by emotionally disturbed and normal adolescents.' *Journal of Music Therapy 18*, 3, 128–136.

Layman, D.L., Hussey, D.L. and Laing, S.J. (2002) 'Music therapy assessment for severely emotionally disturbed children: A pilot study.' *Journal of Music Therapy 39*, 3, 164–187.

Lefebvre, C. (1991) 'All her "Yesterdays": An Adolescent's Search for a Better Today Through Music.' In K. Bruscia (ed.) *Case Studies in Music Therapy.* Gilsum, NH: Barcelona Publishers.

Lehrer-Carle, I. (1973) 'Group dynamics as applied to the use of music with schizophrenic adolescents.' *British Journal of Music Therapy 4*, 2, 2–10.

Liebman, S.S. and MacLaren, A. (1991) 'The effects of music and relaxation on third trimester anxiety in adolescent pregnancy.' *Journal of Music Therapy 28*, 2, 89–100.

Mayhew, J. (2005) 'A Creative Response to Loss: Developing a Music Therapy Group for Bereaved Siblings.' In M. Pavlicevic (ed.) *Music Therapy in Children's Hospices.* London: Jessica Kingsley Publishers.

McFerran, K. (2004) 'Using songs with groups of teenagers: How does it work?' *Social Work with Groups 27*, 2/3, 143–157.

McFerran, K. (2005) 'Articulating the dynamics of music therapy group improvisations.' *Nordic Journal of Music Therapy 14*, 1, 33–46.

McFerran, K., Baker, F., Patton, G. and Sawyer, S.M. (2006) 'A retrospective lyrical analysis of songs written by adolescents with Anorexia Nervosa.' *European Eating Disorder Review 14*, 397–403.

McFerran, K. and Stephenson, J. (2006) 'Music therapy in special education: Do we need more evidence?' *British Journal of Music Therapy 20*, 2, 121–128.

McFerran-Skewes, K. (2000) 'From the mouths of babes: The response of six younger, bereaved teenagers to the experience of psychodynamic group music therapy.' *Australian Journal of Music Therapy 11*, 3–22.

McIntyre, J. (2007) 'Creating order out of chaos: Music therapy with adolescent boys diagnosed with a Behaviour Disorder and/or Emotional Disorder.' *Music Therapy Today 8*, 1. Available at www.musictherapyworld.de/modules/mmmagazine/issues/20070330122710/20070330123242/MTT8_1_Joanne.pdf, accessed on 25 October 2009.

Metzler, R.K. (1973) 'Music therapy at a behavioral learning center, St. Paul Public Schools.' *Journal of Music Therapy 10*, 4, 177–183.

Metzler, R.K. (1974) 'The use of music as a reinforcer to increase imitative behavior in severely and profoundly retarded female residents.' *Journal of Music Therapy 11*, 2, 97–110.

Molyneux, C. (2005) 'Music therapy as a short-term intervention with individuals and families in a child and adolescent mental health service.' *British Journal of Music Therapy 19*, 2, 59–66.

Montello, L. and Coons, E.E. (1998) 'Effects of active versus passive group music therapy on preadolescents with emotional, learning, and behavioral disorders.' *Journal of Music Therapy 35*, 1, 49–67.

Moore, R. and Mathenius, L. (1987) 'The effects of modeling, reinforcement, and tempo on imitative rhythmic responses of moderately retarded adolescents.' *Journal of Music Therapy 24*, 3, 160–169.

Nolan, P. (1989) 'Music as a transitional object in the treatment of Bulimia.' *Music Therapy Perspectives 6*, 49–51.

Parente, A.B. (1989) 'Feeding the hungry soul: Music as a therapeutic modality in the treatment of Anorexia Nervosa.' *Music Therapy Perspectives 6*, 44–48.

Pavlicevic, M. (2002) 'South Africa: Fragile Rhythms and Uncertain Listenings: Perspectives from Music Therapy with South African Children.' In J. Sutton (ed.) *Music, Music Therapy and Trauma: International Perspectives.* London: Jessica Kingsley Publishers.

Pavlicevic, M. (2005) *Music Therapy in Children's Hospices.* London: Jessica Kingsley Publishers.

Pujol, K.K. (1994) 'The effect of vibrotactile stimulation, instrumentation, and precomposed melodies on physiological and behavioral responses of profoundly retarded children and adults.' *Journal of Music Therapy 31,* 3, 186–205.

Ragland, Z. and Apprey, M. (1974) 'Community music therapy with adolescents.' *Journal of Music Therapy 11,* 3, 147–155.

Rees, C. (2005) 'Brief Encounters.' In M. Pavlicevic (ed.) *Music Therapy in Children's Hospices.* London: Jessica Kingsley Publishers.

Rickson, D.J. (2006) 'Instructional and improvisational models of music therapy with adolescents who have attention deficit hyperactivity disorder (ADHD): A comparison of the effects on motor impulsivity.' *Journal of Music Therapy 43,* 1, 39–62.

Rickson, D.J. and Watkins, W.G. (2003) 'Music therapy to promote prosocial behaviors in aggressive adolescent boys: A pilot study.' *Journal of Music Therapy 40,* 4, 283–301.

Rio, R.E. and Tenney, K.S. (2002) 'Music therapy for juvenile offenders in residential treatment.' *Music Therapy Perspectives 20,* 89–97.

Robarts, J. (2006) 'Music therapy with sexually abused children.' *Clinical Child Psychology and Psychiatry 11,* 249–269.

Robarts, J.Z. (2000) 'Music therapy and adolescents with anorexia nervosa.' *Nordic Journal of Music Therapy 9,* 1, 3–12.

Robb, S.L. (1995) 'The effects of music assisted relaxation on preoperative anxiety.' *Journal of Music Therapy 32,* 1, 2–21.

Robb, S.L. (1996) 'Techniques in song writing: Restoring emotional and physical well being in adolescents who have been traumatically injured.' *Music Therapy Perspectives 14,* 30–37.

Robb, S.L. (2003a) 'Coping and Chronic Illness: Music Therapy for Children and Adolescents with Cancer.' In S.L. Robb (ed.) *Music Therapy in Pediatric Healthcare: Research and Evidence-Based Practice.* Silver Spring, MD: The American Music Therapy Association.

Robb, S.L. (2003b) 'Designing music therapy interventions for hospitalized children and adolescents using a contextual support model of music therapy.' *Music Therapy Perspectives 21,* 27–40.

Robbins, C.E. and Robbins, C.M. (1991) 'Creative Music Therapy in Bringing Order, Change and Communicativeness to the Life of a Brain-Injured Adolescent.' In K. Bruscia (ed.) *Case Studies in Music Therapy.* Gilsum, NH: Barcelona Publishers.

Robertson, J. (2000) 'An educational model for music therapy: The case for a continuum.' *British Journal of Music Therapy 14,* 1, 41–46.

Ropp, C.R., Caldwell, J.E., Dixon, A.M., Angell, M.E. and Vogt, W.P. (2006) 'Special education administrators' perceptions of music therapy in special education programs.' *Music Therapy Perspective 24,* 2, 87–93.

Ruutel, E., Ratnik, M., Tamm, E. and Zilensk, H. (2004) 'The experience of vibroacoustic therapy in the therapeutic intervention of adolescent girls.' *Nordic Journal of Music Therapy 13,* 1, 33–46.

Saarikallio, S. (2007) *Music as Mood Regulation in Adolescence.* Jyvaskyla, Finland: University of Jyvaskyla.

Salmon, S. (1981) 'Music therapy with maladjusted children.' *British Journal of Music Therapy 12,* 3, 4–11.

Sausser, S. and Waller, R.J. (2006) 'A model for music therapy with students with emotional and behavioral disorders.' *The Arts in Psychotherapy 33,* 1–10.

Schotsmans, M. (2007) 'Music therapy with youngsters addicted to drugs, alcohol or medication, from the Sirens to Orpheus.' *Music Therapy Today 8*, 3. Available at www.musictherapyworld.de/modules/mmmagazine/issues/20080108093144/20080108100246/MTT8_3_Shotsmans.pdf, accessed on 27 October 2009.

Schwarting, B. (2005) 'The Open Music Therapy Group Session.' In M. Pavlicevic (ed.) *Music Therapy in Children's Hospices*. London: Jessica Kingsley Publishers.

Sheppard, T. (1977) 'Relationship therapy through music with maladjusted boys.' *British Journal of Music Therapy 8*, 3, 6–10.

Silverman, M.J. (2003) 'Music therapy and clients who are chemically dependent: A review of literature and pilot study.' *The Arts in Psychotherapy 30*, 273–281.

Skaggs, R. (1997) 'Music-centered creative arts in a sex offender treatment program for male juveniles.' *Music Therapy Perspectives 15*, 73–78.

Skewes, K. (2001) *The Experience of Group Music Therapy for Six Bereaved Adolescents*. Melbourne, Australia: University of Melbourne.

Slotoroff, C. (1994) 'Drumming technique for assertiveness and anger management in the short-term psychiatric setting for adult and adolescent survivors of trauma.' *Music Therapy Perspectives 12*, 111–116.

Smeijsters, H. (1996) 'Music therapy with Anorexia Nervosa: An integrative theoretical and methodological perspective.' *British Journal of Music Therapy 10*, 2, 3–13.

Spencer, S.L. (1988) 'The efficiency of instrumental and movement activities in developing mentally retarded adolescents' ability to follow directions.' *Journal of Music Therapy 25*, 1, 44–50.

Standley, J.M. and Whipple, J. (2003) 'Music Therapy with Pediatric Patients: A Meta-Analysis.' In S.L. Robb (ed.) *Music Therapy in Pediatric Healthcare: Research and Evidence-Based Practice*. Silver Spring, MD: The American Music Therapy Association, Inc.

Staum, M.J. (1987) 'Music notation to improve the speech prosody of hearing impaired children.' *Journal of Music Therapy 24*, 3, 146–159.

Strange, J. (1999) 'Client-Centred Music Therapy for Emotionally Disturbed Teenagers Having Moderate Learning Disability.' In T. Wigram and J. De Backer (eds) *Clinical Applications of Music Therapy in Developmental Disability, Paediatrics and Neurology*. London: Jessica Kingsley Publishers.

Stuessy, J. (1996) 'A Call for Research on the Effects of Popular Music on Adolescent Behavior.' In R. R. Pratt and R. Spintge (eds) *MusicMedicine*, Volume 2. St Louis, MO: MMB Music, Inc.

Sweeney-Brown, C. (2005) 'Music and Medicine: Music Therapy Within a Medical Setting.' In M. Pavlicevic (ed.) *Music Therapy in Children's Hospices*. London: Jessica Kingsley Publishers.

Tampline, J. (2000) 'Improvisational music therapy approaches to coma arousal.' *Australian Journal of Music Therapy 11*, 38–51.

Tervo, J. (2001) 'Music therapy for adolescents.' *Clinical Child Psychology and Psychiatry 6*, 1, 79–91.

Toyama, B. (1973) 'Experiments with an athetoid girl.' *British Journal of Music Therapy 4*, 2, 15–17.

Trondalen, G. (2003) '"Self-listening" in music therapy with a young woman suffering from anorexia nervosa.' *Nordic Journal of Music Therapy 12*, 1, 3–17.

Tyson, E.H. and Baffour, T.D. (2004) 'Arts-based strengths: A solution-focused intervention with adolescents in an acute-care psychiatric setting.' *The Arts in Psychotherapy 31*, 213–227.

van der Walt, M. and Baron, A. (2006) 'The role of music therapy in the treatment of a girl with Pervasive Refusal Syndrome: Exploring approaches to empowerment.' *Australian Journal of Music Therapy 17*, 35–53.

Viega, M. (2008) *Conceptualizing the Lived Experience of Three Adolescents Through the Interpretation of the Core Metaphors in their Preferred Music*. Philadelphia, PA: Temple University.

Walsh, R. (1997) 'When having means losing: Music therapy with a young adolescent with a learning disability and emotional and behavioural difficulties.' *British Journal of Music Therapy 11*, 1, 13–19.

Whipple, J. (2004) 'Music in intervention for children and adolescents with autism: A meta-analysis.' *Journal of Music Therapy 41*, 2, 90–106.

Whitehead-Pleaux, A.M., Baryza, M. and Sheridan, R.L. (2006) 'The effects of music therapy on pediatric patients' pain and anxiety during donor site dressing change.' *Journal of Music Therapy 43*, 2, 136–153.

Whitehead-Pleaux, A.M., Zebrowski, N., Baryza, M. and Sheridan, R.L. (2007) 'Exploring the effects of music therapy on pediatric pain: Phase 1.' *Journal of Music Therapy 44*, 3, 217–241.

Wolfe, D.E. (1980) 'The effect of automated interrupted music on head posturing of cerebral palsied individuals.' *Journal of Music Therapy 17*, 4, 184–206.

Wooton, M.A. (1992) 'The effects of heavy metal music on affects shifts of adolescents in an inpatient psychiatric setting.' *Music Therapy Perspectives 10*, 93–98.

Wyatt, J.G. (2002) 'From the field: Clinical resources for music therapy with juvenile offenders.' *Music Therapy Perspectives 20*, 80–88.

Wylie, M.E. (1983) 'Eliciting vocal responses in severely and profoundly mentally handicapped subjects.' *Journal of Music Therapy 20*, 4, 190–200.

References

Aasgaard, T. (2000) 'A suspiciously cheerful lady: A study of a song's life in the paediatric oncology ward and beyond...' *British Journal of Music Therapy 14*, 2, 70–82.

Aasgaard, T. (2004) 'A Pied Piper Among White Coats and Infusion Pumps: Community Music Therapy in a Paediatric Hospital Setting.' In M. Pavlicevic and G. Ansdell (eds) *Community Music Therapy*. London: Jessica Kingsley Publishers.

Achenbach, C. (1997) *Creative Music in Group Work*. Bicester: Winslow Press.

Aigen, K. (1991) *The Roots of Music Therapy: Towards an Indigenous Research Paradigm*, Volumes 1 and 2. Unpublished Doctoral dissertation, New York University.

Aigen, K. (2005) *Music-Centered Music Therapy*. Gilsum, NH: Barcelona Publishers.

Ansdell, G. (1995) *Music for Life: Aspects of Creative Music Therapy with Adult Clients*. London: Jessica Kingsley Publishers.

Ansdell, G. (2002) 'Community music therapy and the winds of change.' *Voices: A World Forum for Music Therapy 2*, 2. Available at www.voices.no/mainissues/Voices2(2)ansdell.html, accessed on 27 October 2009.

Ansdell, G. (2005a) 'Being who you aren't; Doing what you can't.' *Voices: A World Forum for Music Therapy 5*, 3. Available at www.voices.no/mainissues/mi40005000192.html, accessed on 27 October 2009.

Ansdell, G. (2005b) 'Community music therapy: A plea for "fuzzy recognition" instead of "final definition".' *Voices: A World Forum for Music Therapy*. Available at www.voices.no/discussions/discm4_07.html, accessed 28 October 2009.

Baker, F. and Bor, W. (2008) 'Can music preferences indicate mental health status in young people?' *Australasian Psychiatry 16*, 4, 284–288.

Baker, F. and McFerran, K. (2006) 'A retrospective lyric analysis of songs written by adolescent girls with disordered eating.' *European Eating Disorder Review 14*, 6, 397–403.

Baker, F. and Wigram, T. (eds) (2005) *Songwriting: Methods, Techniques and Clinical Applications for Music Therapy Clinicians, Educators and Students*. London: Jessica Kingsley Publishers.

Beaumont, P.J., Russell, J.D. and Touyz, S.W. (1993) 'Treatment of Anorexia Nervosa.' *Lancet 341*, 1635–1640.

Becker, C.S. (1992) *Living and Relating: An Introduction to Phenomenology*. Thousand Oaks, CA: SAGE Publications.

Bennett, A. (1999) 'Hip hop am Main: The localization of rap music and hip hop culture.' *Media, Culture and Society 21*, 1, 77–91.

Berk, L.E. (2000) *Child Development*. Fifth edition. Boston, MA: Allyn & Bacon.

Bilides, D.G. (1992) 'Reaching inner city children: A group work program model for a public middle school.' *Social Work with Groups 15*, 129–144.

Bonanno, G.A. (2008) 'Grief, trauma and resilience.' *Grief Matters: The Australian Journal of Grief and Bereavement 11*, 1, 11–17.

Bright, R. (2002) *Supportive Eclectic Music Therapy for Grief and Loss: A Practical Handbook for Professionals.* St Louis, MO: MMB Music, Inc.

Bronfenbrenner, U. (1989) 'Ecological systems theory.' In R. Vasta (ed.) *Annals of Child Development: A Research Annual,* Volume 6. Greenwich, CT: JAI Press.

Bronfenbrenner, U. (2005) *Making human beings human: Bioecological perspectives on human development.* Thousand Oaks, CA: SAGE Publications.

Brooks, D.M. (1989) 'Music therapy enhances treatment with adolescents.' *Music Therapy Perspectives 6,* 37–39.

Brown, E. and Hendee, W.R. (1989) 'Adolescents and their music: Insights into the health of adolescents.' *Journal of the American Medical Association 262,* 12, 1659–1663.

Bruscia, K. (1987) *Improvisational Models of Music Therapy.* Springfield, IL: Charles C Thomas Publishers.

Bruscia, K. (1998a) *Defining Music Therapy.* Gilsum, NH: Barcelona Publishers.

Bruscia, K. (1998b) *The Dynamics of Music Psychotherapy.* Gilsum, NH: Barcelona Publishers.

Bunt, L. (1994) *Music Therapy: An Art Beyond Words.* London: Routledge.

Bushong, D.J. (2002) 'Good Music/Bad Music: Extant literature on popular music media and antisocial behavior.' *Music Therapy Perspectives 20,* 69–79.

Comber, A., Hargreaves, D. and Colley, A. (1993) 'Girls, boys and technology in music.' *British Journal of Music Education 10,* 2, 123–134.

CAIRSS (CAUL Australian Institutional Repository Support Service) (2009) CAIRSS for Music Index. San Antonio: University of Texas. Retrieved on 10 January 2009 from http://ucairss.utsa.edu.

Cresswell, J.W. (2003) *Research Design: Qualitative, Quantitative and Mixed Methods Approaches.* Thousand Oaks, CA: SAGE Publications.

Cross, I. (2006) 'Music and social being.' *Musicology Australia 28,* 114–126.

Cross, I. (2008) 'Musicality and the human capacity for culture.' *Musicae Scientiae, Special Issue: Narrative in music and interaction,* 147–167.

Cross, I. (2009) 'The Nature of Music and its Evolution.' In S. Hallam, I. Cross and M.H. Thaut (eds) *Oxford Handbook of Music Psychology.* Oxford: Oxford University Press.

Dalton, T.A. and Krout, R.E. (2005) 'Development of the grief process scale through music therapy songwriting with bereaved adolescents.' *The Arts in Psychotherapy 32,* 131–143.

Davis, W.B., Gfeller, K.E. and Thaut, M.H. (1999) *An Introduction to Music Therapy: Theory and Practice.* Second edition. New York, NY: McGraw-Hill.

DeNora, T. (2000) *Music in Everyday Life.* Cambridge: Cambridge University Press.

Dileo, C. and Bradt, J. (2009) 'On creating the discipline, profession, and evidence in the field of arts and healthcare.' *Arts and Health 1,* 2, 168–182.

Doak, B. (2003) 'Relationships between adolescent psychiatric diagnoses, music preferences, and drug preferences.' *Music Therapy Perspectives 21,* 69–73.

Duncan, B.L., Miller, S.D. and Sparks, J. (2004) *The Heroic Client: A Revolutionary Way to Improve Effectiveness Through Client-Directed, Outcome-Informed Therapy.* Revised edition. San Francisco, CA: Jossey-Bass.

Duncan, B.L., Miller, S.D. and Sparks, J. (2007) 'Common factors and the uncommon heroism of youth.' *Psychotherapy in Australia 13,* 2, 34–43.

Eccles, J., Wigfield, A., Harold, R.D. and Bulmenfeld, P. (1993) 'Age and gender differences in children's self- and task perceptions during elementary school.' *Child Development 64,* 830–847.

Edwards, J. (2002) 'Debating the winds of change in community music therapy #2.' *Voices: A World Forum for Music Therapy.* Available at www.voices.no/discussions/discm4_02.html, accessed on 29 October 2009.

Epstein, R. (2007) *The Case Against Adolescence: Rediscovering the Adult in Every Teen.* Sanger, CA: Quill Driver Books.

Erikson, E.H. (1963) *Childhood and Society.* New York, NY: WW Norton & Company.

Ferrara, L. (1991) *Philosophy and the Analysis of Music: Bridges to Musical Sound, Form and Reference.* New York, NY: Excelsior Music Publishing Company.

Finnas, L. (1987) 'Do young people misjudge each other's musical taste?' *Psychology of Music 15*, 2, 152–166.

Fitzgerald, M., Jospeh, A.P., Hayes, M. and O'Regan, M. (1995) 'Leisure activities of adolescent schoolchildren.' *Journal of Adolescence 18*, 3, 349–358.

Forinash, M. (ed.) (2001) *Music Therapy Supervision.* Gilsum, NH: Barcelona Publishers.

Forinash, M. and Grocke, D. (2005) 'Phenomenological Inquiry.' In B. Wheeler (ed.) *Music Therapy Research.* Second edition. Gilsum, NH: Barcelona Publishers.

Freeman, W.J. (1997) 'Happiness doesn't come in bottles.' *Journal of Consciousness Studies 4*, 1, 67–70.

Frith, S. (1981) *Sound Effects: Youth, Leisure and the Politics of Rock 'n' Roll.* New York, NY: Pantheon.

Frydenberg, E. (2008) *Adolescent Coping: Advances in Theory, Research and Practice.* London: Routledge.

Frydenberg, E. and Lewis, R. (1993) *Adolescent Coping Scale: Administrator's Manual.* Melbourne, Australia: Australian Council for Educational Research.

Gardstrom, S.C. (2004) 'An Investigation of Meaning in Clinical Music Improvisation with Troubled Adolescents.' In B. Abrams (ed.) *Qualitative Inquiries in Music Therapy: A Monograph Series 1*, 77–160.

Gardstrom, S.C. (2007) *Music Therapy Improvisation for Groups: Essential Leadership Competencies.* Gilsum, NH: Barcelona Publishers.

Gold, C., Voracek, M. and Wigram, T. (2004) 'Effects of music therapy for children and adolescents with psychopathology: A meta-analysis.' *Journal of Child Psychology and Psychiatry 45*, 6, 1054–1063.

Grocke, D.E. and Wigram, T. (2006) *Receptive Methods in Music Therapy.* London: Jessica Kingsley Publishers.

Guba, E.G. and Lincoln, Y.S. (2005) 'Paradigmatic Controversies, Contradictions, and Emerging Confluences.' In N.K. Denzin and Y.S. Lincoln (eds) *The SAGE Handbook of Qualitative Research.* Third edition. Thousand Oaks, CA: SAGE Publications.

Hadley, S. (ed.) (2003) *Psychodynamic Music Therapy: Case Studies.* Gilsum, NH: Barcelona Publishers.

Hadley, S. (ed.) (2006) *Feminist Perspectives in Music Therapy.* Gilsum, NH: Barcelona Publishers.

Hall, G.S. (1904) *Adolescence: Its Psychology and Relations to Physiology, Anthropology, Sociology, Sex, Crime, Religion and Education*, Volume 1. New York, NY: D. Appleton and Company.

Hanser, S. (2005) 'Applied Behavior Analysis.' In B. Wheeler (ed.) *Music Therapy Research.* Second edition. Gilsum, NH: Barcelona Publishers.

Harrison, L. and Harrington, R. (2001) 'Adolescents' bereavement experiences: Prevalence, association with depressive symptoms, and use of services.' *Journal of Adolescence 24*, 2, 159–169.

Hilliard, R.E. (2001) 'The effects of music therapy-based bereavement groups on mood and behavior of grieving children: A pilot study.' *Journal of Music Therapy 38*, 4, 291–306.

Howat, R. (1983) *Debussy in Proportion: A Musical Analysis.* Cambridge: Cambridge University Press.

Howe, M. and Sloboda, J.A. (1991) 'Young musicians' accounts of significant influences in their early lives.' *British Journal of Music Education 8*, 39–63.

Hubble, M.A., Duncan, B.L. and Miller, S.D. (1999) *The Heart and Soul of Change: What Works in Therapy.* Washington, DC: American Psychological Association.

Institute of Education Sciences and US Department of Education (2009) ERIC (Education Resources Information Center). Retrieved on 13 January 2009 from www.eric.ed.gov

James, M. and Freed, B. (1989) 'A sequential model for developing group cohesion in music therapy.' *Music Therapy Perspectives 7*, 28–34.

Jung, C.G. (1956) *Psychological Types, Collected Works*, Volume 6. London: Routledge.

Karcher, M.J. and Lindwall, J. (2003) 'Social interest, connectedness and challenging experiences: What makes high school mentors persist.' *Journal of Individual Psychology 59*, 293–315.

Krout, R. (2009) *Creative Acoustic Guitar Accompaniment Loops for Music Therapy and Music Education: Enhancing the Sound.* Denton, TX: Sarsen Publishing.

Laiho, S. (2004) 'The psychological functions of music in adolescence.' *Nordic Journal of Music Therapy 13*, 1, 47–63.

Larsen, R.J. (2000) 'Toward a science of mood regulation.' *Psychological Inquiry 11*, 129–141.

Lennon, J. and McCartney, P. (1967) 'With a Little Help from my Friends.' The Beatles, *Sgt Pepper's Lonely Hearts Club Band.* London: Parlaphone.

Lomax, A. (1976) *Cantometrics: An Approach to the Anthropology of Music.* Berkeley, CA: University of California.

Lyubomirsky, S. (2001) 'Why are some people happier than others?: The role of cognitive and motivational processes in well-being.' *American Psychologist 56*, 239–249.

Madonna (2000) 'Music' [CD]. Beverley Hills, CA: Maverick Recording Company.

Malekoff, A. (1997) *Group Work with Adolescents.* New York, NY: Guilford Press.

Maslow, A. (1968) *Toward a Psychology of Being.* New York, NY: John Wiley & Sons.

May, B. (1977) 'We will Rock You.' Queen, *News of the World* [CD]. London: Parlophone.

McFerran, K. (2010) 'Tipping the scales: A substantive theory on the value of group music therapy for supporting grieving teenagers.' *Qualitative Inquiries in Music Therapy (A Monograph Series) 5*, 2–26.

McFerran, K., Baker, F., Patton, G. and Sawyer, S.M. (2006) 'A retrospective lyrical analysis of songs written by adolescents with Anorexia Nervosa.' *European Eating Disorder Review 14*, 397–403.

McFerran, K., O'Grady, L., Sawyer, S.M. and Grocke, D.E. (unpublished) 'How teenagers use music to manage their mood: an initial investigation.' Melbourne, Australia: University of Melbourne.

McFerran, K. and Wigram, T. (2002) 'A review of current practice in group music therapy improvisations.' *British Journal of Music Therapy 16*, 1, 46–55.

McFerran-Skewes, K. (2000) 'From the mouths of babes: The response of six younger bereaved teenagers to the experience of psychodynamic group music therapy.' *Australian Journal of Music Therapy 11*, 3–22.

McFerran-Skewes, K. (2003) 'A Brisbane Community Dinkum Experience.' *Voices: A World Forum for Music Therapy.* Available at www.voices.no/discussions/discm25_03.html, accessed on 29 October 2009.

McGuire, M. (2004) *Psychiatric Music Therapy in the Community: The Legacy of Florence Tyson.* Gilsum, NH: Barcelona Publishers.

McLellan, B. (1995) *Beyond Psychoppression: A Feminist Alternative Therapy.* Melbourne, Australia: Spinifex Press.

McNeill, W. (1995) *Keeping Together in Time: Dance and Drill in Human History.* Cambridge, MA: Harvard University Press.

Mead, M. (1973/1928) *Coming of Age in Samoa: A Psychological Study of Primitive Youth for Western Civilisation.* New York, NY: American Museum of Natural History.

Metallica (1991) 'Nothing Else matters.' *Metallica.* New York, NY: Elektra.

Miller, S. (2008) 'What is the Secret of their Success?' Paper presented at the Supershrinks Workshop, Melbourne, Australia, 19 November 2008.

Morgenstern, A. (1982) 'Group therapy: A timely strategy for music therapists.' *Music Therapy Perspectives 1*, 16–20.

National Library of Australia (2008) Meditext (Bibliographic database). Available at www.informit.com.au, accessed on 15 September 2008.

Neimeyer, R.A. and Currier, J.M. (2008) 'Bereavement interventions: Present status and future horizons.' *Grief Matters: The Australian Journal of Grief and Bereavement 11*, 1, 18–22.

Nordoff, P. and Robbins, C.E. (2004/1971) *Therapy in Music for Handicapped Children*. Gilsum, NH: Barcelona Publisher.

North, A.C. and Hargreaves, D.J. (1999) 'Music and adolescent identity.' *Music Education Research 1*, 1, 75–92.

North, A.C., Hargreaves, D.J. and O'Neill, S.A. (2000) 'The importance of music to adolescents.' *British Journal of Educational Psychology 70*, 255–272.

O'Brien, E. (2004) *Living Soul: From the Bedside to the Studio to the Heart*. (Triple CD). Melbourne, Australia: Bakehouse Studios.

O'Brien, E. (2005) 'Songwriting with Adult Patients in Oncology and Clinical Haematology.' In F. Baker and T. Wigram (eds) *Songwriting: Methods, Techniques and Clinical Applications for Music Therapy Clinicians, Educators and Students*. London: Jessica Kingsley Publishers.

O'Grady, L. (2008) 'The role of performance in music-making: An interview with Jon Hawkes.' *Voices: A World Forum for Music Therapy, 8*, 2. Available at www.voices.no/mainissues/mi40008000279. php, accessed on 29 October 2009.

O'Grady, L. (2010) *The Therapeutic Potentials for Women in Prison who Create and Perform Music Together: A Qualitative Case Study*. Unpublished Doctoral dissertation, University of Melbourne.

O'Grady, L. and McFerran, K. (2007) 'Uniting the work of community musicians and music therapists through the health-care continuum: A grounded theory analysis.' *Australian Journal of Music Therapy 18*, 62–86.

Olsson, C.A., Bond, L., Burns, J.M., Vella-Brodrick, D.A. and Sawyer, S.M. (2003). 'Adolescent resilience: A concept analysis.' *Journal of Adolescence 26*, 1–11.

O'Neill, S.A. (1997) 'Gender and Music.' In D. Hargreaves and A. North (eds) *The Social Psychology of Music*. Oxford: Oxford University Press.

Pavlicevic, M. (1997) *Music Therapy in Context: Music, Meaning and Relationship*. London: Jessica Kingsley Publishers.

Pavlicevic, M. (2005) 'Community music therapy: Anyone for practice?' *Voices: A World Forum for Music Therapy*. Available at www.voices.no/discussions/discm4_10, accessed on 10 March 2009.

Pavlicevic, M. and Ansdell, G. (eds) (2004) *Community Music Therapy*. London: Jessica Kingsley Publishers.

Piaget, J. and Inhelder, B. (1958) *The Growth of Logical Thinking: From Childhood to Adolescence*. (trans.) A. Parsons and S. Seagrin. New York, NY: Basic Books.

Plach, T. (1996) *The Creative Use of Music in Group Therapy*. Third edition. Springfield, IL: Charles C Thomas Publishers.

Raz, N. (2006) 'Aging of the brain: Neurobiology and imaging.' *Alzheimer's and Dementia 2*, 3, 5647–5647

Resnick, M.D., Bearman, P.S., Blum, R.W., Bauman, K.E. *et al.* (1997) 'Protecting adolescents from harm: Findings from the National Longitudinal Study on Adolescent Health.' *Journal of the American Medical Association 278*, 10, 823–832.

Roe, K. (1987) 'The school and music in adolescent socialisation.' In J. Lull (ed.) *Pop Music and Communication*. Thousand Oaks, CA: SAGE Publications.

Roe, K. (1999) 'Music and identity among European youth: Music as communication.' *Soundscapes: Journal on Media Culture 2*, July. Available at www.icce.rug.nl/~soundscapes/DATABASES/MIE/Part2_chapter03.shtml, accessed on 2 November 2009.

Rolvsjord, R., Gold, C. and Stige, B. (2005) 'Therapeutic principles for resource-oriented music therapy: A contextual approach to the field of mental health.' *Nordic Journal of Music Therapy 14*, 1. Available at www.njmt.no/appendrolvsjord141.html, accessed on 29 October 2009.

Roth, J.L. and Brooks-Gunn, J. (2003) 'Youth development programs: Risk, prevention and policy.' *Journal of Adolescent Health 32*, 170–182.

Rothenberg, D. (1996) 'Spontaneous effort: Improvisation and the quest for meaning.' *Parabola 8*, 7–12.

Ruud, E. (1980) *Music Therapy and its Relationship to Current Treatment Theories.* St Louis, MO: Magnamusic-Baton.

Ruud, E. (1997) 'Music and identity.' *Nordic Journal of Music Therapy 6*, 1, 3–13.

Ruud, E. (2004) 'Debating the winds of change in community music therapy #4.' *Voices: A World Forum for Music Therapy.* Available at www.voices.no/discussions/discm4_04.html, accessed on 29 October 2009.

Ruutel, E., Ratnik, M., Tamm, E. and Zilensk, H. (2004) 'The experience of vibroacoustic therapy in the therapeutic intervention of adolescent girls.' *Nordic Journal of Music Therapy 13*, 1, 33–46.

Saarikallio, S. and Erkkila, J. (2007) 'The role of music in adolescents' mood regulation.' *Psychology of Music 35*, 1, 88–109.

Schapira, D. (2002) *Musicoterapia: Facetas de lo Inefable [Music Therapy: Facets of the Ineffable].* Rio de Janeiro: Enelivros Editora.

Schapira, D. (2003) 'Review of Wigram, Nygaard Pederson and Bonde: A comprehensive guide to music therapy.' *Nordic Journal of Music Therapy.* Available at www.njmt.no/bookreview_2003034. html, accessed on 2 November 2009.

Schapira, D. and Hugo, M. (2005) 'The plurimodal approach in music therapy.' *Voices: A World Forum for Music Therapy 5*, 2. Available at www.voices.no/mainissues/mi40005000185.html, accessed on 29 October 2009.

Schlaug, G., Norton, A., Overy, K. and Winner, E. (2006) 'Effects of music training on the child's brain and cognitive development.' *Annals of the New York Academy of Sciences 1060*, 219–230.

Schmidt-Peters, J. (1987) *Music Therapy: An Introduction.* Springfield, IL: Charles C Thomas Publisher.

Schwartz, K.D. and Fouts, G.T. (2003) 'Music preferences, personality style, and developmental issues of adolescents.' *Journal of Youth and Adolescence 32*, 3, 205–210.

Shuter-Dyson, R. and Gabriel, C. (1981) *The Psychology of Musical Ability.* Second edition. London: Methuen.

Skånland, M.S. (2009) 'Use of MP3 Players as a Medium for Musical Self-Care.' Paper presented at the Nordic Conference of Music Therapy, Aalborg University, Denmark, April/May 2009.

Skewes, K. (2001) *The experience of group music therapy for bereaved adolescents.* Melbourne, Australia: University of Melbourne.

Small, C. (1998) *Musicking: The Meanings of Performing and Listening.* Middletown, CT: Wesleyan University Press.

Smeijsters, H. and Aasgard, T. (2005) 'Qualitative Case Study Research.' In B. Wheeler (ed.) *Music Therapy Research.* Second edition. Gilsum, NH: Barcelona Publishers.

Solley, B.A. (2005) *When Poverty's Children Write: Celebrating Strengths, Transforming Lives.* Portsmouth, NH: Heinemann.

Spice Girls (1996) 'Wannabe.' *Spice.* London: Virgin Records.

Steinberg, L. (1996) *Adolescence.* Fourth edition. New York, NY: McGraw-Hill.

Stern, D.N., Hofer, L., Haft, W. and Dore, J. (1985) 'Affect Attunement: The Sharing of Feeling States Between Mother and Infant by Means of Inter-Modal Fluency.' In T. Field and N. Fox (eds) *Social Perception in Infants.* New York, NY: Ablex Publishing Corporation.

Stige, B. (2002a) *Culture-Centered Music Therapy.* Gilsum, NH: Barcelona Publishers.

Stige, B. (2002b) 'The relentless roots of community music therapy.' *Voices: A World Forum for Music Therapy 2*, 3. Available at www.voices.no/mainissues/Voices2(3)stige.html, accessed on 30 October 2009.

Stige, B. (2003a) *Elaborations Towards a Notion of Community Music Therapy.* Doctoral thesis, University of Oslo, Norway: Unifob.

Stige, B. (2003b) 'What could music therapy be?' *Voices: A World Forum for Music Therapy 3*, 3. Available at www.voices.no/mainissues/mi40003000125.html, accessed on 30 October 2009.

Stige, B. (2004) 'Debating the winds of change in community music therapy #5.' *Voices: A World Forum for Music Therapy.* Available at www.voices.no/discussions/discm4_05.html, accessed on 30 October 2009.

Stige, B. (2005) 'Participatory Action Research.' In B. Wheeler (ed.) *Music Therapy Research.* Second edition. Gilsum, NH: Barcelona Publishers.

Stige, B. (2008) 'Where Music Helps: Community Music Therapy in Action and Reflection' (keynote address). Paper presented at the XII World Congress of Music Therapy, National University of Buenos Aires, Argentina, July 2008.

Stige, B. (2009) 'So You're Already Doing Community Music Therapy: But Why?' Paper presented at the Free Public Lecture by the Macgeorge Visiting Speaker, University of Melbourne, Australia, 13 February 2009.

Stige, B., Ansdell, G., Elefant, C. and Pavlicevic, M. (2010) *Where Music Helps: Community Music Therapy in Action and Reflection.* Aldershot: Ashgate Publishing.

Stroebe, M. and Schut, H. (2008) 'The dual process model of coping with bereavement: Overview and update.' *Grief Matters: The Australian Journal of Grief and Bereavement 11*, 1, 4–10.

Tarrant, M., North, A.C. and Hargreaves, D.J. (1999) 'Adolescents' intergroup attributions: A comparison of two social identities.' *Journal of Youth and Adolescence 33*, 3, 177–185.

Tarrant, M., North, A.C. and Hargreaves, D.J. (2000) 'English and American Adolescents' reasons for listening to music.' *Psychology of Music 28*, 2, 166–173.

Tarrant, M., North, A.C. and Hargreaves, D.J. (2001) 'Social categorization, self-esteem and the estimated musical preferences of male adolescents.' *The Journal of Social Psychology 141*, 5, 565–581.

Thompson Reuters (2009) ISI Web of Science. Retrieved on 5 January 2009 from http://isiwebofknowledge.com/products_tools/multidisciplinary/webofscience.

Threlfall, C. (1999) 'Community music and music therapy – partnerships and possibilities.' *Australian Music Therapy Association Network*, November, 10–15.

Threlfall, C. (2007) 'Changing the Rhythm: Keeping the Beat' (keynote address). Paper presented at the 33rd Annual National Australian Music Therapy Association Conference, Melbourne, Australia, October 2007.

Trainor, L.J., Shahin, A.J. and Roberts, L.E. (2009) 'Understanding the benefits of musical training: effects on oscillatory brain activity.' *Annals of the New York Academy of Sciences 1169*, 133–142.

Trondalen, G. (2003) '"Self-listening" in music therapy with a young woman suffering from anorexia nervosa.' *Nordic Journal of Music Therapy 12*, 1, 3–17.

Tuckman, B. (1965) 'Developmental sequence in small groups.' *Psychological Bulletin 63*, 384–399.

Turry, A. (1999) 'Performance and product: Clinical implications for the music therapist.' *Music Therapy World.* Available at www.musictherapyworld.de/modules/archive/stuff/papers/perforprod.doc, accessed on 2 November 2009.

UK Encarta Dictionary (2009): available at uk.encarta.msn.com/encnet/features/dictionary/dictionaryhome.aspx, accessed on 30 October 2009.

US National Library of Medicine (2009) Medline (Bibliographic database). Retrieved 12 January 2009 from www.nlm.nih.gov/databases/databases_medline.html

Van Heeswyk, P. (1997) *Analysing Adolescence.* London: Sheldon Press.

Van Wel, F., Linssen, H. and Abma, R. (2004) 'The parental bond and the well-being of adolescents and young adults.' *Journal of Youth and Adolescence 29*, 3, 307–318.

Viega, M. (2008) *Conceptualizing the Lived Experience of Three Adolescents Through the Interpretation of the Core Metaphors in Their Preferred Music.* Philadelphia, PA: Temple University.

Wheatus (2000) 'Teenage Dirtbag.' *Wheatus.* Sydney: Sony.

Wheeler, S. and Austin, J. (2001) 'The Loss Response List: A tool for measuring adolescent grief responses.' *Death Studies 24*, 1, 21–34.

Wigram, T. (2004) *Improvisation: Methods and Techniques for Music Therapy Clinicians, Educators and Students.* London: Jessica Kingsley Publishers.

Wigram, T., Pederson, I.N. and Bonde, L.O. (2002) *A Comprehensive Guide to Music Therapy: Theory, Clinical Practice, Research and Training.* London: Jessica Kingsley Publishers.

Wooten, M.A. (1992) 'The effects of heavy metal music on affects shifts of adolescents in an inpatient psychiatric setting.' *Music Therapy Perspectives 10,* 93–98.

Yalom, I. (1995) *The Theory and Practice of Group Psychotherapy.* Fourth edition. New York, NY: Basic Books.

DNumbers set in *italics* indicate tables and figures

Subject Index

Author Index